CALDERÓN DE LA BARCA STUDIES 1951-69

A CRITICAL SURVEY AND ANNOTATED BIBLIOGRAPHY

General Editors
JACK H. PARKER, University of Toronto
ARTHUR M. FOX, Queen's University at Kingston

Calderón de la Barca Studies 1951-69

1951-69

A CRITICAL SURVEY AND ANNOTATED BIBLIOGRAPHY

© University of Toronto Press 1971
  Printed in Canada by
  University of Toronto Press
  Toronto and Buffalo
  ISBN 0-8020-1762-2

C O M P I L E R S

1951-52
J.C. Castañeda, Rice University

1953-54
A.M. Fox and D.L. Bastianutti, Queen's University

1955-56
H.W. Hilborn, Queen's University

1957-58
Carlos Ortigoza, Universidad Nacional Autónoma de México

1959-60
K.-L. Selig, Columbia University

1961-62
J.H. Parker and Margaret Falconer, University of Toronto

1963-64
Walter Poesse, Indiana University

1965-66
R.W. Tyler, University of Nebraska

1967
F.J. Hernández, Carleton University

1968
R.L. Fiore, Michigan State University

1969
Richard Hildebrandt, Brock University, and
J.G. Renart, University of Toronto

A project of the Research Committee of Spanish Group Three
of the Modern Language Association of America

C O N T E N T S

P R E F A C E

In the section "Cape and Sword" of BCom for April, 1951 (3,
No. 1, p. 4), we find the following editorial comment, under
the heading Cooperative Bibliography: "The very valuable current bibliography of foreign items dealing with the comedia
compiled by Professors Parker and Reichenberger is an excellent
example of cooperative scholarship. It points up, too, the need
of bibliographies for Lope, Calderón and other dramatists of
the Golden Age. Perhaps three or four Comediantes could work
on Lope, several on Calderón, etc. Who will volunteer?"
    Several Lopistas responded to the call, and in 1964 there
was published (University of Toronto Press) Lope de Vega Studies 1937-1962: A Critical Survey and Annotated Bibliography,
in observance of the Quadricentennial Year of the dramatist's
birth. Now, a group of Calderonistas has banded together to
bring forth Calderón de la Barca Studies 1951-1969, as another
response to the editorial challenge enunciated early in 1951,
by coincidence the initial year covered by this study.
    In 1966 the indefatigable bibliographer Warren T. McCready
brought forth his Bibliografía temática de estudios sobre el
teatro español antiguo, covering the years 1850 to 1950. The
decision to date Calderón de la Barca Studies from 1951 to
1969 arose from the desire to continue on from the point where
McCready left off, in imitation, as to format, of the Lope de
Vega Studies of 1964. Several of the bibliographers are the
same persons, some are different; and they are, as can be seen
from the list of Compilers, a group of scholars of the comedia
now domiciled in Canada, the United States and Mexico, repre-
senting various Western European origins.
    For this Calderón volume, preliminary criteria were estab-
lished for the guidance of all, but a certain individuality in
style and method will be observed from unit to unit, according
to resources available in each instance and to personal prefer-
ences and interpretation, especially in the critical surveys
and annotations. The bibliographical system adopted is an al-
phabetical arrangement, going from the general to the particular,

with "Editions" preceding "Studies." To present a picture of
the evolution of editions, book reviews and studies of individual works, the internal treatment in theses cases is chronological. Numerous cross-references are provided within the
various sub-sections, and a limited Index lists editors, translators and critics (but not reviewers of books) in the Annotated
Bibliography (but excluding the Critical Survey). With regard
to the inclusion of unpublished works, it was decided to list
doctoral but not masters dissertations; and in the case of
published works, newspaper material has normally been omitted.

High tribute must be paid to the inspiration received from
the McCready _Bibliografía temática_; and congratulations go to
José Simón Díaz, who published his _Bibliografía de la literatura
hispánica, Tomo VII_, covering "Calderón de la Barca," in 1967.
In addition, compilers have been greatly aided by the serial
bibliographies of a general nature in _NRFH_, _RFE_, _RL_, _ZRP_, etc.,
and, for dissertations, the listings in _Hisp_ and _MLJ_, as well
as the résumés provided by _DA_. Of much help were the _PMLA_ annual compilations, the _SP_ annual bibliography of the Renaissance, the _BCom_ semi-annual bibliography of foreign publications on the _comedia_ and _The Year's Work in Modern Language
Studies_ published by the Humanities Research Association.

The Editors wish to express their appreciation to the Canada
Council for a grant in aid of research and to the Committee on
Humanities and Social Sciences Research of the University of
Toronto for financial assistance for the preparation of the
manuscript for publication. To Professors Warren T. McCready
and Peter B. Bell go our thanks for constant encouragement and
suggestions for the improvement of the bibliography. The fruitful cooperation of Dr. R. M. Schoeffel, Modern Languages Editor
of the University of Toronto Press, is gratefully acknowledged.
Mrs. T. B. Barclay, M.A., who typed the manuscript with great
care for photographic reproduction (and in the process straight-
ened out many inconsistencies and careless errors), receives
the undying gratitude of the Editors for her invaluable support.

Calderonistas are asked to send to the Editors comments,
corrections and additions, to supplement _lacunae_ in the present
work, for in a field as vast as Calderón de la Barca studies
we do not presume to completeness or perfection.

Toronto, Canada
October, 1970

J.H.P.
A.M.F.

ABBREVIATIONS

Acad.	Academia, Academy	Bib.	Biblioteca, Bibliothèque
Anon.	Anonymous	Bol.	Boletim, Boletín
Archiv	Archiv für das Studium der neueren Sprachen und Literaturen	BPIQ	Boston Public Library Quarterly
		BRAE	Boletín de la Real Academia Española
Asoc., Assoc.	Asociación, Association	Bul.	Bulletin
AUC	Anales de la Universidad de Chile	CCLC	Cuadernos del Congreso por la Libertad de la Cultura
BA	Books Abroad		
BAE	Biblioteca de Autores Españoles	CHA	Cuadernos Hispanoamericanos
BBMP	Boletín de la Biblioteca Menéndez Pelayo	Chapt.	Chapter
		CL	Comparative Literature
BCom	Bulletin of the Comediantes	Clás.	Clásica(s), Clásico(s)
		Clás. Cast.	Clásicos Castellanos
BEPIF	Bulletin des Études Portugaises et de L'Institut Français au Portugal	Clav	Clavileño
		CMLR	Canadian Modern Language Review
BFE	Boletín de Filología Española	Col.	Colección, Collection
BH	Bulletin Hispanique	CSIC	Consejo Superior de Investigaciones Científicas
BHR	Bibliothèque d'Humanisme et Renaissance		
		Cuad.	Cuadernos
BHS	Bulletin of Hispanic Studies (until 1948: Bulletin of Spanish Studies)	Cuad. Hisp.	Cuadernos Hispanoamericanos
		DA	Dissertation Abstracts

Dept.	Department	LM	Letterature Moderne
Diss.	Dissertation	LR	Les Lettres Romanes
Doct.	Doctoral	M.-B.	Morley-Bruerton
EAm	Estudios Americanos	MLA	Modern Language Association of America
Ed(s).	Edición(es), edited (by), edition(s), editor(s)	MLF	Modern Language Forum
Edit.	Editorial(es)	MLJ	Modern Language Journal
Fac.	Faculdade, Facultad, Faculty	MLN	Modern Language Notes
		MLQ	Modern Language Quarterly
FiR	Filologia Romanza	MLR	Modern Language Review
FMLS	Forum for Modern Language Studies	MP	Modern Philology
FMod	Filología Moderna	Nac.	Nacional
Govt.	Government	N.d.	No date
GSLI	Giornale Storico della Letteratura Italiana	NL	Les Nouvelles Littéraires
		No.	Number, número
HAHR	Hispanic American Historical Review	n.s.	new series
		NRF	Nouvelle Revue Française
Hisp	Hispania	NRFH	Nueva Revista de Filología Hispánica
Hispanó	Hispanófila		
Hist.	Histoire, Historia, History	NS	Die neueren Sprachen
		O.s.	Old style
HR	Hispanic Review	PMLA	Publications of the Modern Language Association of America
Imp.	Imprenta		
Inst.	Institute, Instituto		
Internac.	Internacional,	PQ	Philological Quarterly
Internat.	International	PSA	Papeles de Son Armadans
Introd.	Introducción, Introduction	Pseud.	Pseudonym
		Pub(s).	Publicación(es), publication(s) (of), published (by), publisher, publishing
KFLQ	Kentucky Foreign Language Quarterly		
Lang(s).	Language(s)		
LanM	Les Langues Modernes	PULC	Princeton University Library Chronicle
Lit(s).	Literario(s), literatura(s), literature(s)	QQ	Queen's Quarterly

RAE	Real Academia Española	RLR	Revue des Langues Romanes
RBFilol	Revista Brasileira de Filologia	RNC	Revista Nacional de Cultura (Caracas)
RBN	Revista de Bibliografía Nacional	RomN	Romance Notes
		RPh	Romance Philology
RBPH	Revue Belge de Philologie et d'Histoire	RR	Romanic Review
		RUBA	Revista de la Universidad de Buenos Aires
Repub(s).	Republication(s), republished (by)	SFr	Studi Francesi
Rev.	Review(s), Revista, Revue	Soc.	Sociedad, Society
		SP	Studies in Philology
RF	Romanische Forschungen	TAE	Teatro Antiguo Español
RFE	Revista de Filología Española	TDR	Tulane Drama Review
RFH	Revista de Filología Hispánica	TLS	Times Literary Supplement
		Trans.	Translated (by), translation, translator
RH	Revue Hispanique	UCPMP	University of California Publications in Modern Philology
RHM	Revista Hispánica Moderna		
RIE	Revista de Ideas Estéticas	Univ.	Universidad(e), University
RJ	Romanistisches Jahrbuch	Unpub.	Unpublished
		Vol(s).	Volume(s)
RL	Revista de Literatura	VR	Vox Romanica
RLC	Revue de Littérature Comparée	ZRP	Zeitschrift für romanische Philologie
RLMC	Rivista di Letterature Moderne e Comparate		

THE YEARS 1951-1969

Critical Survey

1951-1952

Critical and interpretive works constituted a majority of the publications on Calderón for 1951-1952, and included a number of extremely provocative and interesting items. A. L. Constandse, in Le Baroque espagnol et Calderón de la Barca, employed psychological analysis and comparisons with non-literary art forms to enhance his consideration of Calderón's pre-eminence in the Baroque. Everett W. Hesse pointed out convincing biographic and artistic parallelisms between Calderón and Velázquez (Clav, 2, No. 10, 1-10, and Hisp, 35, 74-82). Dámaso Alonso, in the Alonso-Bousoño Seis calas en la expresión literaria española, extended the field of his investigation of correlation to include dramatic art, and concluded that correlation is one of the most characteristic traits of the dramaturgy of Calderón. Edward M. Wilson, in "Gerald Brenan's Calderón" (BCom, 4, No. 1, 6-8), while challenging Brenan's division of Calderón's plays into two chronological groups, convincingly suggested a radical shift in the traditional interpretation of the secret-vengeance plays. Lorenzo Giusso, in Spagna ed Antispagna (pp. 7-19), viewed Calderón's allegory as the poet's method of taking refuge in Biblical prophecy and story in order to avoid describing the sad plight of Spain in her decline. In his short article, "The Calderonian gracioso and Marriage" (BCom, 3, No. 2, 2-3), Harry W. Hilborn pointed out the contrasting attitudes of Calderón's and Lope de Vega's graciosos on the subject of women and marriage.

In the area of biographical studies, interesting documentation on the famous Barca, which became incorporated in the compound patronymic of Calderón's family line, was provided by Constancio Eguía Ruiz, in Cervantes, Calderón, Lope, Gracián. An article by Narciso Alonso Cortés, "Genealogía de D. Pedro Calderón" (BRAE, 31, 299-309), established the paternal line of the poet through seven preceding generations and, in so doing, claimed to have refuted three major theories held by genealogists of Calderón.

On Calderón's _autos_, the most extensive work in this two-year period was that of Eugenio Frutos Cortés, who in an article, "La filosofía del barroco y el pensamiento de Calderón" (RUBA, 9, 173-230), and in the book into which the article was later incorporated, La filosofía de Calderón en sus autos sacramentales, concluded that Calderón is most representative of the Baroque, and therefore an excellent source of documentation on such basic philosophical themes as man, the world, and God. Among four other articles on the autos, two of which were anonymous, Angel Valbuena Prat, in "Los autos calderonianos en el ambiente teológico español" (Clav, 3, No. 15, 33-35), suggested possible doctrinal sources for Calderón's autos.

Max Oppenheimer, Jr., proposed a clarification of chronological order, filiation, and authenticity of the various printings of Volume II of the nine-volume Vera Tassis edition in "A Spurious Edition of the Segunda Parte of the Vera Tassis Edition of Calderón's Comedias" (HR, 19, 346-52). Ada M. Coe's "Unas colecciones de comedias sueltas de Pedro Calderón de la Barca comparadas con Literatur, eine bibliographisch-kritische Übersicht, de Hermann Breymann (München, 1905)," which appeared first in Supplement A, BCom, 2, No. 2, 1950, was reprinted (Estudios, 7, No. 19, 111-69).

The most significant publication in the area of editions was Angel Valbuena Prat's contribution to the Aguilar collection in the form of his edition of seventy-eight Autos sacramentales. In the same collection there appeared Astrana Marín's third edition of Dramas. Two other third editions appeared, in the Clásicos Castellanos series, both editions being of autos and by Valbuena Prat. No critical edition appeared during this period, although there was a book of prose adaptations of three plays, another popular edition of four plays, and editions of single plays by André Nogué and Herbert Koch.

Significant articles on individual works by Calderón were numerous. The philosophical dimensions of La vida es sueño received treatment·from M. F. Sciacca (Humanitas, 6, 472-85) and from L. E. Palacios (Laval Théologique et Philosophique, 7, 123-49). The play was also analysed by an application of categories formulated for the plastic arts by Darnell H. Roaten, first in his doctoral dissertation (Univ. of Michigan, 1951) and then in collaboration with F. Sánchez y Escribano, in Wölfflin's Principles in Spanish Drama. A reprint of an article on the same play by Alfonso Reyes also appeared (Col. Austral, 1020). In addition to articles by Federica de Ritter on El gran teatro del mundo (RNC, 14, 133-53) and by Everett W. Hesse on El mayor monstruo del mundo (Estudios, 8, 395-409), Edward M. Wilson, in his study of A secreto agravio, secreta venganza

(Clav, 2, No. 9, 1-10), presented another aspect of his revision of the traditional interpretation of the secret-vengeance plays, also a concern in his above-mentioned review of Brenan.

Reviews of A. E. Sloman's first book, published prior to our period (The Sources of Calderón's "El príncipe constante"..., Oxford, 1950), heralded the appearance of a truly distinguished Calderonian scholar. Sloman brought out three articles which fall within the limits of our period, two of which convincingly refute charges of plagiary levelled at Calderón in connection with La selva confusa (HR, 20, 134-48) and El mágico prodigioso (HR, 20, 212-22) by H. C. Heaton (PMLA, 44, 243-73; and HR, 19, 11-36, 93-103).

Tangentially, Angel Valbuena Prat, in two articles (Clav, 2, No. 7, 79; Clav, 2, No. 12, 38-40), singled out for praise the contributions to Calderón studies made by Entwistle, Hesse, Oppenheimer, A. A. Parker, Sloman, Wardropper, and Wilson.

José Ayllón (Insula, 7, No. 75, 12) echoed the sentiments of all lovers of the Spanish Golden Age in lamenting the drastically insufficient support given by theatrical companies and the public to the presentation of Spain's classical theatre.

1953-1954

The period 1953-1954 brought forth editions of Calderón from several countries. For example, in Spain, Angel Valbuena Prat published Comedias religiosas and Angel Valbuena Briones his second volume of Comedias de capa y espada in the Clásicos Castellanos series. In addition, the Nicolás González Ruiz Piezas maestras del teatro teológico español was reprinted, in its two volumes, which contain fifteen well-known autos sacramentales and four important comedias religiosas. In Chile, Juan Loveluck included El gran teatro del mundo in a volume of autos by Lope de Vega, Calderón, et al. For Tulane University, New Orleans, William A. Hunter completed his doctoral dissertation: an edition and translation of a Nahuatl version of El gran teatro del mundo (subsequently published). In French translation, there appeared in Paris La Dévotion à la Croix (in a version by Albert Camus) and L'Alcalde de Zalamea (in a version by A. A. Arnoux); in Italian, there appeared in Rome La vita è un sogno (in a version by A. Monteverdi); and in German, in Leipzig, Der Richter von Zalamea (in a version by J. D. Gries).

Roaten and Sánchez y Escribano had published their Wölfflin's Principles in 1952, and the years 1953 and 1954 saw several reviews of the monograph. Alexander A. Parker's very important review article "Reflections on a New Definition of Baroque Drama" (BHS, 30, 142-51) rejects the validity of the application made by Roaten and Sánchez y Escribano of Wölfflin's principles of Baroque art to Baroque drama. For Parker, the unity of La vida es sueño, for instance, is essentially conceptual, and the complex structure that embodies it is strictly logical, not in terms of plot but of unified moral theme, which of its nature cannot be laid bare by the "categories" of formal construction. Wölfflin's principles — concludes Parker — are of no aid to drama, since "drama, because it deals with human acts, manipulates moral values and judgments, thus possessing a dimension in which Wölfflin's principles of plastic art cannot move and to the understanding of which they can offer no clue." Everett W. Hesse was more favourable in his review, seeing in the monograph a very valuable contribution toward an effort to understand and appreciate plot technique in the comedia. From the several reviews, it is clear that the Roaten and Sánchez y Escribano book stimulated discussion through having studied the comedia as a Baroque manifestation.

A high point in our two-year period was Bruce W. Wardropper's Introducción al teatro religioso del Siglo de Oro (La evolución del auto sacramental: 1500-1648). Wardropper gives a complete introduction to the auto, and considers Calderón to be the most intellectual of all auto writers. He reaffirms Bataillon's idea that the auto sacramental is a phenomenon of the Catholic Reformation and not of the Counter-Reformation. Wardropper's volume, even during 1953-1954, was the recipient of many immediate enthusiastic reviews.

Among the other rich offerings of the 1953-1954 period, the Boston Public Library Quarterly (6, 190-91) reproduced a letter (written on April 21, 1875) by James Russell Lowell, in which the American poet-critic advocated the reading of Calderón's plays. Lester G. Crocker dealt exhaustively with Segismundo's final solution of the problem of reality in contrast with the cases of Hamlet and Don Quixote (PMLA, 69, 278-313). La vida es sueño likewise received the attention of Everett W. Hesse (Clav, 4, No. 20, 4-12) and William M. Whitby (in his Yale doctoral dissertation). The structure of La vida es sueño was the subject of a key article by Albert E. Sloman (MLR, 48, 293-300).

Cioranescu's "Calderón y el teatro clásico francés" (in his Estudios de literatura española y comparada) was considered by Joaquín de Entrambasaguas to be the most complete and best written study thus far on the topic; and Eugenio Frutos' La filosofía de Calderón en sus autos sacramentales (of 1952) was designated by Angel Valbuena Prat in his review (Clav, 4, No.

22, 77-78) as "una importantísima aportación al tema a la vez
doctrinal y estético que encarna en el género 'sacramental' de
Calderón." Carlos Ortigoza's <u>Los móviles de la Comedia en Lope,
Alarcón, Tirso, Moreto, Rojas, Calderón</u> was published in Mexico
City, and was the first of the author's two monographs on his
<u>móviles</u> theory.

Angel Valbuena Prat (in "A los veinticinco años de la vuelta
a Calderón," <u>Revista</u>, 3, No. 96, 7) looked back to the year
1927, and was pleased to note that Calderón <u>desiderata</u> mentioned at that time had been underway, in the hands of several
<u>Calderonistas</u>, in a fruitful manner. This brief article in a
Barcelona periodical gives a quick synopsis of important work
done on Calderón between 1927 and 1953, and offers encouragement for future studies of the dramatist and his works.

In retrospect, the two-year period 1953-1954 was a good one
for Calderón.

1955-1956

Except for doctoral dissertations, the years 1955-1956 were
fruitful for Calderonian scholarship. It appears that the only
doctoral thesis recorded for these years was produced in
England at Oxford University, namely, <u>The Code of Honour in
the Spanish Golden Age Drama, with Special Reference to
Calderón</u>, by C. A. Jones. In a by-product of this thesis, Jones
gave particular attention to the two types of honour to be
found in <u>El alcalde de Zalamea</u> (<u>MLR</u>, 50, 444-49).

Outside of the perpetual theme of honour, attention was paid
to the establishing of authentic texts, to dramatic structure,
to sources and influences, to women dressed as men, to the use
of historical material, to Calderonian psychology, to Calderón's
religious concepts, to his use of classical mythology, to his
Baroque style, to performances of his plays in the colonies, to
humour (as expressed in the <u>gracioso</u> and as shown in the <u>autos
sacramentales</u>), to the influence of Segismundo, and to the influence of Calderón on Schiller and other German writers. Particularly conspicuous was interest in the manner in which
Calderón embodies and dramatizes religious dogma. Attention to
minutiae was confined mainly to the collation of manuscripts
and early editions for the purpose of providing reliable texts.

A number of valuable editions were produced in these years.
On the basis of the partly holographic manuscript in the
Biblioteca Nacional, Hesse published a critical edition of <u>El
mayor monstro los çelos</u>. He recorded variants in the text of

the four editions of the play, and described or listed nineteen other editions. Valbuena Briones brought out two more editions of Calderón's plays, his Dramas de honor (A secreto agravio, secreta venganza; El médico de su honra; El pintor de su deshonra) and Volume II (Comedias) of Calderón's Obras completas, which contains 52 plays with commentaries. Less scholarly editions of 1955-1956 were: El alcalde de Zalamea y dos entremeses (El dragoncillo; La rabia), by Durán Cerda; La vida es sueño, El alcalde de Zalamea, El mágico prodigioso and El príncipe constante, by Bergua; and La vida es sueño and El alcalde de Zalamea, by Cortina. Also, a prose translation into French, by Alexandre Arnoux, of Trois comédies (La vida es sueño, El médico de su honra, and El alcalde de Zalamea), was published in Paris.

While Wardropper's Introducción al teatro religioso del Siglo de Oro was published in 1953, four detailed reviews of this important book appeared in 1955: by A. A. Parker (BHS, 32, 49-51), Beatrice P. Patt (HR, 23, 68-73), Edward Sarmiento (MLR, 50, 223-24), and José Montero Padilla (RFE, 39, 365-68). While dramatized religion in Calderón is a topic concerning which incontrovertible conclusions are extremely elusive, the reviews, as well as the book itself, suggested that cultivation of this field was well under way. Hesse's critical edition of El mayor monstro los çelos, already mentioned, did more than establish the text of the play. One important component was the study of plot structure, treated not only in the introduction, but also in a supplementary article, "El arte calderoniano en El mayor monstruo los celos" (Clav, 7, No. 38, 18-30). This study also provided a valuable guide to an understanding of the Baroque dramatic pattern. Hesse's observations concerning psychological struggles portrayed in the play are highly pertinent.

Extending beyond the study of Baroque structure of a single play was Dámaso Alonso's reprinting of "La correlación en la estructura del teatro calderoniano," included in Seis calas en la expresión literaria española (2nd ed., 1956). Here we are given an analysis of Calderón's practice in his plot patterns. Reviews of Constandse, Le Baroque espagnol et Calderón de la Barca, of 1951 (Aubrun, BH, 57, 463-65; Wardropper, HR, 23, 140-43), maintained that, while some startling insights were presented, in general Constandse's Freudian approach fell short of carrying conviction. Another interesting contribution was that of Gallego Morell, who included in his treatment of the Phaeton theme Calderón's use of the myth in El hijo del sol, Faetón and in Apolo y Climene (Clav, 7, No. 37, 13-26; No. 38, 31-43).

The bibliography for Calderonian scholarship in 1955-1956 includes over forty studies or editions. Besides the contributors
mentioned, Bertrand, Bravo-Villasante, Farinelli, Fradejas
Lebrero, Fucilla, Groult, Leavitt, Ley, Mancini, May, Pagés
Larraya, Pietschmann, Rossi, Sage, Shergold, and Sloman, among
others, all merit recognition for their discoveries or hypothe-
ses concerning the work of this fascinating genius. Although
only a few of the studies of the period were of major propor-
tions, interest in Calderón was clearly wide-spread.

1957-1958

The years 1957 and 1958 were rich in Calderonian studies and
bibliographical items, with over 120 entries. The extremely
valuable article by Hans Flasche compels us to begin our survey
with his comprehensive and challenging "Stand und Aufgaben der
Calderónforschung" (Deutsche Vierteljahrsschrift für Literaturwissenschaft und Geistesgeschichte, 32, 613-43). Flasche ren-
dered an invaluable service to Calderón studies by making a
critical review of everything of significance which had
appeared on Calderón from 1940 to 1958, outlining desiderata
regarding aspects and problems requiring further study.
   As for books on Calderón, Ortigoza contributed Los móviles de
la comedia, applied to El príncipe constante, and Sloman The
Dramatic Craftsmanship of Calderón: His Use of Earlier Plays.
Ortigoza states that Calderón based his dramatic technique for
character building on action. Since character is manifested by
action, the author suggests that in order to appreciate the
comedia from within it is essential to penetrate the móviles
which generate the action. The moving springs of the character's
action are easily comprehended as the backbone of the action
but not easy to express as different from the action. La comedia, the author concludes, es la comedia española, meaning that
it is only equal to itself, that it is unique and cannot be
evaluated from points of view foreign to the comedia. With this
as a premise, he follows the protagonist's móviles throughout
the play, verse by verse. This approach to the comedia inspired
Arnold G. Reichenberger to write two masterly review articles
about the móviles theory and the uniqueness of the comedia.
Sloman's book contributed a solid step towards the understanding of Calderón's dramatic art. Using the known sources of
eight Calderón plays, Sloman made a minute comparison between
the early comedias (three of which were written by Calderón
himself in collaboration with others) and the later Calderón

plays; in each case Calderón created a new comedia where we can
clearly observe Calderón's preoccupation with the unity of
theme which ties the play together. Sloman also pointed out
that every action is motivated and there is a concern for unity
of time and place. His careful comparison shows that Calderón
recast new plays from his sources. A third book in this period
was the small volume published by Valbuena Briones entitled
Ensayo sobre la obra de Calderón. Of special interest are his
remarks on "la palabra" and "el demonio y las estrellas."

Although only partly dealing with Calderón, two important
contributions were a large volume by Cioranescu and a small
book by Alexander A. Parker. The first author published his El
barroco o el descubrimiento del drama in 1957. In Cioranescu's
opinion "poco le falta a la teología de Calderón para que la
pudiésemos calificar de jansenista." In spite of this and other
controversial issues, his book throws light on Calderón's Baroque style and dramatic technique. Professor Parker's The
Approach to the Spanish Drama of the Golden Age is an outstanding essay, presenting a novel interpretation. He states that
the plot is the primary thing, and goes on to say that "We can
judge the action in its own right and see what it has to offer
in terms of human values."

Two individual plays, El príncipe constante and El médico de
su honra, received special attention in three important essays.
In 1958 Wardropper contributed two outstanding articles, one
for each of these plays (MLR, 53, 512-20 and RR, 49, 3-11).
Kayser published his essay on the structure of El príncipe
constante, digging deeply into Calderón's dramatic technique.
Of less significance are Anderson Imbert's essay on La vida es
sueño and Capelleti's remarks on the same play. Sloman also
contributed a note of reaction to a previous treatment of El
médico and La amiga de Bernal Francés (BHS, 34, 168-69). As for
textual readings, E. M. Wilson provided the basis for what
could be the definitive text of A secreto agravio, secreta venganza (BHS, 35, 72-82).

The comparative field was also very active. Outstanding among
the contributions was J. Jacquot's "Le Théâtre du monde de
Shakespeare à Calderón" (RLC, 31, 341-72). Of less value were
J. B. Dalbor's "La dama duende, de Calderón, y The Parson's
Wedding, de Killigrew" (Hispanó, No. 2, 41-50) and A. Sánchez's
"Reminiscencias cervantinas en el teatro de Calderón" (Anales
Cervantinos, 6, 262-70). The influence and criticism of Calderón
in Germany occupied J. Wilhelm in an essay intended for the
general public, and of general interest, too, was G. Laplane's
"Calderón et l'Espagne" (Revue de Paris, No. 5, 98-109). How-
ever, special attention should be given to W. Brüggemann's

scholarly article, "Romantisches in Calderóns 'comedia mito-lógica' Eco y Narciso" (in Gesammelte Aufsätze zur Kultur-geschichte Spaniens, 13, 239-58), while some interesting com-parisons are found in Piñera Llera's "¿Descartes en Calderón?" (La Torre, 6, 145-65).

In the special field of the motif of honour, C. A. Jones published "Honor in Spanish Golden-Age Drama" (BHS, 35, 199-210), of which parts are very valuable. There were several important articles in which Calderón was dealt with, but not as the main subject, as for example, Helmut Hatzfeld (Hisp, 40, 261-69). Concerning a Nahuatl translation of El gran teatro del mundo (17th century), Olmedilla and Hunter wrote illuminating notes (in Hist. Mexicana, 7, 237-38 and KFLQ, 5, 26-34, respec-tively).

There were a number of reissues of Calderón's comedias and autos. The only new critical edition was Johanna Schrek's El sitio de Bredá. The frequent reissues of Calderón's works in Austral, Clásicos Castellanos, Ebro, etc., attest to Calderón's popularity. There were also a number of translations. Three autos sacramentales were translated into French by Mathilde Pomès, and La vida es sueño was translated into Elizabethan iambic pentameter by Colford.

Calderón's autos sacramentales and his religious dramas also were given attention by Jeanne Hamelin in her Théâtre chrétien, but the outstanding contribution in the field of autos belongs to Jorge Páramo Pomareda's excellent scholarly study restricted to the "autos mitológicos" (Thesaurus, 12, 51-80). Special note should be made of the reprint of the valuable edition and study of Valbuena Prat in the two volumes of the Clásicos Castellanos (Nos. 69 and 74). D. Taylor and S. Bartina also studied autos; but the most important contribution in this field generally is A. A. Parker's The Theology of the Devil in the Drama of Calde-rón, in which the author studies from the theological viewpoint the Devil as a character on the stage in an early auto and a late one as well as in a religious comedia.

Three articles were published on Calderón's performances. Of top stature is Shergold's "The First Performance of Calderón's El mayor encanto amor" (BHS, 35, 24-27). Of lesser value are Pietschmann's article on German performances (Maske und Kothurn, 3, 317-39) and Pérez Vila's on Venezuelan performances (RNC, No. 127, 95-104).

Lyric poetry was represented by the painstaking contribution of Harry W. Hilborn on culto vocabulary (HR, 26, 223-33), and by Entrambasaguas' publishing of two little-known décimas by Calderón. In Blecua's anthology, however, Calderón is poorly represented.

In the field of reviews there were some outstanding ones like
the review article by Reichenberger on Ortigoza mentioned at
the beginning of this survey. Besides Reichenberger's, Ortigoza's book received a thorough review from J. Brooks (Hisp, 41,
251-52), and Sloman's book received careful consideration from
E. W. Hesse (Hisp, 42, 287-88), E. M. Wilson (MLR, 55, 124-25),
and other important critics noted in this critical bibliography.
Among the books on Calderón of previous years, Hesse's edition
of El mayor monstro received praise in reviews by Crosland
(MLR, 52, 142), Valbuena Briones (Arbor, 38, 326-28), and
Flecniakoska (BH, 59, 344-45). Friedrich's Der fremde Calderón
received the attention of Porqueras-Mayo (RFE, 41, 441-43) and
F. Schürr (RJ, 7, 377-78). Valbuena Briones' edition of Calde-
rón's Obras completas (Aguilar, II) was warmly welcomed by
Sloman (BHS, 35, 180-81). Schrek's edition of El sitio de Bredá
was the subject of a review article by E. M. Wilson (BHS, 34,
227-29), who also gave the same careful attention to Valbuena
Briones' Dramas de honor (BHS, 34, 227-29). A. Rumeau (BH, 69,
472) and P. Groult (LR, 12, 194-95) reviewed Cirot and Darbord's
Littérature espagnole européenne. J. Bourciez (RLR, 72, 380-81)
praised M. Pomès' translation of the autos sacramentales.
Cioranescu's book was reviewed with high acclaim by M. Palomo
(RL, 11, 207-08), and Montero Padilla reviewed D. Poyán's Ame
et esprit du théâtre espagnol (RL, 11, 231-32), but Cesco
Vian's Il teatro "chico" spagnolo received a negative review
from Entrambasaguas (RL, 11, 240-41). Among the reviews of
Calderón translations into French prose, A. Arnoux received a
lukewarm review from W. Mettmann (Archiv, 193, 365). A. A.
Parker had no patience with the erroneous appreciation of
Calderón by Gerald Brenan (MLR, 52, 462-63). Finally we
should note that J. H. Parker's Breve historia received favourable reviews from Alvajar (CCLC, No. 33, 109-10), Aubrun (BH,
61, 460-61), Ortigoza (Hisp, 41, 539-40), Sloman (BHS, 36, 241),
and Storni (Universidad, No. 37, 266-67).
  There were no doctoral dissertations dealing exclusively with
Calderón, but Calderón is included among the dramatists who
wrote plays based on the Old Testament in a dissertation by
R. N. Shervill. Minor mention of Calderón occurs in Hermenegildo's published thesis from the University of Madrid, Burgos
en el romancero y en el teatro de los Siglos de Oro.

1959-1960

In this period, Ana María Martín Andrés discussed editions,
translations, and studies of Calderón in France (RL, 17, 53-100),

and Carmelo Samonà contributed a short monograph on Calderón in Italian criticism. Edward M. Wilson continued his always splendid and exemplary textual and bibliographical studies of various documents relating to Calderón. Another leading British scholar, Alexander A. Parker, contributed a penetrating study of the Coriolanus legend in _Las armas de la hermosura_ in the volume dedicated to Professor Ignacio González Llubera.

American scholars such as Edward Glaser, Arnold G. Reichenberger, Leo Spitzer, Bruce W. Wardropper, and William Whitby, continued their fruitful Calderonian scholarship with sensitive, analytical, and suggestive critical studies. In continental Europe, Calderón activity was pursued in several countries; for example, by Werner Krauss, in his article on Calderón as a poet of the Spanish people (_Studien und Aufsätze_, Berlin, 1959).

1961-1962

In textual work, noteworthy in this two-year period is the splendid number of Calderón translations into several European languages. "Una sólida y elogiosa contribución," in the words of Angel Valbuena Briones, is the Edwin Honig version of _Four Plays_ (1961). (This was a translation, into English, of _A secreto agravio, secreta venganza_, _El alcalde de Zalamea_, _La dama duende_, and _La devoción de la Cruz_.) In Moscow, Paris, Bratislava, Stutgart, London, and New York, there appeared these valuable foreign-language texts, in collections, in individual editions, and in adaptations, from the above-mentioned _A secreto agravio_ through the Calderón canon to _La vida es sueño_. The MacCarthy translation of _Six Plays_ was revised by Henry W. Wells, and Angel Flores included Calderón in his Bantam volume of _Spanish Drama_.

Several critical editions came forth, in Spanish, from the world presses: such as Aubrun's _Eco y Narciso_ and _La estatua de Prometeo_, C. A. Jones' _El médico de su honra_, and A. E. Sloman's _La vida es sueño_. Everett W. Hesse published a school edition of _La vida es sueño_ in the same year as Sloman's abovementioned more scholarly one (1961); and Giacomo V. Sabatelli used his previous doctoral dissertation to publish an edition of _La hidalga del valle_ along with _A María el corazón_. Alexander A. Parker's _No hay más fortuna que Dios_ appeared in a second edition; and Gwynne Edwards edited _La hija del aire_, together with a study of the Semiramis legend, for a doctoral thesis (unpublished) at the University of London.

The most extraordinary Calderonian event of recent times was
the discovery of Václav Černý, in Czechoslovakia, of a manuscript of the lost San Francisco de Borja play, El gran duque
de Gandía. Černý announced his important find in a Prague journal (1961), and John J. Reynolds brought to the attention of
the Comediantes in their Bulletin (13, No. 1, 11) the fact that
Černý was promising a critical edition of the play.

Edward M. Wilson devoted much careful attention to Calderón
in this period, producing at least six articles of distinction.
Calderón's experience with the stage censor was the subject of
one "provisional" (and well developed) article in Symposium
(15, 165-84); Wilson commented on an eighteenth-century copy
of a list of Calderón's plays compiled by the dramatist himself
(MP, 60, 95-102); "Further Notes" on autos appeared in HR (30,
296-303); the Tercera Parte was studied by Wilson in Studies in
Bibliography (15, 223-30); the authorship of a ballad (by
Calderón?) was discussed in the Anuario de Letras (2, 99-118);
and an early "rehash" of El príncipe constante was noted in
MLN (76, 785-94). Another distinguished Calderonista from Great
Britain, Alexander A. Parker, made a distinct contribution to
scholarship in his "Towards a Definition of Calderonian Tragedy"
(BHS, 39, 222-37), where he suggested that "in the drama of
Calderón it is possible to detect an original, significant and
valid conception of tragedy which has hitherto been overlooked."

In monographs dealing with Calderón and his times, "monumental
and definitive" is the Shergold-Varey study of Los autos sacramentales en Madrid en la época de Calderón, 1637-81; and of
considerable interest is Egon Schwarz's Hofmannsthal und
Calderón. Honour was frequently treated in our period; as, for
example, by Américo Castro in his book on De la edad conflic-
tiva; and by Edwin Honig in his articles on "The Seizures of
Honor in Calderón" (Kenyon Review, 23, 426-47) and "Calderón's
Strange Mercy Play" (Massachusetts Review, 3, 80-107). (The
"Strange Mercy Play" is La devoción de la Cruz.) Joaquín de
Casalduero included his "sentido y forma" of La vida es sueño
in his Estudios sobre el teatro español, a study which had
appeared previously in CCLC, 51, 3-13. Calderón and art was
not neglected (by Eunice Joiner Gates, in PQ, 40, 53-67), nor
astrology in Calderón (Erika Lorenz, in RJ, 12, 265-77), and,
among other studies, Menéndez Pelayo's lack of appreciation of
Baroque drama was "corrected" by Francisco Ayala (Quaderni
Ibero-Americani, 28, 193-202).

All in all, 1961-1962 was a very rich two-year period in
Calderón studies, both in quantity and in quality.

1963-1964

The years 1963-1964 saw the appearance of editions of several
Calderonian texts other than the usual La vida es sueño. Perhaps the most interesting was that of Václav Černý, El gran
duque de Gandía, believed to be Calderón's "lost" play about
San Francisco de Borja, a manuscript copy of which was found
in the library of a Czech castle. Although not accepted as
Calderón's without question, the play not only received a good
and informative edition, but its publication gave origin to no
fewer than five articles during the biennium. Other lesser-
known plays of Calderón to receive editions were La desdicha
de la voz (reproduction of the autograph), Eco y Narciso (a
second edition), No hay burlas con el amor (an edition designed
for production), and La dama duende (in Argentina). One of his
plays, Casa con dos puertas, appeared in an English translation,
or, more accurately, adaptation. Several autos were edited: La
hidalga del valle; A María el corazón; El gran teatro del mundo;
La vida es sueño; La cena del rey Baltasar; Los encantos de la
culpa (two); and Tu prójimo como a ti. One auto appeared in a
Brazilian translation and edition as Os mistérios da missa.
    The most prolific contributor to Calderonian scholarship
during the period was Hans Flasche, with some five articles
covering such topics as a suggested critical edition, syntax,
and Calderón as a paraphraser of hymns of the Middle Ages.
    The lyrical element of Calderón inspired, in addition to the
Flasche study, one by Robert Stevenson (in Américas, 16, 33-35)
on Calderón's La púrpura de la rosa, basis of the first opera
to be performed in the New World (Lima), and a fascinating
compilation, by Edward M. Wilson and Jack Sage, of poesías
líricas adapted by Calderón in some of his plays. Professor
Wilson added further to our store of Calderoniana with three
articles on widely different subjects (in BHS, 40, 176-80; MLR,
59, 583-94; and Homenaje a Dámaso Alonso, 3, 605-18), and C. V.
Aubrun also contributed to the subject of lyricism in Calderón
in his study of the beginnings of the lyric drama in Spain.
    The promise of two studies on the man himself, one by Gonzalo
González Román and the other by Harry Lund, proved disappointing, the former because of its inaccessability and the latter
by its flippant tone and careless printing.
    Most of the contributions of these years were by scholars of
English or Spanish speech, with one small item each in Dutch
(van Dam in De Nieuwe Taalgids, 56, 143-45) and in Russian
(Mikhal'chi in Voprosy Literatury, 8, No. 3, 252-54), a translation into Portuguese, a few studies and two editions in

French, and several, as might be expected, in German. Among the last were a dissertation (by Branscheid, University of Cologne) and a study (by Seidler, Vienna) on the literary relationship between Calderón and Grillparzer; an article, more limited in scope, on that between Calderón and Hofmannsthal (Sofer, in Österreich in Geschichte und Literatur, 7, 472-89); and an extensive study on the influence of the Spanish drama and especially Calderón on the romanticists of Germany (Brüggemann, in his Spanisches Theater und deutsche Romantik).

Studies of a more specialized nature were those of Lionel Abel on "metatheatre," T. E. May on the symbolism of El mágico prodigioso (RR, 54, 95-112), A. Irvine Watson on the rôle of Peter the Cruel in El médico de su honra (RJ, 14, 322-46) and on the neo-Aristotelian theory of tragedy in connection with El pintor de su deshonra (BHS, 40, 17-34), Peter N. Dunn's "Patrimonio del alma" (BHS, 41, 78-85), A. A. Parker's "Metáfora y símbolo" in the interpretation of Calderón (delivered before the First International Congress of Hispanists in 1962), C. A. Soons on the problem of aesthetic judgement in El pintor de su deshonra (RF, 76, 155-62), R. W. Truman on the theme of justice in El príncipe constante (MLR, 59, 43-52), and A. Valbuena Briones on "senecanism" in Calderón's theatre (PSA, 31, 249-70).

More information on staging was presented in studies by J. E. Varey, alone, or with N. D. Shergold: two on the auto sacramental and one on palace performances of seventeenth-century plays. Varey and Shergold also collaborated on establishing the date of Troya abrasada (in Studi Ispanici, No. 6, 287-97) and in presenting an autograph fragment of La vacante general (in Symposium, 17, 165-82).

There was the usual spate of editions and studies of La vida es sueño, a play that seems never to lose its attraction and in which scholars continually find something new. There were three new editions and three reprintings of El alcalde de Zalamea in addition to Dunn's article on the patrimony of the soul.

Three dissertations were devoted to Calderón to varying extent: Robert M. ter Horst on La vida es sueño (The Johns Hopkins); John M. La Prade on Golden Age authors, including Calderón, as characters in nineteenth-century drama, and William R. Manson on attitudes, including Calderón's, toward authority (both of the University of North Carolina).

Of the reviews, four stand out from the general run, all of editions: A. G. Reichenberger's (in RR, 54, 223-25) of Aubrun's Eco y Narciso; Wilson's (in BHS, 41, 191-93) of Ebersole's La desdicha de la voz, and those of Varey (in BHS, 40, 190-94) and

W. M. Whitby (in <u>HR</u>, 31, 278-81) of the Hesse and the Sloman editions of <u>La vida es sueño</u> (both appeared in 1961). Professor Whitby also contributed an enlightening review of Samonà's study of Calderón in Italian criticism, in <u>HR</u>, 32 (1964), 270-73.

In bibliography, the description, by B. B. Ashcom (in <u>BCom</u>, 14, No. 2, 19-20), of the <u>Apontes</u> edition in the Wayne State University Library stands almost alone.

1965-1966

In 1965-1966, the repercussions of the intriguing discovery of <u>El gran duque de Gandía</u> were still being felt, as several articles and reviews of Černý's edition show. Predictably, since this is Calderón, there were a number of studies in German on various matters, notably by Hans Flasche, who added a discussion of the Andromeda-Perseus myth to his exhaustive work on the <u>auto</u> version of <u>La vida es sueño</u>.

Reviews of the Wilson-Sage <u>Poesías líricas</u> help to demonstrate the validity of Bruce Wardropper's statement that British and German Hispanists have been the chief non-Spanish Calderón scholars. This is further borne out by such familiar and respected names as A. A. Parker, Shergold, May, Edwards, Varey, Dunn, Wilson, <u>et al</u>. The United States, however, is not left behind. The chief landmark of 1965 was the volume of <u>Critical Essays on the Theatre of Calderón</u>, edited by Wardropper for the New York University Press. The essays antedate 1965, and presenting them in collected form was a service of incalculable value. Worthily following in the same year was Valbuena Briones' <u>Perspectiva crítica de los dramas de Calderón</u>, by a Spanish scholar transplanted to the United States — a reminder of how much the Valbuena family has done for Calderón studies. Also in the United States, another article by Sturgis E. Leavitt on his favourite play showed once again that he deserves to be Honorary Mayor of Zalamea; and Everett W. Hesse directed an edition to <u>Los cabellos de Absalón</u> (dissertation by H. F. Giacoman). This was a good biennium for editions, including also Aubrun's <u>La estatua de Prometeo</u>, Wexler's <u>La devoción de la Cruz</u>, and Dunn's <u>El alcalde de Zalamea</u>. Another treatment of an individual play — the Teatro Español's adaptation of <u>La dama duende</u> — elicited considerable comment, most of it favourable.

It was no surprise to find Calderón's honour plays widely discussed, as in articles by Edwin Honig, T. E. May, Daniel

Rogers, and Amy Sparks. The autos, already mentioned in connection with Flasche's works, came in for their share of attention elsewhere, with articles on such autos as Sueños hay que verdad son and Tu prójimo como a ti, plus the general discussion by Lacosta.

The year 1966 was very important for the publication of Warren T. McCready's Bibliografía temática de estudios sobre el teatro español antiguo, which covered Calderón (and other dramatists) for the 1850-1950 period. The Research Committee's decision to begin our Calderón bibliography in 1951 was due to the years treated, very successfully, by McCready.

The year 1966 also brought with it another announcement by Černý: his second discovery of a Calderón play, No hay que creer ni en la verdad (published in 1968 by CSIC, Madrid).

It is apparent, then, that 1965-1966 afforded a well-balanced diet of approaches, critical and not-so-critical, to the study of Lope de Vega's most brilliant successor.

1967

The year 1967 produced a work of extreme importance for our Calderón studies: José Simón Díaz's Bibliografía de la literatura hispánica, Tomo VII (Autores: Continuación) ("Caballar" to the beginning of "Cervantes"). Items 524 to 3427 are devoted to Calderón, and contain a wealth of bibliographical information. Dr. Simón Díaz is to be congratulated on his successful presentation of data of high significance.

La vida es sueño, so frequently treated throughout the years, continued to draw the attention of several scholars: Rafael de Balbín, who compared lines 1512-17 with Bécquer's Rima XXXII (Atlántida, 5, 365-70); Margaret S. Maurin, who studied related patterns of imagery (HR, 35, 161-78); and Cesáreo Bandera, who interpreted Segismundo's "itinerario" (HR, 35, 69-84). C. V. Aubrun dealt with the dramatic technique used in El sitio de Bredá, and S. A. Vosters studied the same play in his article on "La rendición de Bredá en la literatura española." Aubrun also dedicated some pages to "la télévision magique" in El jardín de Falerina.

Calling the play possibly "Calderón's most moving expression of man's tragic predicament," Gwynne Edwards analysed La hija del aire in relation to the Classical type of tragedy (BHS, 44, 161-94); and Horst Ochse studied the same play in his Studien zur Metaphorik Calderóns. David W. Foster contributed to the study of La torre de Babilonia by connecting the medieval allegory and Calderón's Baroque drama (<u>Criticism</u>, 9, 142-54), and José Subirá related literature and music in <u>Celos aun del aire matan</u> (<u>Anuario Musical</u>, 20, 59-73). The martyr plays were dealt with by Elida Maria Szarota in her monograph on European martyr dramas of the seventeenth century. Slavic themes in Calderón formed the substance of N. J. Balasov's fourteen-page article in a Moscow journal (<u>Izvestija Akademii Nauk</u>, 26, 227-40).

Alan S. Trueblood devoted an important review article to Hatzfeld's <u>Estudios sobre el barroco</u> (Madrid, 1964), in <u>HR</u>, 35, 355-63; and in the <u>In memoriam</u> to Jean Sarrailh, Arturo Serrano Plaja related the absurd in Calderón to the twentieth-century Camus (Vol. II, 389-405). The <u>Actas</u> of the Second Congress of the International Association of Hispanists included E. M. Wilson's "Controversias teatrales: 1650-1681," Angel Valbuena Briones' analysis of "sol" in Calderón, and Wardropper's discussion of "responsabilidad" in the <u>capa y espada</u> plays. It is also very worth while to note that Wardropper's <u>Introducción al teatro religioso del Siglo de Oro</u> was reprinted by Anaya in 1967; and that among other studies there were those of Louis C. Pérez on "preceptiva dramática" in <u>El gran teatro del mundo</u> (<u>Hispanó</u>, 30, 1-6), of Juan Bautista Avalle-Arce on the "cantar" in <u>La niña de Gómez Arias</u> (<u>BHS</u>, 44, 43-58), and of H. Kern on "Ludwig Tiecks Calderonismus" (<u>Gesammelte Aufsätze zur Kulturgeschichte Spaniens</u>, 23, 189-356).

During 1967 E. M. Wilson's significant Taylorian Lecture of May 18, 1966 (which included a consideration of sources of <u>El médico de su honra</u>) was published in Oxford by the Clarendon Press; and Everett W. Hesse's valuable short monograph on the life and works of Calderón de la Barca came forth from Twayne Publishers, New York, in a World Authors Series. For stagecraft, N. D. Shergold's <u>History of the Spanish Stage</u>, of this same year, brought us "an authoritative and indispensable work."

<u>1968</u>

Calderonian scholarship in 1968, although wide in scope, centred primarily on two plays: <u>El alcalde de Zalamea</u> and <u>La vida es sueño</u>. Isasi Angulo prepared an annotated edition of <u>El alcalde de Zalamea</u>, <u>La vida es sueño</u>, and <u>El gran teatro del mundo</u>; Luisa Orioli edited <u>La vita è sogno: Il dramma e l'auto sacramental</u>; and Leonard Mades, in revising Alpern and Martel's <u>Diez comedias del Siglo de Oro</u>, reprinted <u>La vida es</u>

sueño. Ruiz Ramón included in Tragedias: Tomo II, A secreto
agravio, secreta venganza, El médico de su honra, and El pintor
de su deshonra, and Václav Černý edited the recently-discovered
No hay que creer ni en la verdad. Helmy Fuad Giacoman published
his edition and study of Los cabellos de Absalón as No. 9 of
Estudios de Hispanófila. Among translations was the Raine-Nadal
Life Is a Dream. Three unpublished doctoral dissertations,
Weiner's The Spanish Golden Age Theater in Tsarist Russia:
1672-1917, Podol's The Evolution of the Honor Theme in Modern
Spanish Literature, and Gitlitz's The Jew in the Comedia of the
Golden Age, contain critical commentary on a number of Calde-
rón's plays.

Among the major critical works, Hesse's Análisis e interpretación de la Comedia was a high point of the year. It includes
a detailed study of Eco y Narciso and a perceptive essay on
"La reeducación de Segismundo y Basilio." Bodini's book, Segni
e simboli nella "Vida es sueño", contains a detailed analysis
of the play, but unfortunately lacks both an introduction and
a bibliography.

The articles included scholarship on a broad range of topics.
Those dealing with Calderón and his relationship to the arts
were Varey's "Calderón, Cosme Lotti, Velázquez, and the Madrid
Festivities of 1636-1637" (Renaissance Drama, n.s., 1, 253-82)
and Pollin's "Calderón's Falerina and Music" (Music and Letters,
49, 317-28). Grotowski's production of El príncipe constante
was treated in Sipario, 13, 11-13, and in Ouaknine's "Alrededor
de El príncipe constante por Grotowski" (Primer Acto, No. 95,
28-43). Hans Flasche made a notable contribution to Calderonian
scholarship in this year in his two articles and in editing a
Festschrift which included several well written essays by British scholars. Wilson's "La poesía dramática de don Pedro Calderón de la Barca" (pp. 487-500) and Pring-Mill's "Los calderonistas de habla inglesa y La vida es sueño: Métodos del
análisis temático-estructural" (pp. 369-413) are both worth-
while studies. The outstanding article in this distinguished
collection, A. A. Parker's "The Rôle of the Graciosos in El
mágico prodigioso" (pp. 317-30), is highly perceptive in its
analysis of the play and proves to be the most profound article
of the year. Other noteworthy studies were Hall's "Segismundo
and the Rebel Soldier" (BHS, 65, 189-200), Casanova's examination of El alcalde de Zalamea (Hispanó, 11, 17-33), and Cilveti's
"Silologismo, correlación e imagen poética en el teatro de
Calderón" (RF, 80, 459-97).

Two works of special interest were the welcome reprint of A.
A. Parker's The Allegorical Drama of Calderón: An Introduction
to the Autos Sacramentales, probably the most valuable work of

scholarship ever written on the dramatist, and Gerald E. Wade's persuasive review article on the controversial Fernández edition of <u>Tan largo me lo fiáis</u> (<u>BCom</u>, 20, 31-41).

Although much praiseworthy scholarship on Calderón was published in 1968, it was evident that work remained to be done, especially on plays other than <u>La vida es sueño</u> and <u>El alcalde de Zalamea</u>.

1969

The year 1969 brought forth some very significant monographs on the <u>comedia</u> in general and with reference to Calderón in particular. Othón Arróniz's <u>Influencia italiana en el nacimiento de la comedia española</u> naturally deals above all with the pre-Calderón period and pre-Calderón matters, but the contribution to stagecraft of Cosimo Lotti and his assistance to Calderón at the Court of Felipe IV is made very clear by this historian of the drama. Otis H. Green's third volume of the important <u>Spain and the Western Tradition</u> came forth in the translation of Cecilio Sánchez Gil (<u>España y la tradición occidental: El espíritu castellano en la literatura desde "El Cid" hasta Calderón</u>). Margaret Wilson, with rare skill of synthesis and interpretation, brought forth her compact <u>Spanish Drama of the Golden Age</u>, in which she paid due attention and tribute to Calderón. This little manual of a general, popular nature, will serve its purpose very well, in giving a good account of the <u>Siglo de Oro</u> in theatre to an English-reading public. At the same time, in <u>BHS</u> (46, 163-64), Miss Wilson, with knowledgeable understanding, reviewed Everett W. Hesse's <u>Calderón</u> of 1967.

For Calderón and the Baroque, Casalduero found in the movement "una preocupación obsesionante metafísico-moral" (in the Porqueras-Mayo and Rojas volume in honour of Professor Federico Sánchez Escribano). Emilio Orozco Díaz, in a two hundred and fifty page monograph on <u>El teatro y la teatralidad del Barroco</u>, studied, above all, "el sentido teatral que se impone en las artes y, en general, en todas las manifestaciones de la vida de la época." This, it is apparent, is a detailed consideration of the theatrical in the life of the Golden Age, rather than one of drama on stage. For the Baroque theme still, Guillermo de Torre revised some of his essays, written "hace más de veinte años," for <u>Del 98 al barroco</u>; and Benito Brancaforte studied aesthetic theory in "Croce on Lope and Calderón" (<u>Symposium</u>, 23, 101-15). The Dinko Cvitanovic edition of essays on "el sueño" delved into "el barroco español," and, for Calderón, naturally concerned itself a great deal with La vida es sueño.

Elias L. Rivers, in reviewing Bruce W. Wardropper's contribution to Modern Literature, stressed (in MLN, 84, 335-36) the significance and importance of this Calderonista's work in various aspects of American Hispanism. This justified and overdue tribute is similar to that offered by R. D. F. Pring-Mill in his "Los calderonistas de habla inglesa y La vida es sueño" (1968).

In the twentieth century's days of feminist revolt, it is of interest to note that Melveena McKendrick found that very movement in Calderón's La devoción de la Cruz in the person of the lady-bandit Julia (BHS, 46, 1-20). For the international, comparative scene, Jack Weiner continued the field of his doctoral dissertation (Indiana, 1968) to publish an enlightening treatise on "The Introduction of Spain's Golden Age Theater into Russia (1672-1800)" (Annali..., Naples, 193-223); and for comparative literature also J. B. Anderson discussed a Spanish source of Digby's Elvira: No siempre lo peor es cierto (RLC, 43, 108-26). Juan Roca's melancholy in El pintor de su deshonra was treated by Alan K. G. Paterson (in FMLS, 5, 244-61); Elias L. Rivers discussed with acumen Fénix's sonnet in El príncipe constante (in HR, 37, 452-58); and Charles V. Aubrun's article on "chronicle to tragicomedy" (re El sitio de Bredá), from Actes...Montauban, 1967, was translated into Italian for Sipario (24, 5-10). The British scholars, Alexander A. Parker and Edward M. Wilson, continued their valuable studies of Calderón; in this case, the chronology of the autos (HR, 37, 164-88) and Calderón documentation (BRAE, 49, 253-78), respectively.

Alexander A. Parker, in addition, entered into a literary polemic with H. B. Hall concerning the meaning of Segismundo's treatment of the rebel soldier (end of La vida es sueño). Hall's interpretation first appeared in BHS, 1968; Parker did not agree (BHS, 46, 120-27), and Hall replied in the immediately following pages of the same journal.

For doctoral work, Columbia University produced one thesis, Sister María I. Martín Acosta's study of Calderón's mythological autos; and the University of Rochester, Pedro P. Bermúdez's La imaginación escénica del teatro sacramental de Calderón. For the musical side, José Subirá continued his publications on Calderón and music, including the zarzuela, in several Spanish periodicals. A bibliography on "honour," which is of prime concern to Calderón studies, was the contribution to the Sánchez Escribano homenaje by Jenaro Artiles.

For texts, Francisco Ruiz Ramón's third volume of Calderón's tragedies brought us _La devoción de la Cruz_, _El mágico prodigioso_, _Los cabellos de Absalón_, and _La cisma de Inglaterra_. Guillermo Díaz-Plaja provided us with a popular edition of _El gran duque de Gandía_, Černý's amazing find of some years previously. Spain also provided an edition, by Manuel Ruiz Lagos, of _El pintor de su deshonra_, and Germany, in the hands of Manfred Engelbert, gave us _El pleito matrimonial del cuerpo y el alma_.

And last but not least, but rather of supreme importance, let us note that the Dean of Spanish _Calderonistas_, Angel Valbuena Prat, brought forth, in 1969, yet one more volume on the Golden Age theatre: _El teatro español en su Siglo de Oro_. Professor Valbuena Prat gives proper importance to Calderón de la Barca, and makes due reference to the most recent Calderonian scholarship: the Černý discoveries, for example. It is fitting that we students of the _comedia_ should make public note of Valbuena Prat's many writings, and pay high tribute to him as a Calderón scholar and as a fellow-worker. As we close this section of critical survey, let us raise our glasses to Don Angel in a toast, and say "¡Viva el maestro!"

Annotated Bibliography

E D I T I O N S

GENERAL

Calderón de la Barca, Pedro. Obras completas. Tomo I: Dramas.
    Ed. Luis Astrana Marín. 3rd ed. Madrid, Aguilar, 1951. Pp.
    1479. (4th ed., 1959. Pp. 2284.)

The introduction limits itself to problems related to the
early editions of Calderón's comedias, and contains no
analysis of the dramas or of Calderón's dramatic technique.
The plays are not preceded by a nota preliminar.

- Obras completas. Tomo II: Comedias. Ed. Angel Valbuena
    Briones. Madrid, Aguilar, 1956. Pp. 2156.
    Rev: A. E. Sloman, BHS, 35 (1958), 180-81.

Professor Sloman expresses his "gratitude to the publisher
who has provided in a single book no less than fifty-two
plays, together with the editor's introductory remarks and
a brief preface to each of the plays." He regrets, however,
that three plays already printed in Astrana Marín's volume
of dramas are repeated here, while El sitio de Bredá, Saber
del bien y del mal, La exaltación de la Cruz, and La selva
confusa have not been included in either of these two
volumes. Sloman also regrets that Valbuena Briones makes no
reference to the works of scholars (Heaton, Hesse, Maccoll,
Oppenheimer, Shergold, Wilson) who have discussed the problems of the texts and early editions of Calderón's comedias.
He ends his review by deploring "the incorporation of
Hartzenbusch's stage directions," but grants the fact that
Calderón scholars are "indebted to Sr. Valbuena for providing
sound texts of so many plays which have only been available
hitherto in the BAE edition."

- Obras completas. Tomo III: Autos sacramentales. Ed. Angel
    Valbuena Prat. 3rd ed. Madrid, Aguilar, 1952. Pp. 1915. (4th
    ed., 1959. Pp. 2158.)

26

The total of seventy-eight autos includes all of the autos
published by Pando and by Apontes, an occasional additional
one found in an edición extravagante, and three unpublished
manuscripts which constitute first drafts later perfected by
Calderón. The prologue presents a good introduction to the
study of Calderón's religious theatre, and each play is preceded by a helpful nota preliminar. Making available all of
the extant texts of Calderón's autos in a single accessible
volume is in itself meritorious. The fact that the editor is
a scholar of such renown as is Don Angel Valbuena Prat
enhances the value of this edition.

- Autos sacramentales. Tomo I: La cena del rey Baltasar; El
gran teatro del mundo; La vida es sueño. Ed. Angel Valbuena
Prat. 3rd ed. Madrid, Espasa-Calpe, 1951. Pp. lix, 197.
(Clás. Cast., 69.) (Later eds.)

The prologue contains Valbuena Prat's "Clasificación de los
autos de Calderón" in addition to sections on "El teatro de
Calderón" and "El auto sacramental." This volume was first
published in 1926. There is no question but that Professor
Valbuena Prat's excellent contribution has made available
for students as well as for the curious public at large
three of the most famous autos.

- Autos sacramentales. Tomo II: El pleito matrimonial del
cuerpo y el alma; Los encantos de la culpa; Tu prójimo como
a ti. Ed. Angel Valbuena Prat. 3rd ed. Madrid, Espasa-Calpe,
1952. Pp. lxxii, 213. (Clás. Cast., 74.) (Later eds.)

This second volume had its first printing in 1927. Professor
Valbuena Prat's texts are based on several manuscripts to be
found in the Biblioteca Nacional. In the footnotes he tran-
scribes the variants he found in the other manuscripts and
in the princeps edition. The prologue is an excellent introduction to the allegorical and symbolic plays by Calderón.
It is divided into four parts: "Calderón y sus síntesis
teológicas," "El auto en Calderón," "Calderón y el arte
simbólico," and "Los autos incluidos." There is also an
"Indice de materias y nombres contenidos en los tomos I y II."
Erika Lorenz has criticized the readings of Tu prójimo como
a ti (see Studies — Individual Works).

- Autos sacramentales. Barcelona, Plaza y Janés, 1961. Pp. 127.
(Clás. Plaza, 7.)

- Autos sacramentales: El gran teatro del mundo; La vida es
sueño; La cena del rey Baltasar; Los encantos de la culpa;
Tu prójimo como a ti. Barcelona, Iberia, 1964. Pp. 277.
(Col. Obras Maestras.)

- Comedias de capa y espada. Tomo II: La dama duende; No hay
cosa como callar. Ed. Angel Valbuena Briones. Madrid,
Espasa-Calpe, 1954. Pp. xcii, 223. (Clás. Cast., 137.)
(Later eds.)
Rev: J. Montero Padilla, RL, 5 (1954), 404-06; A. Barinaga,
Razón y Fe, 151, No. 689 (1955), 652; C. A. Jones, BHS, 32
(1955), 180-81.

A fine edition, and a valuable study, of this particular
aspect of the theatre of the Golden Age.

- Comedias religiosas. Tomo I: La devoción de la Cruz; El
mágico prodigioso. Ed. Angel Valbuena Prat. Madrid,
Espasa-Calpe, 1953. Pp. 230. (Clás. Cast., 106.) (Later eds.)

- Dramas de honor. Tomo I: A secreto agravio, secreta venganza.
Tomo II: El médico de su honra; El pintor de su deshonra. Ed.
Angel Valbuena Briones. Madrid, Espasa-Calpe, 1956. Pp. civ,
98; 230. (Clás. Cast., 141, 142.)
Rev: E. M. Wilson, BHS, 34 (1957), 227-29.

Professor Wilson calls the three plays "the three tragedies
of honour," and welcomes "the appearance of these three
important and profound plays in a convenient and readable
form." After he notes the few misprints of vol. II and corrects the reading of line 469 on page 69 by using the
Quiñones-Coello edition of 1637 of the Segunda Parte, in
which El médico de su honra was first printed, he regrets
that the editor did not consult this early edition: "It is a
pity that Señor Valbuena had not contrived to consult the
earliest edition of the pre-Vera Tassis Segunda Parte." The
reviewer singles out for praise "the legal details about
honour and adultery printed on pages xxxv-xxxvii and the long
extract from Calderón's own defence of the painter's art on

pp. liii-lv, which is not otherwise very accessible," and concludes this review stating that "All through these two volumes there is some useful material for the critic and for the researcher; unfortunately, it is sometimes badly arranged and often undisciplined."

- _Dramen in der Übertragung von Johann Diederich Gries (weltliche Schauspiele) und Joseph von Eichendorff (geistliche Schauspiele), mit einen Nachwort von Edmund Schramm_. Munich, Winkler Verlag, 1963.

  A reprinting of translations which first appeared in the early 19th century.

- _Eight Dramas of Calderón_. Trans. Edward Fitzgerald. Garden City, New York, Doubleday, 1961. Pp. 440. (Dolphin Master Series.) (There was a London-New York, Macmillan, 1906, edition.)

  Contains: _The Painter of his own Dishonour_; _Keep your own Secret_; _Gil Pérez, the Galician_; _Three Judgments at a Blow_; _The Mayor of Zalamea_; _Beware of Smooth Waters_; _The Mighty Magician_; _Such Stuff as Dreams Are Made of_.

- _Estudio y antología_. Ed. José Inocencio Tejedor Sanz. Madrid, Compañía Bibliográfica Española, 1967. Pp. 239. (Col. Un autor en un libro, 28.)

- _Four Plays_. Trans. Edwin Honig. New York, Hill and Wang, 1961. Pp. xxx, 319.
  Rev: Angel Valbuena Briones, _Arbor_, 52, No. 197 (1962), 102-05 ("Significa una sólida y elogiosa contribución al entendimiento del dramaturgo español en los países de habla inglesa.").

  Contains: _The Phantom Lady_; _The Mayor of Zalamea_; _Devotion to the Cross_; _Secret Vengeance for Secret Insult_.

- _Obra dramática_. Ed. J. Alcina Franch and E. Veres. Barcelona, Elite, 1959. Pp. 183.

- Obras menores (Siglos XVII y XVIII). Cieza, La Fonte que mana y corre, 1969. 55 leaves.

  A facsimile reproduction of 3 poems, an auto, and a pliego suelto by Calderón.

- Obras selectas. Adaptación de Fernando Laina. Madrid, Hernando, 1951. Pp. 143. (Col. Hernando de Libros para la Juventud.)

  Prose adaptations of El alcalde de Zalamea, La dama duende, and La vida es sueño.

- Obras. Teatro doctrinal y religioso. Ed. Angel Valbuena Prat. Barcelona, Vergara, 1965. Pp. 1033.

  The collection contains four comedias (La vida es sueño, La devoción de la Cruz, El mágico prodigioso, El príncipe constante) and eight autos, with a view to showing Calderón's reflective side. After a biographical sketch, the prologue offers "El pensamiento de Calderón," "Calderón y el tema de la muerte," "La estructura dramática de Calderón," "Sobre el estilo de Calderón," and "Calderón y las obras sacras y doctrinales."

- Piesi, per. s ispan. (Plays translated from Spanish.) Introd. by N. B. Tomashevskiy. Moscow, Iskusstvo, 1961. 2 vols.

  Contains twelve plays by Calderón.

- Six Plays. Trans. Denis Florence MacCarthy, and revised by Henry W. Wells. New York, Las Américas, 1961. Pp. 464. Rev: Demetrius Basdekis, RHM, 30 (1964), 54 (A brief statement praising the 19th-century verse translation, reprinted, with many errors, which the reviewer laments, by the Brander Mathews Dramatic Museum.).

  Contains: Life Is a Dream; The Wonderworking Magician; The Constant Prince; The Devotion of the Cross; Love after Death; Belshazzar's Feast.

- <u>Spanische Welttheater</u>. <u>4 Meisterdramen</u>. Ed. Wilhelm von Scholz. Munich, List, 1961. Pp. 389.

- <u>Sus mejores poesías</u>. Barcelona, Bruguera, 1954. Pp. 127. (Col. Laurel, 25.)

- <u>Teatro</u>. Trans. Ferdinando Carlesi. Introd. by Mario Casella. Florence, Sansoni, 1949.
  Rev: G.M.B., <u>Quaderni Ibero-Americani</u>, No. 10 (1951), 62 (The edition contains eight plays, translated from the Hartzenbusch texts. The reviewer, Bertini, praises Carlesi's work, and devotes more than half of the review to Casella's introductory essay, which receives special commendation for the lucid manner in which it succeeds in explaining Calderón and his theatre, with a good analysis of <u>La vida es sueño</u>.).

- <u>Tragedias</u>. Tomo I: <u>La vida es sueño</u>; <u>La hija del aire</u>; <u>El mayor monstruo del mundo</u>. Ed. Francisco Ruiz Ramón. Madrid, Alianza Editorial, 1967. Pp. 609.

- <u>Tragedias</u>. Tomo II: <u>A secreto agravio, secreta venganza</u>; <u>El médico de su honra</u>; <u>El pintor de su deshonra</u>. Ed. Francisco Ruiz Ramón. Madrid, Alianza Editorial, 1968. Pp. 407.

- <u>Tragedias</u>. Tomo III: <u>La devoción de la Cruz</u>; <u>El mágico prodigioso</u>; <u>Los cabellos de Absalón</u>; <u>La cisma de Inglaterra</u>. Ed. Francisco Ruiz Ramón. Madrid, Alianza Editorial, 1969. Pp. 359.

- <u>Trois autos sacramentales</u>. Trans. Mathilde Pomès. Paris, Klincksieck, 1957. Pp. xx, 214. (Col. Témoins de l'Espagne, Textes bilingues, 2.)
  Rev: J. Bourciez, <u>RLR</u>, 72 (1957-58), 380-81; P. Groult, <u>LR</u>, 14 (1960), 159-63.

The three most famous <u>autos sacramentales</u> are translated, with annotation, into French (<u>La vida es sueño</u>, <u>La cena de Baltasar</u>, and <u>El gran teatro del mundo</u>) in a bilingual volume. Bourciez points out that rather than an unbearable ("insupportable") literal translation, "Mme Pomès a préféré

l'heptasyllable blanc qui rend la version beaucoup plus
coulante." For the Spanish texts she reprints "celui qu'a
établi M. Valbuena Prat en 1953 " The problems of translation
and interpretation are explained "dans les notes assez
nombreuses qui suivent chacun des autos." However, as a
result of this freedom in method, the translations receive a
rather negative review from Groult, who feels that the translator has short-changed the French reader by the poor, often
erroneous French renderings. Furthermore, Groult complains
that many of the notes are inadequate.

- Trois comédies: La Vie est un songe; Le Médecin de son
honneur; L'Alcalde de Zalamea. Ed. Alexandre Arnoux. Paris,
Grasset, 1955. Pp. 317. (Club Français du Livre. Théâtre, 21.)
Rev: W. Mettmann, Archiv, 193 (1957), 365.

In his brief review, Mettmann points out that Arnoux made
the prose adaptations of the three plays for modern French
tastes. As a result, the reader must not expect a true rendi-
tion of Calderón texts, not only because of abridgements, but
also because of the modern prose style in which "der
natürlich Wortspiele, Konzeptismen und die barocke Sprache-
gewalt des spanischen Autors sum Opfer fallen müssen." The
reviewer points out that this is not intended as a criticism
of the translator, who undoubtedly has contributed to the
re-kindling in French theatregoers of an interest in Calderón.

- (et. al.). Veinticinco siglos de teatro. Ed. Enrique
Ortenbach. Barcelona, Fomento Internacional de Cultura, 1959.
Pp. 1726.

Includes Calderón.

- El alcalde de Zalamea y dos entremeses: El dragoncillo, La
rabia. Ed. Julio Durán Cerda. Santiago de Chile, Edit.
Universitaria, 1956. Pp. 186. (Col. Bib. Hispana, 8.)

- El alcalde de Zalamea; La vida es sueño. Ed. Jorge Campos.
Madrid, Taurus, 1959. Pp. 365. (Ser y Tiempo, Temas de
España.) (Later eds.)

- <u>El alcalde de Zalamea</u>; <u>La vida es sueño</u>. 11th ed. Madrid, Espasa-Calpe, 1959. Pp. 217. (Col. Austral, 39.) (Later eds.)

- <u>El alcalde de Zalamea</u>; <u>La vida es sueño</u>. Madrid, Edaf, 1964. Pp. 280. (Bib. Edaf, 19.) (Later eds.)

A brief (five-page) introduction. The text is well printed, with a few illustrations, but without other commentary or notes of any kind.

- <u>El alcalde de Zalamea</u>; <u>La vida es sueño</u>; <u>El gran teatro del mundo</u>. Ed. Cipriano Rivas Xerif. Mexico, Ateneo, 1965. Pp. 258.

- <u>El alcalde de Zalamea</u>; <u>La vida es sueño</u>; <u>El gran teatro del mundo</u>. Ed. Amando Isasi Angulo. Barcelona, Bruguera, 1968. Pp. 440.

Includes a preliminary study, notes, and a selected bibliography.

- <u>El alcalde de Zalamea</u>; <u>La vida es sueño</u>; <u>El mágico prodigioso</u>. 3rd ed. Madrid, Aguilar, 1959. Pp. 508. (Col. Crisol, 36 bis.)

- <u>La devoción de la Cruz</u>; <u>El gran teatro del mundo</u>. 3rd ed. Madrid, Espasa-Calpe, 1961. Pp. 147. (Col. Austral, 384.)

- <u>La devoción de la Cruz</u>; <u>El mágico prodigioso</u>; <u>Los cabellos de Absalón</u>; <u>La sibila del Oriente y gran reina de Sabá</u>. In Nicolás Ganzález Ruiz (ed.), <u>Piezas maestras del teatro teológico español</u>, Tomo II: <u>Comedias</u>, 2nd ed., Madrid, Bib. de Autores Cristianos, 1953, pp. 133-360. (Pp. xlv, 924.) (1st ed., 1946.)

- <u>La Dévotion à la Croix</u>; <u>La Vie est un songe</u> (with Lope de Vega's <u>Fontovejuna</u>; <u>L'Enlèvement d'Hélène</u>). In Paul Verdevoye, <u>Les Baroques</u> (trans. and ed.), Paris, Mazenod, 1959. Pp. 224.

- <u>La hidalga del valle y A María el corazón</u>. Ed. Giacomo Vaifro
Sabatelli. Zaragoza, Ebro, 1962. Pp. 171. (Clás. Ebro, 97,
98.)
Rev: Pedro de Alcántara Martínez, <u>Archivum Franciscanum
Historicum</u>, 56 (1963), 363 (Praises the "enjundioso
comentario," but laments the number of typographical errors.);
J. Meseguer Fernández, <u>Archivo Ibero-Americano</u>, 25 (1965),
462-63 ("La presentación es modesta, como corresponde a un
libro escolar para evitar el precio excesivo, pero cuidada
y limpia.").

An adaptation of the editor's doctoral thesis. Calderón's
autograph manuscript of <u>La hidalga del valle</u> has been used
for the first time in conjunction with the first edition
(Granada, 1640). <u>A María el corazón</u> is based on the first
edition (1716), with the aid of two manuscripts from the
Biblioteca Nacional and the Pando text. <u>La hidalga del valle</u>
is a defence of the Immaculate Conception, and clearly
derives from Scotus; <u>A María el corazón</u> is historical-
legendary.

- <u>La hidalga del valle y A María el corazón, dos autos
sacramentales marianos</u>. Ed. Eugenio Frutos Cortés. Madrid,
Aguilar, 1963. Pp. 217.

In his introduction, the editor classifies the <u>autos marianos</u>
of Calderón as to the degree of <u>elementos marianos</u>, and
includes in his edition the first because it is the only one
completely <u>mariano</u> and the second as an example of the
perfect union of the <u>mariano</u> and eucharistic elements. There
is a brief history of Marian <u>autos</u> prior to Calderón and a
discussion of the different types composed by Calderón.
There are 30 pages of notes.

- <u>El mágico prodigioso; Casa con dos puertas mala es de guardar</u>.
4th ed. Madrid, Espasa-Calpe, 1961. Pp. 195. (Col Austral,
289.)

- <u>El mayor monstruo del mundo; El príncipe constante</u>. 3rd ed.
Madrid, Espasa-Calpe, 1961. Pp. 169. (Col. Austral, 496.)

- El médico de su honra; El pintor de su deshonra. Ed. Angel
  Valbuena Briones. Madrid, Espasa-Calpe, 1965. Pp. 232. (Clás.
  Cast., 142.)

- No hay burlas con el amor; El médico de su honra. 3rd ed.
  Madrid, Espasa-Calpe, 1962. Pp. 232. (Col. Austral, 593.)

- El pleito matrimonial del cuerpo y el alma; La cena de
  Baltasar; El gran teatro del mundo; Los encantos de la culpa;
  Tu prójimo como a ti; La vida es sueño. In Autos sacramentales
  eucarísticos, ed. Alejandro Sanvisens, Barcelona, Edit.
  Cervantes, 1952, pp. 119-279.

  "Publicados con motivo del XXXV Congreso Eucarístico
  Internacional."

- El pleito matrimonial del cuerpo y el alma; El veneno y la
  triaca; La cena de Baltasar; La vida es sueño; La hidalga
  del valle; El gran teatro del mundo; Los encantos de la
  culpa; Las órdenes militares; A María el corazón; Sueños hay
  que verdad son; El santo rey don Fernando, I; A Dios por
  razón de estado; El gran mercado del mundo; La devoción de
  la misa; El pintor de su deshonra. In Nicolás González Ruiz
  (ed.), Piezas maestras del teatro teológico español, Tomo I:
  Autos sacramentales, 2nd ed., Madrid, Bib. de Autores
  Cristianos, 1953, pp. 297-792. (Pp. lxxi, 923.) (1st ed.,
  1946; 3rd ed., 1968.)

- Der standhafte Prinz; Der Arzt seiner Ehre. (El príncipe
  constante; El médico de su honra.) Trans. August Wilhelm
  Schlegel and Johann Diederich Gries. Munich, Goldmann, 1961.
  Pp. 175.

- El príncipe constante; La vida es sueño; El alcalde de
  Zalamea; Los encantos de la culpa. Ed. José María Pemán.
  Barcelona, Exito, 1951. Pp. xxiii, 389. (Clás. Jackson, 15.)
  (Later eds.)

  The selection of plays was based on the following criteria:
  El alcalde de Zalamea, as the most popular of Calderón's
  plays, having derived from Lope de Vega; La vida es sueño,

as the most intellectual and metaphysical; El príncipe constante, as falling between the two extremes; Los encantos de la culpa, as a representative auto. The "estudio prelimi- nar" devotes very little space to the first two because they are such well known plays. The comments on El príncipe constante are more extensive. There follows a section on the auto in general. There is a short bibliography. Each play is preceded by a two-page introduction.

- La vida es sueño; El alcalde de Zalamea. Ed. Augusto Cortina. Madrid, Espasa-Calpe, 1955. Pp. lxi, 238. (Clás. Cast., 138.) (Nueva ed., 1960. Pp. 248.) (Later eds.)

- Das Leben, ein Traum; Der Richter von Zalamea. Trans. Johann Diederich Gries. Munich, Goldmann,1960. Pp. 183.

- La vida es sueño; El alcalde de Zalamea. Ed. Sturgis E. Leavitt. New York, Dell, 1964. Pp. 256.

An inexpensive and convenient edition based on the Vera Tassis publication of the Séptima Parte (1683), with a brief introduction and some notes.

- La vida es sueño; El alcalde de Zalamea; El mágico prodigioso. 4th ed. Ed. Federico Sainz de Robles. Madrid, Aguilar, 1961. Pp. 505. (Col. Crisol, 36 bis.) (Later eds.)

- La vida es sueño; El alcalde de Zalamea; El mágico prodigioso. New York, Doubleday, 1961. Pp. 312.

- La vida es sueño; El alcalde de Zalamea; El mágico prodigioso; El médico de su honra; El gran teatro del mundo. In Antonio Espina (ed.), Las mejores escenas del teatro español e hispanoamericano desde sus orígenes hasta la época actual, Madrid, Aguilar, 1959. Pp. 1172.
Rev: José Montero Padilla, Arbor, 46, Nos. 175-76 (1960), 410-11.

- La vida es sueño; El alcalde de Zalamea; El mágico prodigioso; El príncipe constante. Ed. José Bergua. Madrid, Ibéricas, 1955. Pp. 380.

- La vida es sueño; El alcalde de Zalamea; El médico de su honra. Barcelona, Maucci, 1961. Pp. 642.

- Life Is a Dream; Love after Death; The Wonder-Working Magician. In Eric Bentley (ed.), The Classic Theatre, Vol. III: Six Spanish Plays, Garden City, N. Y., Doubleday, 1959, pp. 314-507.
Rev: V. Oelschlager, Américas, 16 (1959-60), 412-13; A. del Río, RHM, 27 (1961), 57-58; A. Valbuena Briones, Arbor, 48, No. 184 (1961), 147-49.

The first two plays are in the Roy Campbell English versions; the third is Shelley's translation of several scenes.

- La Vie est un songe; La Dévotion à la croix (also L'Etoile de Séville and Cervantes' Le Retable des merveilles). In Calderón, Lope de Vega, et Cervantes, Théâtre espagnol, trans. Alexandre Arnoux, Albert et Jules Supervielle, et Dominique Aubier, Paris, Club des Libraires de France, 1957.

- La vida es sueño; El príncipe constante; El alcalde de Zalamea; La cena del rey Baltasar. In Vicente Gómez-Bravo (ed.), Silva dramática. Asuntos del teatro español dispuestos para estudio literario, 4th ed., Madrid, Razón y Fe, 1957. Pp. 334.

This class text for grade school or junior high school devotes a large number of pages to reprint from the Hartzenbusch (BAE) edition numerous fragments of Calderonian plays. The few critical comments are of low calibre.

E D I T I O N S

INDIVIDUAL WORKS

A secreto agravio, secreta venganza

Calderón de la Barca, Pedro. **A secreto agravio, secreta venganza**. 3rd ed. Madrid, Espasa-Calpe, 1964. Pp. 168. (Clás. Cast.)

- **A secreto agravio, secreta venganza**. Ed. Edward Nagy. Zaragoza, Ebro, 1966. Pp. 120. (Col. Clás. Ebro.)

  After the usual Ebro tables of important dates in the author's life and in his era in general, the editor treats "El honor y el teatro calderoniano," the play's title, plot, and character, sources, versification, and first edition. Next comes a bibliography and then the texts, based on Hartzenbusch (1848), but collated with that of Valbuena Briones (Dramas de honor, I, Clás. Cast., 141). The lines of each act are numbered separately, and there are footnotes and illustrations. Finally, there are critical judgments on honour and on this play in particular, followed by ten "Temas de trabajo escolar," and an index.

El alcalde de Zalamea

Calderón de la Barca, Pedro. **El alcalde de Zalamea**. Ed. André Nougé. Toulouse-Paris, Privat-Didier, 1952. Pp. 244. (Col. Privat, Classiques Espagnols.)
Rev: A. Baradet, Bul. de l'Univ. de Toulouse, 62 (1952-53), 45.

Although this edition does not have scholarly pretensions, it is preceded by a generally sound twenty-six page introduction

in French, which should help students to understand Calderón
and his theatre in general and El alcalde de Zalamea in
particular. The text is based on the editions of Kressner and
Hartzenbusch. It is followed by three short appendices:
"I. - Lope de Vega, El alcalde de Zalamea, extraits;
II. - Calderón, Amar después de la muerte, extrait (scenes in
which Calderón invokes the figure of don Lope de Figueroa);
III. - Pellicer, Avisos (accounts of trouble caused by
soldiers in Calderón's times). The end notes are primarily
concerned with explaining vocabulary considered to be
difficult for French readers.

- L'Alcalde de Zalamea. Trans. Alex. André Arnoux. Paris,
  Illustration, 1953.

- El alcalde de Zalamea. Ed. Fermín Estrella Gutiérrez. Buenos
  Aires, Kapelusz, 1954.

  A shortened, school edition, with prologue and notes.

- El alcalde de Zalamea. (Extracts.) Paris, 1954. Pp. 32. (Col.
  Mil renglones.)

- Der Richter von Zalamea. Trans. J. D. Gries. Leipzig, Reclam,
  1954. Pp. 96.

- El alcalde de Zalamea. Madrid, Escelicer, 1959. Pp. 112. (Col.
  Teatro.)

- L'Alcalde de Zalamea. Trans. Robert Marrast. Paris, Aubier,
  1959. Pp. 206. (Col. bilingue.) (Later eds.)
  Rev: Noël Salomon, BH, 61 (1959), 457-58.

  Salomon states that the edition is well done, with a clear
  introduction, dealing first with Calderón's theatre in
  general and then providing an analysis of the play itself.

- Alcadele din Zalamea. Trans. Emanuel Avilar. Ed. Paul
  Alexandru Georgescu. Bucharest, Editura de Stat Pentru
  Literatura si Arta, 1959. Pp. 174. (Bib. Pentru Foti.)

- The Mayor of Zalamea. Trans. William E. Colford. Great Neck, N. Y., Barron's, 1959. Pp. 128.

- Zalamejský Rychtár. Trans. Jaroslav Pokorny. Ed. Milos Fiala. Prague, Orbis, 1959.

- L'Alcalde de Zalamea. Trans. Georges Pillement. Paris, T.N.P., 1961. Pp. 64. (Col. du Théâtre National Populaire.)

Performed, Avignon, Palais des Papes, XVe Festival d'Art Dramatique, July 15, 1961. (Also pub. with André Camp's French adaptation of Sancho Pansa dans son île, Paris, L'Avant-Scène, 1962.)

- El alcalde de Zalamea. Ed. Gabriel Espino. 7th ed. Zaragoza, Ebro, 1962. Pp. 134. (Bib. Clás. Ebro. Clás Españoles, Serie Teatro, 14.)

- Zalamejský Richtár. Ed. Víťazoslav Hečko. Bratislava, Czechoslovakia, Diliza, 1962. Pp. 114.

- El alcalde de Zalamea. Ed. Peter N. Dunn. Oxford, Pergamon, 1966. Pp. viii, 140.
Rev: Gwynne Edwards, BHS, 44 (1967), 294-95; James A. Castañeda, MLJ, 52 (1968), 236 (Favourable. The reviewer considers the introduction to be extremely helpful and an interesting résumé of literary history and criticism. "The notes following the text are excellent, many going beyond simple clarification of a textual difficulty to relate a specific word, construction or concept to the full context of Golden Age tradition and technique."); Arnold G. Reichenberger, HR, 26 (1968), 362-65 ("Professor Dunn's pages...present us with a new and true insight into the ideological and religious background of the Alcalde. His metaphysical concerns lead him to judge the world of Rebolledo and La Chispa only as 'shady', omitting reference to humor and relief. The 'realism' of the soldiers' life reminds one of Schiller's Wallenstein Lager. Professor Dunn also goes too far in throwing traditional critical opinions overboard when he concludes: 'Honour then, is not the central theme of the plays, but one aspect of the characters' urge to arrange appearances to suit their own desires'.").

The editor uses Alfay's texts of 1651 and 1653, and discusses
any departure therefrom, as he seeks to "reconcile scholarly
standards with readability." His introduction discusses
"Calderón and the Spanish Drama," "The two Alcaldes," the
date of composition, and the play itself — its plan and its
themes. Also discussed are "The idea of 'Honra'," "The
Co-ordinating Ideas," the play's reputation, and the text.
Then comes the text of the play, followed by extensive notes.

- El alcalde de Zalamea (El garrote más bien dado, según el
  texto de 1651). Ed. Everett W. Hesse. Buenos Aires, Plus
  Ultra, 1967. Pp. 147.

La aurora en Copacabana

Calderón de la Barca, Pedro. La aurora en Copacabana. Ed.
  Antonio Pagés Larraya. Estudio preliminar by Ricardo Rojas.
  Buenos Aires, Hachette, 1956. Pp. 224. (Col. El pasado
  argentino.)
  Rev: Edward M. Wilson, BHS, 24 (1957), 229.

The reviewer declares that Rojas' "introduction to the play
is not very illuminating; it is mainly concerned with the
autos sacramentales, and he has rather an old-fashioned view
of them." The text of the comedia is based on Hartzenbusch.
Professor Pagés Larraya's notes "will help those who wish to
assess Calderón's use of historical material from the New
World."

Los cabellos de Absalón

Calderón de la Barca, Pedro. Los cabellos de Absalón. Ed. Helmy
  Fuad Giacoman. Doct. diss., Univ. of Southern California,
  1966. (DA, 27, 4251A.) (See next item.)

- Los cabellos de Absalón. Ed. Helmy Fuad Giacoman. Valencia,
  Castalia (Chapel Hill, Univ. of North Carolina), 1968. Pp.
  183. (Estudios de Hispanó, 9.)

In this critical edition, the play is analysed, and compared with its literary and Biblical sources and analogues (<u>II Samuel</u> through Faulkner), as well as with Tirso's <u>La venganza de Tamar</u>. Tirso's main concern: Amon's passion for Tamar; Calderón's: Absalón's lust for power, especially for King David's throne. This is symbolized by Dionysus, the sun, while Narcissus represents Absalón's self-worship. Given the play's quality, it is puzzling that critics had previously neglected it.

Casa con dos puertas mala es de guardar

Calderón de la Barca, Pedro. <u>A House with Two Doors Is Difficult to Guard</u>. Trans. Kenneth Muir. <u>TDR</u>, 8 (1963), 157-217.

A rather free translation in prose and blank verse; one that reads well but scarcely conveys the spirit of the original. The translator omits a long soliloquy of Calabazas and shortens and changes other speeches. There is a brief introduction.

- <u>Casa con due porte mal si guarda</u>. Trans. Antonio Gasparetti. Rome, Paoline, 1966. Pp. 124.

La cisma de Inglaterra

Calderón de la Barca, Pedro. <u>Le Schisme d'Angleterre</u>. Trans. Robert Marrast and André Reybaz. Paris, L'Arche, 1960.

La dama duende

Calderón de la Barca, Pedro. <u>La dama duende</u>. Ed. Herbert Koch. Halle, Max Niemeyer Verlag, 1952. Pp. 119.
Rev: C. V. A(ubrun), <u>BH</u>, 54 (1952), 96-97. (A slightly negative review, critical of punctuation in general, of some notes, and of the fact that many passages are unjustifiably passed by without notes.).

In a four-page introduction in German, Koch indicates the great popularity which <u>La dama duende</u> must have enjoyed in

seventeenth century Spain, and touches upon some theories
concerning its possible source. Koch principally follows
Keil's edition (Leipzig, 1827).

- *La dama duende*. Ed. Pilar Díez y Jiménez de Castellanos. 2nd
ed. Zaragoza, Ebro, 1957. Pp. 134. (Clás. Ebro, 83.) (Later
eds.)

This small volume of Calderón's *La dama duende*, reprinted
without changes in the several editions it has had, provides
a handy text, notes, a "resumen cronológico" of Calderón's
life, the important events of his epoch, an introduction to
his dramas, and an analysis of *La dama duende*; all of which
make it valuable for class use.

- (*La dama duende*.) *Drilledjaevelen*. Danish adaptation by Jens
Louis Petersen. Copenhagen, Gyldendal, 1959. Pp. 123.

("The teasing devil.")

- *La dama duende*. Ed. Eugenio Castelli. Buenos Aires, Edit.
Huemul, 1965. Pp. 175. (Col. Clás. Huemul.)

- *La dama duende*. Ed. José Luis Alonso. Madrid, Editora Nacional,
1966. Pp. viii, 135. (Obras del Teatro Español.)

Calderón's *capa y espada* plays can still be staged with only
slight modifications, as was the case at the 1966 Teatro
Español performance. Authentic seventeenth-century guitar
music, recorded by Andrés Segovia and Narciso Yepes, was
used. See Studies — Individual Works (*La dama duende*) —
Acerete, Aragonés, Quinto, and Santaló.

La desdicha de la voz

Calderón de la Barca, Pedro. *La desdicha de la voz*. Ed. A. V.
Ebersole. Valencia, Castalia, 1963. Pp. xxiv, 139. (Estudios
de Hispanó, 3.)
Rev: Edward M. Wilson, BHS, 41 (1964), 191-93 (The reviewer
speaks well of the reproduction of the text, but finds a

number of errors in the treatment of the printed texts of the play.); Jean-Louis Flecniakoska, <u>BH</u>, 67 (1965), 203 (The editor is praised for his meticulous work with a MS, 1639, in poor condition, helped by seven printed texts of 1650-80. While some might prefer an eclectic text chosen from among the variants, the reviewer commends the editor for presenting the materials wherewith we can solve textual problems for ourselves.); Henry W. Hilborn, <u>Hisp</u>, 48 (1965), 610-11 (The reviewer finds several errors in Acts I and II, but praises the editor's patience in coping with a very difficult MS, and insists that "the corrections and criticism offered are in no way intended to detract from the reviewer's high opinion of this edition. Long, persistent work has obviously gone into its preparation."); Juan M. Rozas, <u>Segismundo</u>, 1 (1965), 203.

A reproduction of the autograph now in the Biblioteca Nacional, with a "nota preliminar," some data concerning the actors, synopsis of the plot, a brief description of the manuscript with respect to what has been crossed out or rewritten, variants with the first printed edition, and a list of editions. The notes are limited to those relating to the variants. The text restores numerous lines omitted in the earlier printed editions.

La devoción de la Cruz

Calderón de la Barca, Pedro. <u>La devoción de la Cruz</u>. Ed. Sidney F. Wexler. Doct. diss., New York University, 1952. (See below.)

- <u>La Dévotion à la Croix</u>. Trans. Albert Camus. Paris, Gallimard, 1953. Pp. 176.
Rev: D. McPheeters, <u>Symposium</u>, 12 (1958), 52-64 (Camus turned to the translation or adaptation of foreign dramatic works for two reasons: one, because he felt that new versions designed for actors, rather than those made by scholars for scholars, were needed; and two, because the Golden Age plays present basic problems of life in its great spectacle, which can compete with the cinema, and they do not require heavy cerebration on the part of the audience.).

- *La devoción de la Cruz.* Ed. Isidoro Montiel. 4th ed. Zaragoza, Ebro, 1961. Pp. 132. (Bib. Clás. Ebro, Clás. Españoles, Serie Teatro, 26.)

- *La devoción de la Cruz.* Ed. Sidney F. Wexler. Salamanca, Anaya, 1966. Pp. 156. (Bib. Anaya, Serie Textos Españoles.) Rev: Robert L. Hathaway, *Hisp*, 51 (1968), 939-40 (Favourable.).

After sections on "Vida y obras de Calderón," and "Clasificación y publicación de las comedias," the play in question is discussed as to "Paternidad literaria y fecha de composición," versification, sources, technique and style, characters, and imitations and translations. The text follows a bibliography, and is in turn followed by an appendix of 120 lines from *La Cruz en la sepultura*, considered the primitive, shorter version of *La devoción de la Cruz.*

La divina Filotea

Calderón de la Barca, Pedro. *La divina Filotea, auto sacramental.* Ed. José Carlos de Torres Martínez. *Segismundo*, 3 (1967), 203-365.

Eco y Narciso

Calderón de la Barca, Pedro. *Eco y Narciso.* Ed. Charles V. Aubrun. Paris, Centre de Recherches de l'Institut d'Etudes Hispaniques, 1961. Pp. xxxi, 78. (Chefs d'Oeuvres des Lettres Hispaniques, I.) (2nd ed., 1964.)
Rev: Pierre Groult, *LR*, 16 (1962), 103-13 (The reviewer sets out to prove that Aubrun has completely misinterpreted this play. His imagination has converted it from the magnificent fable which it is into an exalted hymn to the Christian religion. The reviewer also takes exception to the statement that the play offers modern man the mirror in which he will recognize his psychological complexes.); Mireya Jaimes-Freyre, *Hisp*, 45 (1962), 173-74 (A brief review concerning itself entirely with the introduction and Aubrun's contribution and points of view. Although favourable, the reviewer is not entirely in accord with Aubrun's opinions. This review also appeared, in Spanish translation, in *RHM*, 29, 1963, 78-79.);

Edward M. Wilson, <u>BHS</u>, 39 (1962), 107-10 (A highly favourable
review: "He gives us a whole series of thoughtful criticisms
to help us read this beautiful work with comprehension.");
Arnold G. Reichenberger, <u>RR</u>, 54 (1963), 223-25 (The reviewer
considers the preface the chief merit of the work, and
believes that the play has grandeur because of an "underlying
serious and valid religiosity" and that it is not a true
tragedy in the Aristotelian sense.); Everett W. Hesse, <u>HR</u>,
32 (1964), 268-70 (The reviewer concerns himself mainly with
the preface, which he calls "stimulating and provocative."
There is a brief summary of each of nine sections into which
the preface is divided, but the text itself is dismissed in
one short paragraph.).

- <u>Eco y Narciso</u>. Ed. Charles V. Aubrun. 2nd ed. Paris, 1964.

A reissue of the edition first published in 1961. A second,
short (four-page) preface has been added to the first, in
which Aubrun defends his presentation of the text, a method
different from "historical documentation, social information,
psychoanalytical testimony, technical dissection and the good
old prestige of the school pedant." "There is necessary a
direct contact with the truth of the poem, a truth which
reveals it and, at the same time, reveals ourselves."

En la muerte de la señora doña Inés Zapata

Calderón de la Barca, Pedro. <u>En la muerte de la señora doña
Inés Zapata, dedicada a doña María Zapata</u> (poem). In José
Manuel Blecua (ed.), <u>Floresta lírica española</u>, Madrid, Gredos,
1957, pp. 276-78; and in Arthur Terry (ed.), <u>An Anthology of
Spanish Poetry, 1500-1700. Part II: 1580-1700</u>, Oxford, Perga-
mon Press, 1968, pp. 168-72.

The source of this "poema de circunstancias" is the <u>Cancionero
de 1628</u>. It is regrettable that in these anthologies this
unfortunate <u>silva</u> should represent the marvellous poet that
Calderón is.

La estatua de Prometeo

Calderón de la Barca, Pedro. <u>La estatua de Prometeo</u>. Ed. Charles

V. Aubrun. Paris, Centre de Documentation Universitaire, 1961.
Pp. 66.
Rev: Edward M. Wilson, <u>BHS</u>, 39 (1962), 107-10 (Although Wilson
notes doubtful interpretations in one or two places, he concludes that "on the whole this introduction is very relevant
to the play, and very well written." The notes elucidate
difficulties of syntax and vocabulary very well.).

The text is a photographical facsimile of a corrected copy of
Keil's text, while the introduction and notes are in the form
of mimeographed typescript, consequently rather difficult to
read.

- <u>La estatua de Prometeo</u>. Ed. Charles V. Aubrun. Paris, Centre
de Recherches de l'Institut d'Etudes Hispaniques, 1965. Pp.
xxxiv, 71.
Rev: Andrés Amorós, <u>CHA</u>, 66 (1966), 618-20 (The reviewer
praises Aubrun for not piling up erudition for its own sake,
though providing the necessary textual notes and analysis of
versification. He finds the edition "muy correcta, clara,
bien ordenada, y bellamente impresa." What he finds most
admirable in the edition is its "claridad, sencillez, orden.").

In addition to the usual features, the introduction contains
discussions of such matters as "Contenus et couches de
significations," and some interesting suggestions as to
possible difficulties of staging. The text is followed by two
appendices on Prometheus: "Teatro de los dioses de la
gentilidad" and "Los emblemas de Alciato."

El gran duque de Gandía

Calderón de la Barca, Pedro. <u>El gran duque de Gandía</u>. Ed.
Václav Černý. Prague, Editions de l'Académie Tchécoslovaque
des Sciences, 1963. Pp. 208.
Rev: Ramón Barce, <u>Indice de Artes y Letras</u>, No. 183 (Madrid,
April, 1964), 21 (A brief review which does not question the
attribution to Calderón.); <u>TLS</u>, No. 3296 (London, April 29,
1965), 330 ("One more for the Canon?": the reviewer points
out the difficulties in accepting it conclusively as Calderón's); Miguel V. Olivera Giménez, <u>Cuad. del Idioma</u>, No. 3
(1965), 170-73 (The handling of this "drama de santo," with
many examples of Calderón's thought and style at their best,

shows Černý's "cuidadosa y sobria labor de Documentación y
comentario." There are some mistakes, e.g. in the treatment
of versification; but the notes are excellent, and "La his-
panística no puede menos que agradecer calurosamente este
regalo."); Ricardo Domenech, CHA, 70 (1967), 419-25.

An edition of a play which Černý believes to be the lost play
of Calderón about St. Francis Borja, a manuscript copy of
which was found in Czechoslovakia in 1958. The introduction
discusses the date and reasons for composition, and how it
came to the library of the château of Mladá Vožice. Also, it
analyses the work and its sources. Included with the text are
the loas and two entremeses of the manuscript and notes. The
edition, in French, is well done. Titta Brunetti, in Il
Dramma, No. 361 (Dec., 1966), 93-94, reviews a performance
of a German translation of the play (Die Welt ist Trug) in a
Vienna festival, and recalls the history of the Spanish MS.
See Studies — Individual Works (El gran duque de Gandía).

- El gran duque de Gandía. Ed. Guillermo Díaz-Plaja. Madrid,
  Guadarrama, 1969. Pp. 167. (Col. Punto Omega, 59.)

A popular edition, without critical apparatus.

El gran teatro del mundo

Calderón de la Barca, Pedro. El gran teatro del mundo. Ed. Juan
  Loveluck M. In Autos sacramentales por Lope de Vega y otros,
  Santiago de Chile, Zig-Zag, 1953. (Serie verde, 84-85.)

- The Great Theater of the World. Trans. Mack H. Singleton. In
  Masterpieces of the Spanish Golden Age. ed. Angel Flores, New
  York, Rinehart, 1957, pp. 368-95.
  Rev: Irving P. Rothberg, Hisp, 41 (1958), 256-57 (The reviewer
  points out that "This book is not a smorgasbord of literary
  apogees but a concentrated offering made up of six full
  selections translated by several people." Referring to this
  auto sacramental, Rothberg observes that "The last selection,
  The Great Theater of the World, is a free translation in which
  Calderón's tremendous grasp of his medium does not at all
  suffer. His modernity may confound today's undergraduate,
  which is all the more reason for its inclusion in this
  anthology.").

- <u>El gran teatro del mundo</u>. Ed. Eugenio Frutos Cortés. Salamanca, Anaya, 1958. Pp. 75. (Bib. Anaya, 5.)

The small volume published by Anaya provides a good text of the <u>auto</u>. The excellent background and scholarly works of Frutos Cortés make this edition a highly valuable one for use in Spanish literature classes. The availability of the Anaya series and the careful edition by Frutos Cortés have put this Calderón <u>auto</u> within popular reach.

- <u>Das grosse Welttheater</u>, Trans. (and arranged for staging) by Hans Urs von Balthasar. Einsiedeln, Johannes, 1959. Pp. 82.

- <u>Das Einsiedler grosse Welttheater</u>. Trans. Joseph von Eichendorff. Music by Heinrich Sutermeister. Einsiedeln, Gesellschaft der geistlichen Spiele, 1960. Pp. 51.

- <u>El gran teatro del mundo</u>. An edition and translation of a Nahuatl version by William A. Hunter. In <u>Middle American Research Institute</u>, Publication 27, New Orleans, 1960, pp. 107-221. (Doct. diss., Tulane Univ., 1954; Tulane <u>Abstracts</u>, Series 55, No. 14, p. 94.)

- <u>El gran teatro del mundo</u>. Adaptation "a lectura dialogada." Madrid, Gráficas Ibarra, 1962. Pp. 16.

- <u>Das grosse Welttheater</u>. Ed. Joseph von Eichendorff and Fritz Schalk. Stuttgart, Reclam, 1962. Pp. 54.

<u>Guárdate del agua mansa</u>

Calderón de la Barca, Pedro. <u>Stille Waters habben diepe Gronden</u>. Oudenbosch, Plesef, Wim Kubbenga, 1962. Pp. 140.

<u>La hija del aire</u>

Calderón de la Barca, Pedro. <u>La hija del aire</u>. <u>A Critical</u>

Annotated Edition of the "Primera Parte", with a Study of the Semiramis Legend and its Dramatic Treatment by Calderón in Relation to Earlier Dramatizations of the Theme. Ed. G. Edwards. Unpub. doct. diss., Univ. of London (King's College), 1960-61.

El mágico prodigioso

Calderón de la Barca, Pedro. El mágico prodigioso. Ed. Angel Valbuena Prat. Zaragoza, Ebro, 1953. Pp. 126. (Clás. Ebro, 87.) (Later eds.)

This edition of El mágico prodigioso, which has been reprinted several times without change, provides a handy text for class usage. It follows the pattern of the other Ebro editions: a chronological table of Calderón's life, main events during his lifetime, which is published without change in other volumes of different Calderonian plays, a "Prólogo," divided by Valbuena Prat into three parts: "Las comedias de santos," "El mágico prodigioso," and "Lo teológico," which are followed by some remarks about "Técnica y versificación," "El lenguaje, el estilo," "Los personajes," "Nuestra edición," and a "Bibliografía."

- Der wundertätige Magier. Ed. Eugen Gürster. Stuttgart, Reclam, 1962. Pp. 96.

- Le Magicien prodigieux. Trans. and ed. Bernard Sesé. Paris, Editions Montaigne, 1969. Pp. 288. (Col. Bilingue.)

El mayor monstruo los celos (El mayor monstruo del mundo)

Calderón de la Barca, Pedro. El mayor monstro los celos. A Critical and Annotated Edition from the Partly Holographic Manuscript. Ed. Everett W. Hesse. Madison, Univ. of Wisconsin Press, 1955. Pp. xi, 249.
Rev: Ramon Rozzell, Hisp, 38 (1955), 512-14; José Ares Montes, Clav, 7, No. 40 (1956), 73-74; John M. Hill, HR, 24 (1956), 325-28; A. E. Sloman, BHS, 33 (1956), 227-29; E. M. Wilson, MP, 54 (1956), 61-63; Margaret Crosland, MLR, 52 (1957), 142;

J.-L. Flecniakoska, <u>BH</u>, 59 (1957), 344-45; Angel Valbuena
Briones, <u>Arbor</u>, 38, Nos. 141-44 (1957), 326-28.

The reviewers praise this painstaking and valuable editorial
service, but would have welcomed an extension, and some corrections, of commentary and notes. Professor Crosland particularly welcomes the Hesse edition, and describes in detail
the contents of the volume; Professor Flecniakoska states
that the editor "nous donne une très bonne édition critique
du <u>Mayor monstruo los celos</u> d'après le manuscrit N° 79 de la
Bibliothèque Nationale de Madrid." After describing the edition and recognizing its scholarly value, the reviewer gives
his own opinion about this Calderón drama: "Malgré ses efforts
(Hesses's), le commentateur n'arrive pas à nous convaincre de
la valeur de cette pièce ... les conflits tragiques ne nous
sollicitent pas, la pièce reste froide, non seulement parce
que l'ensemble est inhumain, mais aussi parce que la technique
dramatique est souvent défectueuse." The reviewer ends by
regretting that all of Professor Hesse's time and effort
"n'ait pas été consacré à une oeuvre de Calderón de plus de
relief." Professor Valbuena Briones praises very highly the
critical edition published by Dr. Hesse: "Precede la edición
un fino trabajo en el que el erudito estudia el sentido
aristotélico de la tragedia. Se trata de una imitación
escénica de una acción que produce miedo y piedad en el
ánimo del espectador... El final, sorprendente e imprevisto,
es de un típico senequismo español." The reviewer, in
presenting the history of the ups and downs of the play,
recalls that "El siglo XIX, finalmente, la condena a través
de la incomprensión, en este caso, de Menéndez Pelayo. En el
XX, <u>El monstruo...</u> vuelve a ser alabado, después de la
revalorización que mi padre, el profesor Valbuena Prat, hace
del teatro calderoniano."

El médico de su honra

Calderón de la Barca, Pedro. <u>The Surgeon of His Honour</u>. Trans.
Roy Campbell. Introd. by Everett W. Hesse. Madison, Univ. of
Wisconsin Press, 1960. Pp. xxx, 82.
Rev: C. A. Jones, <u>HR</u>, 29 (1961), 171-72 (The translation does
not consistently live up to the high hopes raised by this
noted Hispanophile. However, Dr. Hesse contributes "an
excellent introduction, brief and business-like, and, while
clearly aimed at the popular reader, reliable and scholarly.");

J. E. Varey, <u>MLR</u>, 57 (1962), 617-18 ("Whilst the version reads well the reader familiar with the original is bound to be conscious of a certain constraint.").

- <u>El médico de su honra</u>. Ed. C. A. Jones. Oxford, Oxford Univ. Press, 1961. Pp. xxvi, 111.
Rev: Robert Marrast, <u>BH</u>, 64 (1962), 324 (The reviewer states that with this edition we possess the best, most carefully edited version of <u>El médico de su honra</u>, which will henceforth be the authoritative one.); J. E. Varey, <u>MLR</u>, 57 (1962), 617-18 (Laments the lack of any reference to the staging of the play, other than one cursory note at the beginning, but concludes that "Dr. Jones' edition has clearly been prepared with the utmost care and is presented with the greatest clarity."); A. Irvine Watson, <u>BHS</u>, 39 (1962), 106-07 (Points out drawbacks: "falls between two stools: it is too expensive for the student and not quite adequate for the scholar." However, he qualifies the text as the most trustworthy to date. "We shall be grateful to Dr. Jones for having given us the first edition based firmly on the 'princeps' of this fine play."); Everett W. Hesse, <u>Symposium</u>, 17 (1963), 146-47 (A brief review in which the author regrets that Jones did not give his own interpretation of the play and the rôle of honour.); Eberhard Leube, <u>RJ</u>, 14 (1963), 368-70 (Criticizes the limitation of the bibliography to English and Spanish titles and the scarcity of truly clarifying footnotes, and questions some devoted to classical references. Nevertheless, the reviewer considers it a carefully prepared and useful edition. He accepts Jones' approach to the honour theme, in which he accepts earlier Calderonian criticism, as legitimate and even necessary, but not the only approach.); J. H. Parker, <u>HR</u>, 31 (1963), 89-90 (A favourable review, but points up such small details as overlapping in two parts of the introduction and inconsistency in bibliographical procedure.).

<u>Los misterios de la misa</u>

Calderón de la Barca, Pedro. <u>Os mistérios da missa</u>. (<u>Auto sacramental alegórico</u>.) Trans. João Cabral de Mello Neto. Rio de Janeiro, Editora Civilização Brasileira, 1963. Pp. 95. (Col. Universitária de Teatro, Series 1, Livros de Texto, 1.)

A verse translation of <u>Los misterios de la misa</u>, but not

always in the original metres or rhymes. The translation
follows the original closely but not exactly. There is a
brief commentary on Calderón and his <u>auto</u> by Martim Gonçalves.

No hay burlas con el amor

Calderón de la Barca, Pedro. <u>No hay burlas con el amor</u>. Adaptation by José Hierro. Madrid, Edit. Nacional, 1963. Pp. 137.

A printing of the text as used in a performance in September,
1963, with brief remarks by the adapter and the director. The
text has been modernized and some allusions, not understood
by modern audiences, eliminated. The play is divided into two
acts, and each has both <u>cuadros</u> and scenes. Although nicely
printed and a souvenir of the performance, it is of little
value to scholars. There are no notes.

No hay más fortuna que Dios

Calderón de la Barca, Pedro. <u>No hay más fortuna que Dios</u>. Ed.
Alexander A. Parker. Manchester, Manchester Univ. Press, 1949.
Pp. xl, 92. (2nd ed., 1962.)
Rev: Courtney Bruerton, <u>NRFH</u>, 5 (1951), 332-33 (Bruerton
praises the solid and useful erudition with which Parker has
edited the text of one of Calderón's best <u>autos</u>. Although the
edition initiates a series designed to reach beyond the
limited range of specialists in the Golden Age, Bruerton
states that the careful, complete, and erudite notes will be
"apreciadas" by all of the specialists, not only of the <u>auto
sacramental</u>, but also of the <u>comedia</u>. Only on the question of
dating does Bruerton take exception to Parker's work. Parker
suggests that the <u>auto</u> was written either in 1652 or 1653,
probably in the latter year. Bruerton is not convinced by the
evidence adduced by Parker, and ends his review by pointing
out that Hilborn, on the basis of his study of versification,
dates the <u>auto</u> towards 1675.); Esteban Pujals, <u>Arbor</u>, 18, No.
61 (1951), 148-49 (This edition is the first fruit of a selection of <u>autos</u> announced by Parker in 1943 in <u>The Allegorical
Drama of Calderón</u>. The reviewer gives a résumé of the allegorical significance of the <u>auto</u>. He provides little critical
comment on this specific edition, but expresses great praise
of Parker as a leader in Calderonian studies.); Fritz Schalk,
<u>RF</u>, 65 (1953), 196-97.

No hay que creer ni en la verdad

Calderón de la Barca, Pedro. No hay que creer ni en la verdad.
Ed. Václav Černý. Madrid, CSIC, 1968. Pp. 160. (Anejos de
Segismundo, 1.)

Another MS found by Černý in the same Czechoslovakian castle
as El gran duque de Gandía. The text includes a critical
study. See Studies — Individual Works.

No siempre lo peor es lo cierto

Calderón de la Barca, Pedro. No siempre lo peor es cierto. In
John M. Hill and Mabel M. Harlan (eds.), Cuatro comedias,
New York, Norton, 1941, pp. 483-614. (Re-issue: 1956.)
Rev: Arnold G. Reichenberger, HR, 25 (1957), 77-78.

Professor Reichenberger writes a brief note stating that "It
is with great satisfaction and pleasure that we bring to the
attention of our readers the re-issue of this scholarly work."

El pintor de su deshonra

Calderón de la Barca, Pedro. El pintor de su deshonra. Ed.
Manuel Ruiz Lagos. Madrid, Ediciones Alcalá, 1969. Pp. 240.

La plazuela de Santa Cruz

Calderón de la Barca, Pedro. La plazuela de Santa Cruz. In
Cesco Vian (ed.), Antologia breve del teatro "chico" spagnolo,
Milan, La Goliardica, 1953, pp. 81-98. (Pp. 240.)

- La plazuela de Santa Cruz. In Cesco Vian (ed.), Il teatro
"chico" spagnolo, Milan, 1957. Pp. 192.
Rev: Joaquín de Entrambasaguas, RL, 11 (1957), 240-41.

Professor Entrambasaguas' review is highly adverse to Vian's
book. It is an anthology, containing eight one-act comic plays,

each by a different author. The reviewer objects to the
grouping of such a wide range of authors, from Rueda to the
Quinteros, and questions the omission of several leading
entremesistas. Entrambasaguas closes his review with a polite
thanks for the difusión of these short plays in Italy, "no
obstante la ligereza y el afán de interpretación original
errónea."

El pleito matrimonial del cuerpo y el alma

Calderón de la Barca, Pedro. El pleito matrimonial del cuerpo
y el alma. Ed. Manfred Engelbert. Hamburg, Kommissionsverlag
Cram, de Gruyter und Co., 1969. Pp. 320. (Hamburger
Romanistische Studien. B, Ibero-Amerikanische Reihe, 31.)

El príncipe constante

Calderón de la Barca, Pedro. El príncipe constante. Ed.
Alexander A. Parker. 2nd ed. (with corrections). Cambridge,
Eng., Cambridge Univ. Press, 1957. Pp. vii, 94. (Cambridge
Plain Texts.) (1st ed.: 1938.)
Rev: Edward M. Wilson, BHS, 36 (1959), 58-59.

Professor Wilson, in his review, points out that "The book
went to press before the bibliography of the three editions
of D. Joseph Calderón's Primera parte had been clarified.
These are dated 1636, 1640, and 1640. The ... Vera Tassis
appeared in 1685. Professor Parker based his edition on what
is now thought to be the falsely dated edition of 1640 (really
of c. 1670) and on that of 1685." However, it is the best
edition we have of the play, and includes the sarcastic gibe
against Paravicino not found in other editions.

- Der standhafte Prinz. Trans. and ed. by Eugen Gürster.
Stuttgart, Reclam, 1960. Pp. 80.

El sitio de Bredá

Calderón de la Barca, Pedro. El sitio de Bredá. Ed. Johanna R.

Schrek. The Hague, 1957. Pp. 259. (Pubs. of the Inst. of
Hispanic Studies, Univ. of Utrecht, 1.)
Rev: F. López Estrada, Archivo Hispalense, Nos. 84-85 (1957),
97-99; Edward M. Wilson, BHS, 34 (1957), 227-29; P. Groult,
LR, 14 (1960), 285-87.

Professor Wilson writes in his review that Johanna R. Schrek
"has based her text on the manuscript copy made in 1632 by
Diego Martínez de Mora, which she has collated with the
editions of the Primera Parte of 1636 and that falsely dated
1640, as well as with an unidentified suelta. As far as I
have been able to test her transcription, it seems accurate
and reliable; it will be useful to serious students of
Calderón's texts. Her work on the sources of the play and on
its historical background seems thorough and fairminded.
Unfortunately her notions of literary criticism are elementary.
The chapter of her introduction entitled Estilística leaves
a good deal to be desired. A word of caution must be said
about the purely learned aspect of her work." Professor Wilson
also mentions that "like many other scholars she also is
unaware of what Maccoll knew in 1888: that there were two
editions of the Primera Parte dated 1640." The reviewer also
criticizes the edition's "ignorance of bibliographical
niceties."

Tan largo me lo fiáis

Calderón de la Barca, Pedro. Tan largo me lo fiáis. Ed. Xavier
A. Fernández. Madrid, Revista Estudios, 1967. Pp. xlix, 233.
(Appeared in Revista Estudios, 23, No. 79, 1967, pp. 503-784;
"Número monográfico.").

See review article, Gerald E. Wade, BCom, 20, No. 2 (1968),
31-41; Studies — Individual Works (Wade).

El verdadero Dios Pan

Calderón de la Barca, Pedro. El verdadero Dios Pan. Ed. José M.
de Osma. Lawrence, Univ. of Kansas Press, 1949. Pp. ix, 149.
Rev: Bruce W. Wardropper, HR, 19 (1951), 274-76.

Professor Osma is to be congratulated for having undertaken

the initial edition of a series designed to include <u>autos</u>
inaccessible in modern texts. He is commended for his masterly
discussion of the mythological background of the <u>auto</u>, but the
reviewer laments the extremely limited explanation of the dogma involved, stating that "mythology in the <u>autos</u> is never
more than a vehicle for the conveyance of dogma." It is not
clear whether Professor Osma's publication is intended as an
<u>edición escolar</u> or as a critical edition, but the reviewer
notes its inadequacies on both counts, pointing out the
absence of critical apparatus and documenting several instances of carelessness.

La vida es sueño

Calderón de la Barca, Pedro. <u>Y los sueños sueños son</u>. Bogotá,
Espiral, 1951. Pp. 91.

A modernized version of <u>La vida es sueño</u>.

- <u>La vita è un sogno</u>. Trans. A. Monteverdi. In C. Pavolini (ed.),
<u>Tutto il teatro di tutti i tempi</u>, Rome, 1953, pp. 615-50.

- <u>La vida es sueño</u>. Ed. Rafael Gastón. Zaragoza, Ebro, 1954.
Pp. 142. (Bib. Clás. Ebro, 13.) (Later eds.)

- <u>La vida es sueño</u>. Ed. Martín de Riquer. Barcelona, Juventud,
1954. Pp. 174. (Col. Para Todos.) (Later eds., including New
York, Las Américas, 1966. Pp. 187.)

- <u>Life Is a Dream</u>. Trans. William E. Colford. Great Neck, N. Y.,
1958. Pp. xx, 102. (Barron's Educational Series.)

This translation is preceded by an "Introduction," which is
divided into five parts: "The Period," "The Author," "The
Work," "The Translation," and "Bibliography." It also has 29
footnotes mostly clarifying proper names. Professor Colford's
purpose is to provide "The American student of Comparative
Literature with a complete verse translation into the meter
of the Elizabethan dramatists' iambic pentameters." Colford's
version successfully attains its goals.

- *La vida es sueño*. Ed. Everett W. Hesse. New York, Scribner, 1961. Pp. 168.
Rev: Carlos Ortigoza, <u>Hisp</u>, 44 (1961), 577-78 ("The edition is intended for use at the junior-graduate level and in our opinion Professor Hesse succeeds in satisfying this varied range because of his psychological, modern approach ... the chapter on 'analysis and interpretation' is in itself an excellent essay."); Bruce W. Wardropper, <u>MLN</u>, 77 (1962), 199-202 (Compares this edition to Sloman's of 1961. Finds fault with the introduction to Hesse's edition for being eclectic, thus giving a too brief account of several attempts to explain the meaning of <u>La vida es sueño</u>. Re the explanation of the symbolism of the play, Wardropper qualifies it as audacious: "Hesse is just guessing." Conclusion: "Each of these editors helps one a little towards a better understanding of the play. The pity of it is that it is so little."); J. E. Varey, <u>BHS</u>, 40 (1963), 190-94 (Compares the edition with Sloman's. Objects to Hesse's "post-Freudian" treatment of the play and the attempt to "impose a pattern ... from without," and insists that the play is built on "sure foundations of authority and precedent," thus invalidating Hesse's approach. The appearance of the edition is praised.); William M. Whitby, <u>HR</u>, 31 (1963), 281-84 (Praises the text as a combination of scholarly editing and more popular editing to arouse the interest of the beginning reader of Spanish literature. The reviewer makes a number of useful corrections and disagrees with some of Hesse's symbolism.)

- *La vida es sueño*. Ed. Albert E. Sloman. Manchester Univ. Press, 1961. Pp. 137.
Rev: See Hesse ed. above; H. Hinterhauser, <u>Archiv</u>, 198 (1961), 347 (Highly recommended for use by students.); Wardropper, <u>MLN</u>, 77 (1962), 199-202 (See Hesse ed. above; prefers Sloman's text and introduction, but is not entirely satisfied.); Everett W. Hesse, <u>Symposium</u>, 17 (1963), 146 (A brief and favourable review which speaks highly of the edition and corrects two errors.); J. E. Varey, <u>BHS</u>, 40 (1963), 190-94 (See Hesse ed. above; prefers Sloman's limiting himself to the <u>princeps</u> for his text as well as his interpretation, which is that the play is "essentially a moral one." Considers the text well presented.); William M. Whitby, <u>HR</u>, 31 (1963), 278-81 (Praises it as a "carefully wrought contribution to scholarship," and discusses some differences between the Zaragoza text, 1636, and other earlier texts.).

- *Das Leben ist ein Traum*. Ed. Eugen Gürster. Stuttgart, Reclam, 1962. Pp. 96.

- *Life Is a Dream*. Trans. Edward and Elizabeth Huberman. In Angel Flores (ed.), *Spanish Drama*, New York, Bantam Books, 1962, pp. 191-242.

- *La vie est un songe*. Adaptation by M. C. Valène and André Charpak. Paris, L'Avant-Scène, No. 258, 1962. Pp. 54.

- *La vida es sueño*. Buenos Aires, Edit. La Mandrágora, 1963. Pp. 159. (Bolsi Clás., 11.)

- *La vida es sueño*. Madrid, Alfil, 1964. Pp. 167. (Col. Teatro, 435, especial.)

- *La vida es sueño*. Buenos Aires, Losada, 1965. Pp. 259.

- *La vida es sueño*. Ed. Carmelo Samonà. Rome, De Santis, 1966. Pp. 184. (Pub. dell'Univ. degli Studi di Roma, Facoltà di Magistero.)

- *La vita è sogno*. *Il dramma e l'auto sacramental*. Ed. Luisa Orioli. Milan, Adelphi, 1967. Pp. xvi, 364.
Rev: *Libri e Riviste d'Italia*, 20 (1968), 792-93; Giacomo V. Sabatelli, *Vita e Pensiero*, 51 (1968), 161-66; Cesare Sughi, *Il Verri*, 28 (1968), 111-12.

- *La vida es sueño*. In José Martel, Hymen Alpern and Leonard Mades (eds.), *Diez comedias del Siglo de Oro*, New York, Harper and Row, 1968, pp. 607-700.

An improved edition of the anthology of 1939 (revised by Leonard Mades), with a bibliography of reference works. The introduction and the section on versification have been augmented. A new glossary of terms and stage directions has also been added.

- <u>Life's a Dream</u>. Trans. Kathleen Raine and R. M. Nadal. London, Hamish Hamilton, 1968. Pp. 116.
Rev: Gwynne Edwards, <u>BHS</u>, 46 (1969), 275-76 (Fails to produce an accurate picture of the drama; the translators have neglected to use a reliable critical text and have therefore continued the faults of cheap, popular editions.).

STUDIES

GENERAL

(Anon.) "Los autos sacramentales en España. Teología al aire libre." Mundo Hispánico, Nos. 50-51 (May-June, 1952), 37.

An illustrated note on the timelessness of Calderón's autos.

(Anon.) "La tradición eucarística en los autos sacramentales." Estudios, 8 (1952), 227-33.

In connection with the XXXV Congreso Eucarístico Internacional in Barcelona, this non-literary article discusses the Eucharistic significance of the autos in the light of the "pure" Catholic tradition of Spain. Having cited the revival of scholarly interest (manifest largely in the work of foreign, i.e., non-Spanish scholars) which dates from post-Menéndez Pelayo days, the article affirms a corresponding revival of popular interest in the autos which, in Spain, "florece ahora con nueva pujanza como acontece a las semillas cuando tienen clima más apropiado, el hecho es que la España de Franco reúne la mayor concentración de católicos que jamás haya existido, en un Congreso Eucarístico Internacional de trascendentes resultados, y remoza la españolísima afición popular por los españolísimos Autos Sacramentales."

(Anon.) "James Russell Lowell on Calderón." BPLQ, 6 (1954), 190-91.

Reproduces a letter of 21 April, 1875, by Lowell, advocating the reading of Calderón's plays.

Abirached, Robert. "Le Théâtre dans la cité: Aristophanes, Calderón, Behan." Etudes, 313 (1962), 99-103.

Alonso, Dámaso. "La correlación en la estructura del teatro
calderoniano." In Dámaso Alonso and Carlos Bousoño, Seis calas
en la expresión literaria española, Madrid, Gredos, 1951, pp.
115-86. (2nd ed., "aumentada y corregida," 1956. Calderón:
pp. 119-91.)
Rev: G. B., Clav, 2, No. 11 (1951), 70-71 (Lavish praise for
the ensemble, and very special distinction for the section on
Calderón: "Este primer estudio que, con el dedicado a aplicar
el método estilístico al teatro de Calderón, constituye, a mi
juicio, la clave del libro y la más importante aportación de
Dámaso Alonso — en esta ocasión — a un nuevo enfoque de la
crítica literaria, sitúa al lector plenamente en el ambiente
de toda la obra."); E. Allison Peers, BHS, 28 (1951), 217-19
("The fourth and longest (chapter), which many readers will
find the most fruitful, treats of correlation in the structure
of Calderón's plays." Peers objects to the lack of an index;
otherwise his review is a straightforward report on content,
with no further judgment expressed.); Sergio Ferraro, Quaderni
Iberoamericani, No. 12 (1952), 214-15 (The reviewer is
unfavourably disposed towards the scientific approach employed
by the authors in the study of poetry. He relaxes his criticism somewhat with regard to the chapter on Calderón precisely
because Dámaso Alonso there studies the playwright "nel suo
lato meno poetico, appunto in quello che ci appare molto
adatto alla catalogazione e risolvibile, assai spesso, in
equazioni.").

Not considered in this chapter on Calderón is the correlation
which is found throughout Calderón's theatre in lyrical
incrustations such as the famous first monologue of Segismundo.
In this study, Dámaso Alonso concentrates on the correlation
found in the structure of Calderón's plays. From the comedia
de capa y espada, undergirded by a natural spirit of
bimembración, to the autos, where the dramatization of the
elements leads naturally to cuadrimembración, and even to
correlación pentamembre when dramatizing the senses, correlation is discovered in great abundance, and classified. The
study of correlation had previously been limited to literature.
Dámaso Alonso has now extended the field of investigation to
dramatic art and his analyses prove that correlation is one
of the most characteristic traits of the dramaturgy of
Calderón.

- "Los versos trimembres en España." In Libro de homenaje a
Luis Alberto Sánchez en los 40 años de su docencia universitaria, Lima, Univ. Nac. Mayor de San Marcos, 1967, pp. 11-13.

Examples are drawn from Calderón's poetry.

Alonso Cortés, Narciso. "Genealogía de D. Pedro Calderón."
BRAE, 31 (1951), 299-309.

Alonso Cortés establishes the paternal line of the poet
through seven preceding generations. In so doing, he categor-
ically claims to have refuted three major theories held by
genealogists of Calderón; and he only slightly more timidly
proposes a fourth rectification. The refuted theories are:
1. to suppose that Pedro Calderón, "vecino del Sotillo," is
the same Pedro Calderón who was the grandfather of the poet
(Pedro Calderón, "vecino del Sotillo," precedes the poet by
five generations); 2. to suppose that the same Pedro Calderón,
"vecino del Sotillo," was the first member of the family to
move to Boadilla (in the documentation prepared by the poet
for his entrance into the Orden de Santiago, he claims this
distinction for his great-grandfather, Diego); and 3. to
suppose that an Alonso Sánchez Calderón was the son of Hernán
Sánchez and father of Pedro Calderón, "vecino del Sotillo"
(Alonso Cortés considers the very existence of this Alonso
Sánchez Calderón improbable, and documents Alvaro Calderón's
right to the cited filial and paternal relationships). The
testament of Diego Calderón, great-grandfather of the poet,
in which he mentions "Isabel Calderón, mi madre," seems to
refute the theory that Diego was the son of Pedro "del
Sotillo." In a second section, on the basis of a "pleito de
hidalguía" filed in 1583 by the poet's grandfather, Diego de
Henao, Alonso Cortés establishes the maternal line of the
poet through his great-great-grandparents.

Ammer, Floriar. Die Nachtwachen des Don Pedro Calderón de la
Barca. Ein Vermachtnis. Freiburg, Heider, 1952. Pp. 292.
Rev: A. Baldus, Welt und Wort, 8 (1953), 58.

The reestablishment of Calderón. A legacy; with prose versions,
in German, of some of the dramatist's plays.

Anderson, Vernon Lockwood. Hugo von Hofmannsthal and Pedro
Calderón de la Barca: A Comparative Study. Unpub. doct. diss.,
Stanford Univ., 1954. (DA, 14, 523.)

The objectives of the study are first the comparison of the

work of the two authors with respect to plot, characterization, theme, influence, dramatic structure, etc.; and secondly, to interpret the principal differences in terms of personality, artistic talent, and taste, and philosophic viewpoint of each. The essential difference is found in Hofmannsthal's interpretation of Calderón's characterization and language, reflecting the social, political, and philosophical convictions of 20th century Europe.

Arauz, Alvaro. <u>Notas sobre Lope de Vega y Calderón</u>. Mexico, Ediciones Atlántico, 1951. Pp. 79. (Published in a 2nd ed., Mexico, B. Costa Amic, 1959, Col. Panorama, 16, as <u>Lope de Vega y Calderón de la Barca</u>. <u>Ensayo</u>. Pp. 64. No change.)

A series of extremely subjective and oversimplified notes which result in a superficial comparison of Lope and Calderón. Arauz uses all of the stock epigrammatic comparisons ("Lope es espontáneo; Calderón, reflexivo") and adds many others ("Calderón es la celda, Lope es la calle." "Norte o sur de la dramática. Perfectos."). Some of the better comparisons indicate a certain perceptiveness in Arauz's contrastive analysis. Such oversimplification normally runs the risk, however, of obscuring the many differences in degree alone which mark the work of the two dramatists simply as different stages in an evolutive process. Typographical errors abound.

Arjona, J. H. "The Use of Autorhymes in the XVII Century <u>Comedia</u>." <u>HR</u>, 21 (1953), 273-301.

The author studies the autorhyme (identical rhyme in form) in over one hundred plays from twenty-two different dramatists, and describes the elaborate system of rules which governed its usage in the Golden Age. The study leads the author to hope that the variation in usage of the autorhyme may be a future aid in the investigation of authorship and chronology of <u>comedias</u>.

Arróniz, Othón. <u>La influencia italiana en el nacimiento de la comedia española</u>. Madrid, Gredos, 1969. Pp. 339. (Bibl. Románica Hisp., II, Estudios y ensayos, 133.)

There are a few references to the work of Cosimo Lotti and the staging of Calderón's plays; but, as the title indicates, this monograph deals above all with the pre-Calderón periods.

Artiles, Jenaro. "Bibliografía sobre el problema del honor y la honra en el drama español." In Filología y crítica hispánica: Homenaje al Prof. Federico Sánchez Escribano, ed. Alberto Porqueras-Mayo and Carlos Rojas, Madrid-Atlanta, Ediciones Alcalá-Emory Univ., 1969, pp. 235-41.

Ashcom, B. B. "The WSU-Apontes." BCom, 14, No. 2 (1963), 19-20.

A description of a set of six volumes of Calderón's plays, some sueltas and some of the edition of Fernández de Apontes (1760-63), in the possession of the Wayne State University Library, Detroit.

- A Descriptive Catalogue of the Spanish Comedias Sueltas in the Wayne State University Library and the Private Library of Professor B. B. Ashcom. Detroit, Wayne State Univ. Libraries, 1965. Pp. vii, 103.

Lists a large number of Calderón items.

Atkins, Stuart. "Goethe, Calderón und Faust: Die Tragödie zweiter Teil." Germanic Review, 28 (1953), 83-98.

Describes the long-disregarded influence of Calderón on Goethe in the field of dramatic symbolism.

Aub, Max. "Lo más del teatro español en menos que nada." PSA, Año 5, Tomo 19, No. 55 (1960), 11-38.

A running personal commentary on the entire Spanish theatre, with only brief mention of Calderón.

Aubrun, Charles V. "Les Enfants terribles dans la Comedia (1600-1650)." RJ, 8 (1957), 312-20.

Includes "le conflit des générations," with reference to Curcio and his daughter Julia of La devoción de la Cruz.

- "Abstractions morales et références au réel dans la tragédie lyrique." In Réalisme et poésie au théâtre, Paris, Centre

National de la Recherche Scientifique, 1960, pp. 53-59. (2nd
ed., 1967.)

References to Calderón.

- "Determinismo y libertad humana en la dialéctica calderoniana."
Tareas (Panama), 1, No.2(1961), 3-14.

- "Le Déterminisme naturel et la causalité surnaturelle chez
Calderón." In Le Théâtre Tragique, Paris, Centre National de
la Recherche Scientifique, 1962, pp. 199-209.
Rev: Léon Chancerel, Rev. d'Hist. du Théâtre, 14 (1962),
248-49.

A discussion of such problems as free will and grace. El
mayor monstruo los celos is used to illustrate the author's
points. Calderón considered his plays as instruments for the
service of God and the King, rather than as works of purely
literary value. Therefore·we see these works as instruments
for bringing Augustinian theology closer to Spanish society.
Calderón's treatment of honour, love, incest, and jealousy
was, then, a dramatic enactment of contemporary Roman Catholic
theology.

- "Les Débuts du drame lyrique en Espagne." In Le Lieu Théâtral
à la Renaissance, Paris, Centre National de la Recherche
Scientifique, 1964.

Calderón: pp. 423-36 and 436-44. Only in 1661 did Calderón
definitely fix the form and conventions of the new genre (the
lyric drama): a tragicomedy of mythological theme for
"représentation en musique." Aubrun describes a performance
of La gloria de Niquea of Villamediana, Lope's eclogue La
selva sin amor, and Calderón's El mayor encanto amor at a
great celebration held in the Buen Retiro. He mentions other
attempts of Calderón, and then says that in 1661 the dramatist
fixes the genre with three works "coup sur coup": Faetonte,
El monstruo de los jardines and Eco y Narciso, "un spectacle
chanté et déclamé."

- "Realismo y poesía en el teatro: Abstracciones morales y
referencias a lo real en la tragedia lírica de Calderón."

Rev. de la Univ. Nac. de la Plata, 18 (1964), 297-305. (Trans. Saul Yurkievich.)

The study deals with Calderón's La estatua de Prometeo as the basis of the author's theory that although the spectator cannot completely identify himself with the protagonist of a real tragedy or of a farce, in a tragicomedia he believes that what happens on the stage can happen, or has happened, to him. Aubrun then analyses the Calderón play, showing how its events could be interpreted in the events of the day; for example, the reconciliation of the Titan brothers reflects that of Carlos and his son Juan of Austria, made enemies by the intrigues of the queen mother. Today, Prometeo might be identified with an atomic scientist.

- Histoire du théâtre espagnol. Paris, Presses Universitaires de France, 1965. Pp. 124. (Que sais-je?, 1179.)

Chapt. 5: "Un nouveau tournant et l'art de Calderón (1635-1680)."

- La Comédie espagnole (1600-1680). Paris, Presses Universitaires de France, 1966. Pp. viii, 1960. (Trans. Julio Lago Alonso, Madrid, Taurus, 1968.)
Rev: Andrés Amorós, CHA, 72 (1967), 380-88; Leonard Mades, RHM, 33 (1967), 148-49; Juan Manuel Rozas, Segismundo, 3 (1967), 402-06; J. H. Parker, Hisp, 51 (1968), 363 ("The volume is an excellent presentation and comprehension of the seventeenth-century Spanish theater. Prof. Aubrun is to be congratulated on publishing the book."); A. Vermeylen, LR, 23 (1969), 283-84.

Calderón is given full and proper treatment.

Ayala, Francisco. "Sobre el punto de honor castellano." Rev. de Occidente, 2a. Epoca, 1, No. 5 (1963), 151-74.

In the course of discussing the honour code from its seriousness of purpose to mocking treatments of it, the author cites Calderón, along with Alemán, Cervantes, Lope de Vega, Quevedo, Tirso and others.

Ayllón, José. "La interpretación de los clásicos." Insula, 7,
No. 75 (1952), 12.

Although no specific mention is made of Calderón, the author's
reference is clearly to the Golden Age in his indictment of
the contemporary public, theatrical companies, and actors for
the drastically insufficient support given to the presentation
of Spain's classical theatre.

Azanza Nieto, Rosa María. Bibliografía de los dramas de honor
de Calderón de la Barca. Unpub. thesis, Univ. de Madrid, 1960.

Baeza, José. Pedro Calderón de la Barca: Su vida y sus más
famosos autos sacramentales relatados a los niños. 4th ed.
Barcelona, Edit. Araluce, 1956. Pp. 173. (1st ed., 1929.)
(Los grandes hechos de los grandes hombres, 11.)

Balasov, N. J. "Slavjanskaja tematika u Kal'derona i problema
Renessans-Barocco v ispanskoj literature." Izvestija Akademii
Nauk S.S.S.R., Otdelenie Literatury i Jazyka (Moscow), 26
(1967), 227-40.

Slavic themes in Calderón and the Renaissance-Baroque problem
in Spanish literature.

Le Baroque au Théâtre et la Théâtralité du Baroque. Actes 1966
de la 2e session des Journées internationales d'étude du
Baroque. Montauban, Centre National de Recherches du Baroque,
1967. Pp. 151.
Rev: Marc Fumaroli, XVIIe Siècle, No. 79 (1968), 117-22.

"On ne saurait trop recommander à tous la lecture attentive
de ces Actes, riches de suggestions et de rapprochements
féconds entre les différents arts et les diverses traditions
nationales. Un tel travail collectif, conçu dans le même
esprit que les belles publications du C.N.R.S. dont M. Jacquot
est l'initiateur, augure bien de l'avenir des rencontres
montalbanaises sous le signe du baroque."

Bataillon, Marcel. Varia lección de clásicos españoles. Madrid,
Gredos, 1964. Pp. 443.

Rev: Robert Ricard, <u>Rev. d'Ascétique et de Mystique</u>, 41 (1965), 210-11; C. A. Jones, <u>MLR</u>, 62 (1967), 540-41.

References to Calderón.

- <u>Défense et illustration du sens littéral</u>. Leeds, Maney and Son, 1967.

The Presidential address of the Modern Humanities Research Assoc. References to Calderón.

Baur-Heinhold, Margarete. <u>Theater des Barock</u>. Munich, Verlag G. D. W. Callwey, 1966. Pp. 296. (And as <u>Baroque Theatre</u>, London, Thames and Hudson, 1967. Pp. 292.)

Calderón (in both editions), pp. 91-92.

Bermúdez, Pedro Pablo. <u>La imaginación escénica del teatro sacramental de Calderón</u>. Unpub. doct. diss., Univ. of Rochester, 1969.

Bertrand, J. J. A. "Los comienzos del hispanismo alemán." <u>Clav</u>, 3, No. 14 (1952), 11-14.

Unsystematized but enthusiastic interest in Spain, her language, culture, and literature during the pre-romantic period, documented by Bertrand as far back as 1770. Cervantes, Lope de Vega, and Calderón are cited as the literary figures who received most attention.

- "Encuentros de F. Schiller con España." <u>Clav</u>, 6, No. 35 (1955), 38-42.

Schiller saw in Calderón "un arte sumo y toda la reflexión de un maestro; aun hasta lo irregular que salta a la vista está dominado por las leyes de una unidad superior."

Beysterveldt, A. A. van. <u>Répercussions du souci de la pureté de sang sur la conception de l'honneur dans la "Comedia nueva" espagnole</u>. Leiden, E. J. Brill, 1966. Pp. 239.

Rev: Luis V. Aracil, Rev. de Estudios Políticos, No. 158
(1968), 300-02; André Gloesener, Rev. Belge de Philologie et
d'Histoire, 46 (1968), 667-68.

Bomli, P. W. La Femme dans l'Espagne du Siècle d'Or. The Hague,
Martinus Nijhoff, 1950. Pp. viii, 390.
Rev: G. B., Clav, 2, No. 8 (1951), 70-71 (Favourable review.);
A. A. Parker, BHS, 28 (1951), 62-64 (The reviewer gratefully
acknowledges the usefulness of this book, but is surprised
that Bomli does not mention La devoción de la Cruz, as an
illustration of a daughter's revolt against her father's
authority. The discussion of the question of honour is cited
as the least satisfactory section of the book. In the study
of the mother, Parker notes the absence of any reference to
a very significant type of mother: the sad and tragic Doña
Blanca in Las tres justicias en una. He concludes his review
with a correction to Bomli's interpretation of the word
divorcio as used in Golden Age plays.); Otis H. Green, HR,
20 (1952), 255-57 (Cited as an outgrowth of a doctoral dissertation on the pícara, this work receives negative criticism
because of severe bibliographical limitations and because of
sketchy treatment, or no treatment at all, accorded to significant areas. Green points out that the vast literature on
the subject has not been adequately exploited. He laments the
complete lack of mention of the mujer sabia in literature,
the inadequate treatment received by marriage, and the way in
which the author lightly passes over the religious, philosophical, and legal aspects of the subjects.); E. F. Jareño, Rev.
Internac. de Sociología, 10 (1952), 512-14; K. L. Selig, Hisp,
36 (1953), 127 (The examination of the topic centred primarily
on the drama, with serious gaps in the investigation. The
monograph serves as an introduction to further studies on the
topic.)

Boughner, Daniel C. The Braggart in Renaissance Comedy.
Minneapolis, Univ. of Minnesota Press, 1954. Pp. ix, 328.
Rev: K. L. Selig, RBPH, 35 (1957), 834-35.

Chapter IX treats "The Renaissance and the Golden Age in
Spain," and makes reference to Calderón. However, says the
reviewer, the author does not show a thorough knowledge of
the plays he discusses, and the character of the braggart
lack a sufficiently critical approach.

Braig, Friedrich. "Kleist und Calderón." Literaturwissenschaft-liches Jahrbuch der Görresgesellschaft, n.s., 2 (1961), 41-54.

Parallels are drawn between the plays of the two dramatists. Goethe's opinions of Calderón are also touched upon.

Brancaforte, Benito. "Croce on Lope and Calderón: The Applica-tion of an Aesthetic Theory." Symposium, 23 (1969), 101-15.

Brancaforte points out that although Croce did not favour comparisons between authors, he was unable to resist the temptation of comparing Lope de Vega and Calderón. However, his purpose was other than that of conventional critical practices: he intended to show that such a comparison is impossible on aesthetic grounds. "...Croce's committed approach, however dangerous, must be recognized as a meaning-ful step in the history of literary criticism."

Branscheid, Waltraud. Grillparzer und Calderón. Inaugural-Dissertation zur Erlangung des Doktorgrades, Faculty of Phi-losophy, Univ. of Köln. Zentral-Verlag für Dissertationen, Triltsch, Düsseldorf, 1963.

Traces the literary relationship between Germany and Spain from the Renaissance to the Enlightenment, the interest of the Romantics in Calderón, translations, reworkings, and productions of his works, Grillparzer's introduction to Spanish culture and Spanish spirit and the difficulties in the way of learning the language and studying the literature. References are made to his Spanische Studien and to the mention of Calderón therein. The thesis then takes up those plays which show Calderonian traces, ending with the turning of Grillparzer's interest from Calderón to Lope. The opinion of the study is that, in spite of his acquaintance with Calderón, Grillparzer worked independently.

Bravo-Villasante, Carmen. La mujer vestida de hombre en el teatro español (Siglos XVI-XVII). Madrid, Rev. de Occidente, 1955. Pp. 238.
Rev: Alfredo Carballo Picazo, RFE, 39 (1955), 403-08; José Luis Cano, Clav, 7, No. 38 (1956), 75; Margaret Wilson, BHS, 33 (1956), 235-36; María Alfaro, Indice de Artes y Letras, 11 (1957), 28 ("La autora ha realizado un estudio muy completo...");

J. Campos, _Insula,_ 12, No. 131 (1957), 8 ("Trabajo interesante
y cuidadoso."); G. E. Wade, _BCom_, 9, No. 2 (1957), 19-20 (Exploration of the literary sources of the device, mainly
Italian, constitute a significant contribution. The author
traces its development and decline from Lope de Rueda on.);
and, an outstanding review article: B. B. Ashcom, "Concerning
'la mujer en hábito de hombre' in the _Comedia,_" _HR_, 28 (1960),
43-62.

The sixth chapter deals with Calderón and indicates that he
showed less interest in disguised women than other dramatists
of the Golden Age. (See also the author's _La mujer vestida de
hombre en la literatura española_, unpub. doct. diss., Univ.
of Madrid, 1957.)

Brenan, Gerald. _The Literature of the Spanish People_. Cambridge,
Univ. Press, 1951. Pp. xxii, 495. (2nd ed., 1953.)
Rev: E. M. Wilson, _Clav_, 2, No. 12 (1951), 76-77 (Wilson's
comments on Brenan's treatment of Calderón are basically
favourable, although he takes exception to certain details:
"El bosque está bien visto, aunque no siempre logre distinguir
los diversos árboles." Rather surprisingly, there is no hint
in this review of the rather severe criticism which Wilson
was later to direct at this section of the book in _BCom_,
1952); A. Valtierra, _Rev. Javeriana_, 37 (1952), 128; Glen D.
Willbern, _Hisp_, 35 (1952), 371-72 (Very complimentary in
every way. "The whole book is characterized by sympathetic
appreciation coupled with a sense of proportion."); E. M.
Wilson, _BCom_, 4, No. 1 (1952), 6-8 (Wilson challenges the
theory advanced by Brenan according to which Calderón's plays
seem to be divided into two chronological groups. According
to Brenan, during the first period, up to 1640, when Calderón
"led the roistering, duelling life of the _galán_ of the period,"
he wrote realistic (cloak-and-sword comedies, tragedies of
honour) and poetical plays. After 1655, he specialized in
zarzuelas and _autos_, during which time "theology, which he
got from books, weakened his interest in conduct." The intervening period is one of transition in which few masterpieces
are produced, except for _El alcalde de Zalamea_. Taking _A
secreto agravio, secreta venganza_ and _El médico de su honra_
as illustrations, Wilson suggests a radical shift in the
traditional interpretation of these secret-vengeance plays.
He feels that they should be seen as an honest presentation
by Calderón of the prevalent code of honour without our
reading into the frankness of the treatment Calderón's

approval of the code. This theory unveils a hitherto unnoticed identification of spirit between the earlier and later plays and indicates to Wilson that Brenan's theory of Calderón's conversion must be considerably modified.); E. M. Wilson, <u>MLR</u>, 47 (1952), 595-96 (Incrusted in an otherwise generally favourable review are the following comments: "The great defect of this most interesting volume is the treatment of the theatre ... Calderón is better served (than Lope), but even there Mr. Brenan has been unable to penetrate the deeper meaning of the dramas he describes."); Rev. of 2nd ed.: A. A. Parker, <u>MLR</u>, 52 (1957), 462-63 (In the chapter referring to Calderón's theatre, Professor Parker comments that "the most unsatisfactory part of the book is the treatment of Calderón... Mr. Brenan's unfamiliarity with seventeenth century intellectual preoccupations and modes of thought is not due to any lack of general treatment of the subject, nor is his inadequate knowledge and understanding of Catholic dogmatic and moral theology due to any lack of sources for proper information. The failure to understand Calderón is due as much to misunderstanding of his dramatic and stylistic technique...").

In Chapter XII of the book, "Calderón and the Late Drama," the brevity imposed by the nature of the volume is perhaps responsible for forcing Brenan into some unfortunate generalizations, such as his reaction to the dénouement of <u>El médico de su honra</u>: "This secret, premeditated murder of an innocent wife is held up to us as a course to be followed." His analyses of the poetic dimension of Calderón's theatre and of some individual plays are far superior to his comments on honour. In the preface to the second edition, Brenan states: "I have been criticized too by several people whose knowledge and judgment I respect for my interpretation of Calderón. If I have erred here, as I think I have.... But I do not see how anyone can interpret his <u>comedias</u> in a satisfactory way while we remain in our present state of ignorance upon his intellectual background ... a young Hispanist scholar, Mr. Pring-Mill, has suggested to me that the key to a great deal of what I found obscure lies in the Jesuit-Dominican controversy over free-will and predestination, and I think it probable that he is right."

Brüggemann, Werner. <u>Spanisches Theater und deutsche Romantik</u>. Münster-Aschendorff, 1964. Pp. 275.
Rev: Juan M. Díez Taboada, <u>Segismundo</u>, 1 (1965), 428-29; G. Orton, <u>BHS</u>, 42 (1965), 266-68; R. Ayrault, <u>Etudes Germaniques</u>,

21 (1966), 300-01; Hans Juretschke, FMod, Nos. 21-22 (1965-66),
59-73; B. Llorca, Razón y Fe, 173 (1966), 327.

The first volume of a study of the influence of the Spanish
theatre on German Romanticism. The first two parts of the
book deal with the development of the theatre in Spain, the
disfavour among the "élite" (critics) into which it fell in
the 18th century, its revival and the interest of the Germans
in it. Although Calderón is frequently mentioned here, it is
only the third part that deals more specifically with him as
the most important and influential dramatic poet of the Siglo
de Oro in Romantic Germany.

Cain, Virgil J. "The Spanish Classical Theatre." A.U.M.L.A.
(Journal of the Australian Universities Language and Literature Association), No. 10 (1959), 71-80.

Camón Aznar, José. "Teorías pictóricas de Lope y Calderón."
Velázquez, 1 (1964), 66-72.

Carilla, Emilio. El teatro español en la Edad de Oro (Escenarios
y representaciones). Buenos Aires, Centro Editor de América
Latina, 1968. Pp. 96.

 "El teatro en la época de Calderón (I)," pp. 67-74; "El teatro
 en la época de Calderón (II)," pp. 75-83; "Epoca de Calderón.
 Literatura dramática," pp. 85-88.

- El barroco literario hispánico. Buenos Aires, Edit. Nova,
1969. Pp. 179.

Includes some previously published essays.

Casalduero, Joaquín de. "Algunas características de la literatura española del Renacimiento y del Barroco." In Filología
y crítica hispánica: Homenaje al Prof. Federico Sánchez
Escribano, ed. Alberto Porqueras-Mayo and Carlos Rojas,
Madrid-Atlanta, Ediciones Alcalá-Emory Univ., 1969, pp. 87-96.

 "La última generación (del Barroco: Quevedo, Gracián y
 Calderón) tiene una preocupación obsesionante metafísico-
 moral."

Castañeda, James A. "El impacto del culteranismo en la edad de
oro." In <u>Hispanic Studies in Honor of Nicholson B. Adams</u>,
Chapel Hill, North Carolina, 1966, pp. 25-36. (University of
North Carolina Studies in Romance Languages and Literatures,
59.)

Castro, Américo. <u>La realidad histórica de España</u>. Mexico, Porrúa,
1954. Pp. 684.

Passim about Calderón and some of his works, with reference
to "limpieza de sangre," the "hidalguismo," and the "creencia
entrañable en la tierra." (A new, revised ed. of <u>España en
su historia</u>, Buenos Aires, 1948.)

- "El drama de la honra en España y en su literatura." <u>CCLC</u>,
No. 38 (1959), 3-15; No. 39 (1959), 16-28.

Fragments of his book, <u>De la edad conflictiva</u>, Madrid, 1961.
Based on his thesis of the Judaic influence on the Spanish
spirit in the 16th and 17th centuries. Castro declares that
the concern with honour in the theatre is a reflection of the
preoccupation with the intangible purity of blood, and with
man as an individual. Antijudaism and neoplatonism made
possible the development of the concept of honour in the
Spanish classic theatre.

- <u>De la edad conflictiva</u>. I: <u>El drama de la honra en España y
en su literatura</u>. Madrid, Taurus, 1961. Pp. 221. (Col.
Persiles, 18.)
Rev: <u>Year's Work in Modern Language Studies</u>, 23 (1961), 175
("Less concerned with the theatre than its title suggests,
and advances a rather too ingenious theory linking the honour
plays with the contemporary obsession with 'limpieza de
sangre,' and people's fears that they might not really be
'cristianos viejos.'"); Ramón de Garciasol, <u>CHA</u>, 144 (1961),
429-43 ("Un libro de entendimiento y esperanza, una lectura
atenta e imprescindible de la que dependen muchas posibili-
dades de convivencia. Dentro de la meditación general
castriana, fundamental para valorar realidades hispánicas,
quizá sea éste el trabajo más decisivamente probatorio, no
de unas tesis previas ... sino de unas conclusiones en vista
de unos hechos."); Manuel Durán, <u>MLN</u>, 77 (1962), 195-99 ("Can
be fully understood only as a part of Castro's effort to offer

a new interpretation of Spanish history and culture ...
Briefly, Castro's book is a must for all Hispanists, especially of course for Golden Age specialists.").

A noteworthy addition to Castro's scholarly achievements,
which supersedes his old article, "Algunas observaciones
acerca del concepto del honor en los siglos XVI y XVII"(in
RFE, 1916), and develops certain ideas contained in his The
Structure of Spanish History. It also deals with the Spanish
concept of "la honra" and "el honor" in 16th and 17th century
society: — what it was, what produced it, and how it influenced literature, as well as the economic and cultural life
of Spain.

Černý, Václav. "Wallenstein, héros d'un drame de Calderón."
RLC, 36 (1962), 179-90.

A lost play (no title given) of Calderón and Coello, which
was the first to deal with this historical personage (a Czech
nobleman, who was at the head of the Imperial armies). Presents an over-simplified and false picture due to the fact
that Calderón had no idea of the infinitely complicated
personality of Wallenstein, nor of the local, national, and
religious circumstances which formed his character.

- "Barokní divadlo v Europe. I, Co je baroko?; II, Baroko a
divadlo; III, Barokní drama, I: Spanely a Portugalsko."
Slovenské Divadlo, 16 (1968), 502-34; 17 (1969), 87-113,
225-47.

The Baroque theatre in Europe. I, What is the Baroque?; II,
Baroque and the theatre; III, Baroque drama, I: Spain and
Portugal.

Chandler, Richard E., and Kessel Schwartz. A New History of
Spanish Literature. Baton Rouge, Louisiana State Univ. Press,
1961. Pp. xiii, 696.

Calderón is discussed as a dramatist on pages 91-94.

Chapman, W. G. "Las comedias mitológicas de Calderón." RL, 5
(1954), 35-67.

Rightly calls attention to the little-known but substantial mythological plays of Calderón's later years. These are shown to closely parallel the <u>autos</u> in their allegorical presentation of moral philosophy.

Chevalier, Maxime. <u>L'Arioste en Espagne (1530-1650)</u>. <u>Recherches sur l'influence du "Roland furieux"</u>. Bordeaux, Féret et Fils, 1966. Pp. 539. (Bib. de l'Ecole des Hautes Etudes Hispaniques, 39.)
Rev: G. C. Rossi, <u>L'Italia che Scrive</u>, 50 (1967), 33.

Pp. 405-38, especially, are devoted to the <u>Comedia</u>.

Ciesielka-Borkowska, Stefania. <u>Calderón w tworczosci Slowackiego</u>. Warsaw, Organiz, 1959. Pp. 61.

Cilveti, Angel L. "Silogismo, correlación e imagen poética en el teatro de Calderón." <u>RF</u>, 80 (1968), 459-97.

A detailed study of the structure, function and correlation of Calderón's use of the syllogism, and its relation to poetic imagery.

Cioranescu, Alejandro. "Calderón y el teatro clásico francés." In <u>Estudios de literatura española y comparada</u>, La Laguna, 1954, pp. 137-95.
Rev: Joaquín de Entrambasaguas, <u>RL</u>, 6 (1954), 408-10 (Considers this study to be the most complete and best written thus far on the topic.).

- <u>El barroco o el descubrimiento del drama</u>. La Laguna, Univ. de La Laguna, 1957. Pp. 445.
Rev: María del Pilar Palomo, <u>RL</u>, 11 (1957), 207-08 (María del Pilar Palomo briefly describes Cioranescu's important contribution to baroque studies. In her opinion, the book is an "obra fundamental para estudiar la esencia del barroco, por sus aportaciones críticas, sus novísimas y originales teorías, su documentación y estructuración perfecta de su desarrollo."); V. G. S., <u>Rev. di Letterature Moderne e Comparate</u>, 11 (1959), 308-09.

The scope of Cioranescu's book is very wide, and covers a
large territory in both space and time. His examples are
drawn from the wide range of European and classical authors.
Calderón, however, occupies much of his attention, but no
more than any other of the great Spanish, English, French or
Italian authors of the Renaissance and baroque periods. Of
Calderón, Cioranescu says, among other things, "Calderón es
quizá el mejor maestro de la descripción y del retrato en
movimiento. Sus imágenes son siempre en lucha." Since it is
common knowledge that so many critics have praised the women
characters in Tirso while they belittle those of Calderón,
the following words by Cioranescu strike hard because of his
antagonistic view: "De una manera más general, se puede decir
que todo el teatro español del Siglo de Oro, y más particular-
mente el teatro de Calderón, está en manos de las mujeres,
quienes hacen y deshacen la intriga de la comedia, mientras
los galanes no hacen más que seguir el camino que ellas les
indican." We disagree with his view. As for Calderonian style,
Cioranescu points out the baroque techniques of the duality
of the unity to which the authors add, by the use of metaphors,
comparisons and repetitions, a second presence to the object;
and he proposes the terminology "progresión en abanico" for
the characteristic "resumen calderoniano." For him, a perfect
example of this "progresión en abanico" is Segismundo's famous
monologue in the first act of La vida es sueño. Another device
dear to Calderón is the "enigma." The sixth chapter, which
deals with "el conflicto" also offers some interesting
remarks: "Tanto en Calderón como en Racine, los conflictos
llegan a complicarse y a multiplicarse de tal modo, que la
conducción y la construcción del edificio dramático viene a
ser una difícil empresa estratégica...." The most important
contribution in Cioranescu's book is found in Chapter 7, "El
drama," which contains refreshing and suggestive subtitles:
"La duda solucionada por la voluntad: Corneille," "La duda
suprimida por la fe: Tirso de Molina y Calderón," "La duda
reducida por la pasión: Racine," and "La duda sin solución:
Shakespeare." With respect to Calderón, the author points out
that "La vida es sueño es la solución por medio de la fe, y
con exclusión de cualquier influencia de la duda o de la
vacilación, del mismo dualismo antinómico del alma...." In
conclusion, let us quote once more from this interesting book,
which is of uneven quality and contains quasi-controversial
issues: "El arte barroco encuentra su expresión en lo sublime
o, si no, en lo burlesco; pero no le es dado encontrarla en
lo simplemente natural. Alguna vez, como por ejemplo en
Shakespeare o en Calderón, no vacila en reunir los dos tonos ...

sin que se encuentren alguna vez a mitad del camino.... En
los casos en que la naturalidad gana terreno, el barroco
desparece.... Así se explica, por ejemplo, que en la inmensa
producción dramática de Lope de Vega, y en general en el
teatro del Siglo de Oro, los rasgos genuinamente barrocos no
sean tan evidentes como en la demás producción literaria."
Also, we should note that Cioranescu handles a limited number
of Calderón's plays, and that his "Bibliografía del barroco"
is uneven and disconcerting, mainly because of omissions of
works printed in the United States and Great Britain. Probably
these books did not reach the libraries accessible to him.

Cirot, C. and M. Darbord. <u>Littérature espagnole européenne</u>.
Paris, Colin, 1956. Pp. 213.
Rev: A. Rumeau, <u>BH</u>, 69 (1957), 472 ("Offre ce que nous
demandons à un manuel ... bon instrument d'information pour
le non-spécialiste."); Pierre Groult, <u>LR</u>, 12 (1958), 194-95
(Professor Groult points out the innumerable defects and
shortcomings of this book, which was finished by Darbord
after Cirot's death. As for the <u>autos sacramentales</u>, the
reviewer, without being sarcastic, offers some rather
humorous quotations from the book; for example, "quand on
lit, p. 109, qu'un 'auto était un acte, de durée assez courte,
deux ou trois heures, avec la <u>loa</u>, qui précédait en manière
de prologue,' on se raillie sans hésiter à la théorie de la
relativité.").

Coe, Ada M. "Unas colecciones de comedias sueltas de Pedro
Calderón de la Barca comparadas con <u>Literatur, eine
bibliographisch-kritische Übersicht</u>, de Hermann Breymann
(München, 1905)." <u>Supplement A</u>, to <u>BCom</u>, 2, No. 2 (1950).
Pp. 42; and <u>Estudios</u>, 7, No. 19 (1951), 111-69.

A helpful catalogue which supplements Breymann's list with
titles found in the following libraries: Professor Coe's own,
at Wellesley College; Mt. Holyoke College Library; Oberlin
College Library; The Ticknor Collection in the Boston Public
Library; University of Toronto Library; and the Wellesley
College Library. All entries include, in addition to the
bibliographical essentials, the opening and closing lines of
each <u>comedia</u>, and several are followed by interesting notes.
The cross-referencing is confusing in the <u>Estudios</u> publication,
because the page indications refer to the original version.

- "Sueltas en la biblioteca de Ada M. Coe, Professor Emeritus of Wellesley College." BCom, 10, Nos. 1 and 2 (1958), 12-15 and 9-16.

    In the Spring issue (No. 1) of BCom, there is a list of comedias sueltas, which includes 46 Calderón titles. The Fall issue (No. 2) contains 59 Calderón titles. Most of them are 18th century printings, and there are many repetitions of title.

Colomès, Jean. "La Révolution catalane de 1640 et les écrivains espagnols du temps." In IVᵉ Congrès des Hispanistes Français, Poitiers, 1968, pp. 45-58.

    Reference to Calderón's anonymously published Conclusión defendida por un soldado del campo de Tarragona del ciego furor de Cataluña.

(Comediantes.) "A Current Bibliography of Foreign Publications Dealing with the Comedia." In BCom, from 2, No. 2 (Nov., 1950) on.

    Contains a systematic semi-annual bibliography of Calderón publications outside of U.S.A. and Canada. The present compiler is Peter B. Bell.

Connor, Patricia Josephine. The Music in the Spanish Baroque Theatre of Don Pedro Calderón de la Barca. Unpub. doct. diss., Boston Univ., 1964.

Constandse, A. L. Le Baroque espagnol et Calderón de la Barca. Amsterdam, Boekhandel "Plus Ultra"; Oxford, Dolphin; 1951. Pp. 144.
Rev: C. V. A., BH, 54 (1952), 230 (The reviewer has reservations concerning the general validity of the study, which he describes as follows: "Ce curieux petit essai conjugue la méthode freudienne d'interpretation de l'oeuvre littéraire avec un appareil notionnel emprunté à l'histoire de l'art (ou des styles)." The reviewer does concede, however, that owing to the high incidence of such thematic elements as incest, revolt, jealousy, father-son conflicts, etc., in his plays, Calderón is the playwright who lends himself best to the

method of study employed by Constandse.); A. H., Insula, 7, No. 81 (1952), supplement, p. 4 (This short review emphasizes the importance given to the Baroque by Constandse as an expression of the anguish and the morbid vitality of the Spain of the seventeenth century and to the fact that the Baroque, as the art of the Counter Reformation, had a predilection for symbols which revealed eternal and spiritual values. No judgment of Constandse's book.); Angel Valbuena Prat, Clav, 3, No. 14 (1952), 77-78 (A very favourable review, with special commendation to Constandse for having enhanced his provocative analyses of Calderón and the Spanish Baroque by the most perceptive consideration of Freud, non-literary art forms, and other topics and perspectives not normally employed to such a degree in literary study. "Esto hace que, junto a lo acertado y preciso, sea este libro tan ampliamente sugestivo y rico en horizontes."); C. V. Aubrun, BH, 57 (1955), 463-65 and Bruce W. Wardropper, HR, 23 (1955), 140-43 (In the opinion of these two reviewers, this Freudian approach to Calderón's drama, with some startling insights, is fundamentally not successful.).

This provocative study is designed to show to what extent the character of the Baroque corresponds to the character of sixteenth and seventeenth century Spain, composed largely of "âmes fendues," represented by the great protagonists of artistic creation (Don Quijote, Don Juan, Segismundo, etc.), all symbols of the most complicated internal conflicts. Constandse's intention is also to explain how the Spain of the seventeenth century was more inclined than any other nation to accept the Baroque as the most pure expression of its distress, anguish, dreams, and morbid vitality. He also presents the thesis that Calderón is, above all, the representative of the Spanish Baroque. His study of the Baroque, as reflected in Calderón, is intended to show to what point our culture has made of man an "animal triste" — but also, to what extent man's grandeur, terrible beauty, creative force, and permanent revolution are attributable to the unending Baroque effort to draw away from nature. Constandse's extensive use of psychological analysis and his perceptive comparisons with non-literary art forms contribute greatly to the provocative nature of this interesting volume.

Cordaso, Francisco. "Spanish Influence on Restoration Drama: George Digby's Elvira (1663?)." RLC, 27 (1953), 93-98.

It is not a translation or adaptation of any particular play. Its origins are suggested by three Calderón plays: <u>No siempre lo peor es cierto</u>, <u>Mejor está que estaba</u>, <u>Peor está que estaba</u>.

Cruickshank, D. W. "A Contemporary of Calderón." <u>MLR</u>, 63 (1968), 364-68.

Pedro Ignacio de Arce y Tofiño.

Curtius, Ernst Robert. <u>European Literature and the Latin Middle Ages</u>. Trans. Willard R. Trask. New York, Pantheon, 1953. Pp. xv, 662. (<u>Europäische Literatur und lateinisches Mittelalter</u>, Bern, A. Francke, 1948. Pp. 601.)

Calderón is frequently mentioned.

- "La teoría del arte en Calderón y las artes liberales." In <u>Literatura europea y Edad Media latina</u>, trans. Margit Frenk Alatorre and Antonio Alatorre, Vol 2, Mexico, Fondo de Cultura Económica, 1955, pp. 776-90. ("Calderóns Kunsttheorie und die 'artes liberales'." In <u>Europäische Literatur und lateinisches Mittelalter</u>, Bern, 1948, pp. 543-53.)

- "Georges Hofmannsthal y Calderón." In <u>Ensayos críticos acerca de literatura europea</u>, I, Barcelona, 1959, pp. 213-50. ("Georges Hofmannsthal und Calderón." In <u>Corolla Ludwig Curtius zum sechzigsten Geburtstag dargebracht</u>, I, Stuttgart, Kohlhanmer, 1937, pp. 20-28; and in <u>Kritische Essays zur europäische Literatur</u>, Bern, 1950, pp. 170-201, and Bern, 1954, pp. 128-51.)

- "Calderón und die Malerei." In <u>Gesammelte Aufsätze zur romanischen Philologie</u>, Bern, Francke, 1960, pp. 376-411. (Previously pub. in <u>RF</u>, 50, 1936, 89-136.)

Cvitanovic, Dinko (ed.). <u>El sueño y su representación en el barroco español</u>. Bahía Blanca, Univ. Nac. del Sur, 1969. Pp. 188.

See individual items.

Cvitanovic, Dinko. "Hipótesis sobre la significación del sueño en Quevedo, Calderón y Shakespeare." In Cvitanovic (ed.), El sueño..., 1969, pp. 9-89. (See above.)

Dalmasso, Osvaldo B. Calderón de la Barca. Buenos Aires, Centro Editor de América Latina, 1969. Pp. 64.

Davies, R. Trevor. The Golden Century of Spain. London, Macmillan, 1954. Pp. 327. (Reprint of 1937 ed.)
Rev: A. M. Fox, QQ, 62 (1955), 131-33.

The intellectual achievements of the period (with reference to Calderón) are included.

Derla, Luigi. "Voltaire, Calderón e il mito del genio eslege." Aevum, 36 (1962), 109-40.

Voltaire's opinions of Calderón, whom he was unable to appreciate, are partly due to his hatred of Catholic and reactionary Spain. For Voltaire, Calderón, like Shakespeare and Lope de Vega, was a primitive poetic genius, uncultivated and undisciplined.

Díaz-Plaja, Guillermo (ed.). Historia general de las literaturas hispánicas. III: Renacimiento y Barroco. Barcelona, Barna, 1953. Pp. 1036.

Includes: Angel Valbuena Prat, "Calderón" and Federico Carlos Sainz de Robles, "Rojas Zorrilla, Moreto, Cubillo y otros dramaturgos del 'Ciclo de Calderón'."

- (ed.). El teatro: Enciclopedia del arte escénico. Barcelona, Noguer, 1958. Pp. 648.
Rev: J. L. C., Insula, 14 (1959), 147; José Montero Padilla, BBMP, 35 (1959), 393-96.

Díaz-Plaja contributes Chapter I: "Introducción histórica," which covers Greek tragedy to Romanticism in a very incomplete manner. The Spanish comedia receives four pages; Calderón one-half page. The autos sacramentales receive less than twenty lines. What is most surprising, however, is that

Calderón is not even mentioned in the chapter on "El teatro musical," by Antonio Fernández-Cid, which covers from the "primeros brotes" to the "zarzuela."

Díez Echarri, Emiliano. <u>Teorías métricas del Siglo de Oro. Apuntes para la historia del verso español</u>. Madrid, 1949. Pp. 355. (<u>RFE</u>, Anejo 47.)
Rev: Dorothy Clotelle Clarke, <u>HR</u>, 20 (1952), 84 (The reviewer sums up her very favourable opinion as follows: "This work furnishes background material necessary in any study of Golden Age versification and will henceforth undoubtedly rank as one of the key works in the field.").

Dilthey, Wilhelm. <u>Die grosse Phantasiedichtung und andere Studien zur vergleichenden Literaturgeschichte</u>. Göttingen, Vandenhoek und Ruprecht, 1954. Pp. 324.

Passim about Calderón and the <u>comedia</u> in general in the lead article "Die grosse Phantasiedichtung." (Written in the 1890's, but hitherto unpublished.) Also includes "Das Volksschauspiel und Calderón" and "Satan in der christlichen Poesie."

Dunn, Peter N. "Honour and the Christian Background in Calderón." <u>BHS</u>, 37 (1960), 75-105. (Also pub. in Wardropper, <u>Critical Essays</u>, 1965, pp. 24-60.)

Dunn makes an interesting and convincing case for considering honour the equivalent of a religion in the minds of 17th century men, which will include the ritual sacrifice of blood. Dunn next analyses <u>El alcalde de Zalamea</u>, to show how the play "presents a possible Christian solution to the personal problem of the loss of worldly honour." Crespo, in effect, resolves his situation by renouncing his worldly honour, thus retaining the higher honour given by God ("patrimonio del alma"). The death of the Captain does not represent personal vengeance, but rather justice demanded by the law which Crespo represents as the Alcalde.

Durán, Manuel. "Camus and the Spanish Theatre." <u>Yale French Studies</u>, No. 25 (1960), 123-31.

Camus' translation and adaptation of some of Calderón's dramas.

Eguía Ruiz, Constancio. Cervantes, Calderón, Lope, Gracián. Nuevos temas crítico-biográficos. Madrid, C.S.I.C., 1951. Pp. 162. (Anejos de Cuad. de Lit., 8.)

Calderón, pp. 47-61. Having traced the poet's line back to the famous house of the Calderón de la Barca family in Santillana (during which process he perpetuates the inclusion of Alonso Sánchez Calderón, whose very existence is considered doubtful by Narciso Alonso Cortés, "Genealogía de D. Pedro Calderón," BRAE, 31, 1951, 299-309), Eguía Ruiz then relates two other branches of the family to the genealogical line of the poet. In a pleito de hidalguía, dated 1570, is established the relationship with the Calderón de Aguilar de Campo branch, and in another ejecutoria, won in 1652 by Juan Velarde against the Cabildo y Concejo de Santillana, the Velardes are identified genealogically with the playwright. Both documents provide interesting and descriptive comment on the famous Barca which became incorporated into the compound patronymic of the family line.

Entrambasaguas, Joaquín de. "Dos olvidadas décimas de Calderón." In Miscelánea erudita: Serie primera, Madrid, Jura, 1957, pp. 144-46.

Entrambasaguas reproduces two of Calderón's décimas which appeared among other poems by various authors in the preliminary pages of Arias de Quintanadueñas, Antigüedades, and Castro y Anaya's Auroras de Diana. Entrambasaguas does not include commentary or criticism. The Castro y Anaya work was reprinted as recently as 1948 in the Biblioteca de antiguos libros hispánicos; and Entrambasaguas chides the editor, A. González Palencia, who brought forth an edition which, "aprovechando la ausencia del director titular (Entrambasaguas), que hubo de cumplir un viaje oficial de conferenciante y profesor, por América del Sur, abunda en errores, no sigue las normas habituales de La Biblioteca citada, y va precedida en un prólogo sin interés."

Escobar López, Ignacio. "Teatro sacramental y existencial de Calderón de la Barca." CHA, No. 134 (1961), 219-34. (Also in Rev. de la Univ. de los Andes, 3, 1960, pp. 50-62; and Bol. de la Acad. Colombiana, 10, 1960, pp. 313-28.)

Part I is concerned with the development of medieval mystery

plays in Europe, and especially in Spain. Calderón's <u>autos</u>
are considered superior to those of other Spanish dramatists
("Calderón los supera a todos en profundidad de concepto, en
la manera de dar vida artística a la especulación didáctica,
en el lirismo al hablar de principios teológicos y en el
emblema plástico de lo más incórporeo y sutil que imaginarse
pueda."). Part II is concerned with Calderón's <u>teatro
existencial</u>, in particular <u>El gran teatro del mundo</u>, which
poses the problem of death in a manner not unlike that of
20th century writers. The article is a rather general,
personal, and emotional evaluation.

Esquer Torres, Ramón. "Las prohibiciones de comedias y autos
sacramentales en el siglo XVII." <u>Segismundo</u>, 2 (1965), 187-
226.

Estrella Gutiérrez, Fermín. <u>Historia de la literatura española
con antología</u>. Buenos Aires, Kapelusz, 1957. Pp. 758.

A re-issue of earlier printings (1945, for example). The
chapter on "Siglo de Oro: El teatro," devotes 67 pages to
drama from Torres Naharro to Moreto, including some seventeen
pages on Calderón. Half of this reprints numerous fragments
from Calderón plays. This text, for high school use, provides
a good introduction to Calderón; and the "Juicios sobre el
teatro de Calderón" are good. Of Segismundo the author writes:
"Semejante a Hamlet, se asoma por un momento al vértigo del
ser y del no ser, y sale de la experiencia con el alma y la
razón cambiadas. El simboliza, por consiguiente, la idea
tenaz y enloquecedora de la caducidad y la fragilidad de los
bienes materiales."

Farinelli, Arturo. <u>Poesía y crítica</u>. <u>Temas hispánicos</u>. Madrid,
CSIC, 1954. Pp. 298.
Rev: B. Moreno Quintana, <u>Arbor</u>, 30 (1955), 344-45; A. Veloso,
<u>Brotéria</u>, 60 (1955), 736; Rodolfo Oroz, <u>AUC</u>, 114, No. 102
(1956), 118-19; M. Darbord, <u>BH</u>, 60 (1958), 266 (Darbord
acknowledges the publication of a number of Farinelli's
scattered articles: "Malgré le style trop facilement
emphatique de Farinelli, on les lira avec intérêt.").

Contains: "Pirandello y Calderón," pp. 109-15.

Ferdinany, Magdalena de. Sprache und Gebärde. Untersuchungen zur mimischen Interpretation Calderóns und seiner deutschen Übersetzer. Berlin, Universität, 1965. Pp. 119. (Dissertation.) Rev: Juan María Díez Taboada, Segismundo, 3 (1967), 414-17.

Fernández, Américo. "La escena rusa y nuestro teatro clásico." CHA, No. 121 (1960), 55-80.

Includes reference to Calderón.

Ferraro, Sergio. "Bibliografia di Benedetto Croce ispanista. IV: 1926-1955." Quaderni Ibero-Americani, No. 21 (1957), 403-04.

Among Croce's bibliographical items of interest to Calderón studies are: "1943. Calderón, I, La hija del aire. II, Sulla critica calderoniana, ne La Critica, XLI, pp. 173-88." Also a few of Croce's reviews.

Fiore, Robert Luis. Neo-Scholasticism in Calderón's Autos: "No hay más fortuna que Dios," "El gran teatro del mundo," "A Dios por razón de estado." Unpub. doct. diss., Univ. of North Carolina, 1967. (DA, 28, 3108A.)

Flasche, Hans. "Stand und Aufgaben der Calderónforschung (Ergebnisse der Jahre 1940-1958)." Deutsche Vierteljahrsschrift für Literaturwissenschaft und Geistesgeschichte, 32 (1958), 613-43.

These thirty pages which Flasche contributed to Calderonian studies were a landmark, offering a most comprehensive "Stand und Aufgaben." The point of departure for his critical survey was Valbuena Prat's "vuelta a Calderón," with the two volumes of Autos sacramentales (Clás. Cast., 1927), and the book, Calderón. Su personalidad... (1941). The years 1940-1958, however, are those on which Flasche concentrates; and the coverage is global. Flasche finds an incomplete and imperfect image of the dramatist; and research needs pointed out are, among others: Calderón's knowledge (or lack of knowledge) of history, geography, botany, zoology, etc., of the classics, of Platonic and Neoplatonic ideas, of Patristic and Scholastic literature, ... Flasche notes clashes in

chronology between Hilborn and Valbuena Prat; that many texts
still are in an unsatisfactory state; that many problems, for
example, in structure and interpretation, remain. The intent
of this excellent critical review seems to be summed up in
the following words: "Aus der Tatsache, dass in allen bisher
dargebotenen Abschnitten des Forschungsberichtes immer wieder
gesagt werden müsste, die Calderonforschung habe dort eine
Lücke zu füllen und hier ein Desiderat zu verwirklichen geht
schon hervor, wie seit wir noch von der Möglichkeit entfernt
sind, eine umfassende und repräsentative Calderonmonographie
zu schreiben. Eine Reihe von Büchern, die jene repräsentative
Monographie vorbereiten, sind erschienen."

- "Das aus - mente = Adverb und Adjektiv bestehende Syntagma
(Zur Sprache Calderóns)." In Saggi e ricerche in memoria di
Ettore Li Gotti, Vol. II, Palermo, 1962, pp. 18-37. (Centro
di Studi Filologici e Linguistici Siciliani, Bolletino, 7.)

A study of Calderón's use of the adverb-adjective syntagma
(such as "piadosamente importuna").

- "Calderón als Paraphrast mittelalterlicher Hymen." In Medium
Aevum Romanicum (Festschrift für Hans Rheinfelder), ed.
Heinrich Bihler and Alfred Noyer-Weidner, Munich, Max Hueber
Verlag, 1963, pp. 87-119.

Flasche analyses some twelve autos sacramentales by Calderón,
showing his acquaintance with medieval hymns and how he
incorporated them in his works. The citations range from
lengthy translations to fragments and phrases of a few words.

- "Problemas de la sintaxis calderoniana (la transposición
inmediata del adjetivo)." Archivum Linguisticum, 16 (1964),
54-68.

Discusses the use by Calderón, especially in his autos sacramentales, of the construction lo + adjective as a noun (lo
alegórico, etc.). He divides Calderón's use into three
aspects: a simple abstract term, its use indicating a quality
tied to its possessor but without mentioning the possessor,
and the quality tied to the possessor, which is bound
syntactically (lo inmortal del alma). He believes that
Calderón chose such terms not only for their unexpectedness

88

and attractiveness, but also as a result of a premeditated
decision of his intellectual and philosophical character
(índole).

- "Studie zur Negation mit no im Sprachgebrauch Calderóns." In
  Linguistic and Literary Studies in Honor of Helmut A. Hatzfeld,
  Washington, 1964, pp. 129-48.

  The article takes up first earlier studies on the use of "no,"
  and then gives examples of Calderón's use of the negative in
  positions other than before the verb: at the beginning of the
  sentence, before past participles and adjectives, adverbs,
  infinitives, and prepositions, and between article and
  adjective plus noun.

- "Antiker Mythos in christlicher Umprägung: Andrómeda y Perseo
  bei Calderón." RJ, 16 (1965), 290-317. (Re-pub., 1968.)

  A detailed study of how an auto (Andrómeda y Perseo) and a
  comedia (Fortunas de Andrómeda y Perseo) show Calderón's
  remarkable talent for blending Christian and mythological
  themes.

- (ed.). Litterae hispanae et lusitanae. Munich, Max Hueber
  Verlag, 1968. Pp. vii, 511. (Festschrift zum fünfzigjahrigen
  Bestehen des Ibero-Amerikanischen Forschungsinstituts der
  Universität Hamburg.)

  Includes: Alexander A. Parker, "The Rôle of the graciosos in
  El mágico prodigioso"; R. D. F. Pring-Mill, "Los calderonistas
  de habla inglesa y La vida es sueño: Métodos del análisis
  temático-estructural"; Edward M. Wilson, "La poesía dramática
  de don Pedro Calderón de la Barca."

- "Zu Semantik und Syntax des Wortes acción in Corpus
  Calderonianum." In Verba et Vocabula: Ernst Gamillscheg zum
  80. Geburtstag, ed. Helmut Stimm and Julius Wilhelm, Munich,
  W. Fink, 1968, pp. 221-39.

Franco, Angel. El tema de América en los autores del Siglo de
  Oro. Unpub. doct. diss., Univ. of Madrid, 1954.

Fredén, Gustav. La cena del amor (Estudios sobre Calderón de la Barca). (Versión española de Matilde Goulard de Lima.) Madrid, Insula, 1954. Pp. 55. (2nd ed., Inst. Iberoamericano de Gotemburgo; and Madrid, Insula, 1962.)
Rev: J. Montero Padilla, RL, 8 (1955), 358-59; and see Spanish Cultural Index, No. 113 (June 1, 1955), 635.

Advances a slenderly supported theory about Calderón's interest in Orphic religion; the rôle of love in several plays.

Freund, Markéta Lily. Baroque Technique, Thought and Feeling in Certain Representative Comedias of Calderón. Unpub. doct. diss., Univ. of Colorado, 1966. (DA, 28, 1433A.)

The plays discussed in detail are: La hija del aire, El médico de su honra, and El gran duque de Gandía.

Friedrich, Hugo. Der fremde Calderón. Freiburg, Hans Ferdinand Schulz Verlag, 1955. Pp. 44. (Freiburger Universitätsreden, Neue Folge, 20.) (Re-issued 1966.)
Rev: H. L., Archiv, 193 (1956), 98; H. Weinrich, RF, 67 (1956), 453-55; A. Porqueras-Mayo, RFE, 41 (1957), 441-43 (Translates the title as "el extraño Calderón," explaining that Friedrich insists that "A pesar de los románticos y Goethe, a pesar de los esfuerzos de los que vienen después, como Immermann, incluso Hofmannstahl, y recientemente Kommerell, Calderón no se ha aclimatado entre nosotros." This is explained by Calderón's "acusado 'extranjerismo' y concretamente su 'españolismo histórico'."); Friedrich Schürr, RJ, 7 (1957), 377-78 (Presents an excellent summary of the booklet; and, among other things, points out Calderón's three perspectives of the world: "die Welt als Nichtigkeit — die Welt als Macht — und die Welt als Heiterkeit." This three-fold perspective allows us to comprehend the inner unity of the whole of Calderón's dramatic works.).

Froldi, Rinaldo. Il teatro valenzano e l'origine della commedia barroca. Pisa, Ed. Tecnico Scientifico, 1962. Pp. 112.
Rev: Eduardo Juliá Martínez, RL, 21 (1962), 181-83; Joseph G. Fucilla, Hisp, 47 (1964), 866-67; Edwin S. Morby, HR, 32 (1964), 265-68.

Frutos Cortés, Eugenio. "La filosofía del barroco y el pensamiento de Calderón." <u>RUBA</u>, 9 (1951), 173-230.

The three sections of this article (I: Los problemas filosóficos del siglo XVII; II: El barroquismo de Calderón; III:
"La filosofía calderoniana") correspond to three identically
titled sections (C, D, and E, of Parte I) of Frutos' book,
Zaragoza, 1952 (see item following). The article includes
nineteen subtitles which are not found in the corresponding
sections of the book, although the material itself is essentially the same.

- <u>La filosofía de Calderón en sus Autos sacramentales</u>. Zaragoza,
Institución "Fernando el Católico," CSIC, 1952. Pp. 346.
Rev: G. Bravo, <u>Pensamiento</u> (Madrid), 10 (1953), 504-06;
Garciasol, <u>Insula</u>, No. 90 (1953), 6; C. Láscaris Comneno,
<u>RIE</u>, 11 (1953), 90-93; A. Valbuena Prat, <u>Clav</u>, 4, No. 22
(1953), 77-78 ("Una importantísima aportación al tema a la
vez doctrinal y estético que encarna en el género 'sacramental'
de Calderón...").

Parte I ("Calderón en su época y su carácter filosófico")
deals principally with the baroque and with philosophical
trends in the seventeenth century, and concludes that
Calderón is very representative of his epoch and therefore an
excellent source of documentation on such basic philosophical
themes as <u>man</u>, <u>the world</u>, and <u>God</u>. The volume is completed by
an extensive Parte II ("Los temas filosóficos de Calderón en
sus autos sacramentales"). Quotes from the <u>autos</u> illustrate
in a schematic fashion the poet's philosophical thinking in
connection with the three principal themes and their subdivi-
sions. Of particular interest are the sections in which Frutos
analyses Calderón's presentation of his allegorical figures.

Fucilla, Joseph G. <u>Relaciones hispanoitalianas</u>. Madrid, CSIC,
1953-54. Pp. 238. (<u>RFE</u>, Anejos 59-60.)

Italian MS versions of <u>La vida es sueño</u>, and a passing
reference to rhyming devices in an octave of <u>La cena del rey</u>
<u>Baltasar</u>.

- "Etapas en el desarrollo del mito de Icaro en el Renacimiento
y en el Siglo de Oro." <u>Hispanó</u>, No. 8 (1960), 1-34.

Calderón and Tirso, pp. 27-29.

Gallego Morell, Antonio. "El mito de Faetón en la literatura española." <u>Clav</u>, 7, No. 37 (1956), 13-26; No. 38 (1956), 31-43.

Refers to the original treatment of this myth by Calderón in <u>El hijo del sol, Faetón</u> and in <u>Apolo y Climene</u>, which he believes to be the first part of the former play.

Gallo, Ugo. <u>Storia della letteratura spagnola</u>. Milan, Academia, 1952. Pp. 750.
Rev: Annamaria Gallina, <u>Quaderni Ibero-Americani</u>, No. 14 (1953), 376-77 ("Serie di impressioni sui vari momenti o ... sulle maggiori figure della letteratura castigliana.").

Garasa, Delfín Leocadio. "Teatro y sociedad en el Siglo de Oro español." <u>Universidad</u> (Santa Fe, Argentina), No. 48 (1961), 107-28.

- "Circe en la literatura española del Siglo de Oro." <u>Bol. de la Acad. Argentina de Letras</u>, 29 (1964), 227-71.

Includes: "Una versión barroca: <u>El mayor encanto amor</u> de Calderón," pp. 257-65; and "Versión alegórico-sacramental," pp. 266-71 (re <u>Los encantos de la culpa</u>).

Gates, Eunice Joiner. "Calderón's interest in Art." <u>PQ</u>, 40 (1961), 53-67.

A brief description of Calderón's private art collection is followed by an analysis of his theories on art as seen in the <u>Deposición</u> (1677) in which he defends the nobility of painting. The author then explores Calderón's use of a portrait "as a theme or as a supporting element in the delineation of character, the development of plot, and the unification of structure." Concludes that Calderón's interest in art was an integral part of his drama, reflecting both the taste of his era and his own feelings with respect to portrait painting and religious art.

Gérard, Albert. "Pour une phénoménologie du baroque littéraire. Essai sur la tragédie européenne au XVIIe siècle." In <u>Publications de l'Université de l'Etat à Elizabethville</u>, No. 5 (1963), 25-65.

A study of the Baroque that ranges over the dramatic literature of England, France, Germany, Holland, Italy, and Spain, introducing only incidentally Calderón, his plays <u>El príncipe constante</u> and <u>El mágico prodigioso</u> and the play and <u>auto La vida es sueño</u>, as well as the honour theme.

Gerstinger, Heinz. <u>Calderón</u>. Velber (bei Hannover), Friedrich Verlag, 1967. Pp. 138. (Friedrich Dramatiker des Welttheaters, 32.)

Particular attention is given to the staging of German translations of Calderón.

- <u>Spanische Komödie</u>. <u>Lope de Vega und seine Zeitgenossen</u>. Velber (bei Hannover), Friedrich Verlag, 1968. Pp. 152. (Friedrich Dramatiker des Welttheaters, 48.)

Special interest is shown in <u>comedias de capa y espada</u>.

Gilman, Stephen. "The <u>Comedia</u> in the Light of Recent Criticism Including the New Criticism." <u>BCom</u>, 12, No. 1 (1960), 1-5.

Rejects the possibility of applying the "New Criticism" to the <u>Comedia</u>.

Gitlitz, David Martin. <u>The Jew in the Comedia of the Golden Age</u>. Unpub. doct. diss., Harvard Univ., 1968.

Mentions Calderón in the last chapter.

Giusso, Lorenzo. "Calderón e la poesia dell'allegoria." In <u>Spagna ed Antispagna</u> (<u>Saggisti e Moralisti spagnuoli</u>), Mazara, Società Editrice Siciliana, 1952, pp. 7-19.

Giusso detects, even in the works of Calderón's youth, a tendency to avoid the concrete and historical in favour of

an allegorical superstructure which was developed constantly
in the <u>comedias</u> and which received its definitive form in the
<u>autos</u>. Calderón's allegory is viewed by Giusso as the poet's
method of taking refuge in the world of Biblical prophecy and
story in order to avoid describing the sad plight of Spain in
her decline. "Calderón è veramente un epigono, un postumo. E
la su opera è una vasta epigrafe murata sopra un tempio della
fama. Il tempio della grandezza spagnuola ormai lesionato e
scosso nei suoi pilastri. È come se questa enorme vicenda si
proiettasse già nelle teatrali fluorescenze dell'allegoria."

- "Calderón. Gli <u>autos sacramentales</u> e il secondo <u>Faust</u>." In
  <u>Autoritratto spagnolo</u>, Turin, 1959, pp. 80-96.

Gómez Fernández, Catalina. <u>Bibliografía crítica de las ediciones</u>
  <u>y estudios de autos sacramentales de D. Pedro Calderón de la</u>
  <u>Barca</u>. Diss., Univ. de Madrid, 1960.

Gómez Martín, Hilarión Bernardo de María Virgen. "La Inmaculada
  en la dramatúrgica clásica española." <u>Estudios Marianos</u>, No.
  116 (1955), 329-59.

  Includes Calderón among others.

González de la Riva, David. "Cristocentrismo en los autos
  sacramentales de Calderón, por Gabriel de Sotiello." <u>Estudios</u>
  <u>Franciscanos</u>, No. 306 (1959), 321-44.

González García, Aurora. <u>Bibliografía crítica de las ediciones</u>
  <u>y estudios de las comedias religiosas de Calderón</u>. Diss.,
  Univ. de Madrid, 1959.

González Román, Gonzalo. <u>Calderón de la Barca</u>. Plasencia
  (Cáceres), Sánchez Rodrigo, 1964. Pp. 126. (Hijos Ilustres de
  España, 32.)

  A short account, pitched on a rather sombre note, of the life
  of Calderón for young readers. It touches on but a few plays
  and ends with a brief, general chapter on his work, the
  criticism taken mainly from Menéndez Pelayo.

González Ruiz, Nicolás. "Idealismo y espíritú de combate por la fe en los autos sacramentales." Mundo Hispánico, Nos. 50-51 (1952), 35-36.

Reflections on the route of the "procesión del Corpus" in Madrid and on the presentation of Calderón's autos in the seventeenth century. Praise not only for Calderón, but also for the "pueblo que supo sentir e interpretar tan honda manifestación de arte religioso."

Granados, Juana. "La actitud de Menéndez Pelayo frente al barroco." Quaderni Ibero-Americani, No. 23 (1959), 507-13.

Menéndez Pelayo's criticism of the theatre of Calderón is clearly negative, for in it he sees a certain superficiality and lack of faith in Calderón's Catholicism.

Green, Otis H. Spain and the Western Tradition: The Castilian Mind in Literature from "El Cid" to Calderón. 4 vols. Madison, Univ. of Wisconsin Press, 1963-66. Pp. xii, 329; vii, 365; vi, 507; vii, 345. (Trans., underway, by Cecilio Sánchez Gil, Madrid, Gredos: España y la tradición occidental: El espíritu castellano en la literatura desde "El Cid" hasta Calderón. Vol. I, "En prensa;" Vol. II, pp. 412; Vol. III, 1969, pp. 596; Vol. IV, "En prensa.")

Monographs of great importance, making an outstanding contribution to Spanish criticism, and frequently mentioning Calderón.

Gustafson, Donna. "Un díptico barroco: Calderón y Sor Juana." Universidad de México, 9, No. 12 (1955), 17 and 26.

Hamelin, Jeanne. Le Théâtre chrétien. Paris, Arthème Fayard, 1957. Pp. 126.

Two of the six chapters of the book are devoted to the theatre of Spain's Golden Age. Calderón is given a prominent part. Autos as well as comedias are dealt with. In general, the book lacks criticism, the few critical statements being from the 19th century (Hartzenbusch, Vieil-Castel, etc.), and the point of view of the author is limited by religious prejudice.

Hamilton, John W. "América en las obras de Calderón de la Barca." <u>Anuario de Letras</u> (U.N.A.M.), 6-7 (1966-67; pub. 1969), 213-15.

Hampejs, Zdeněk. <u>Prehled dějin spanelské literatury</u>. I. Prague, 1957. Pp. 118.

A "Survey of Spanish literature."

- "Vrchlicky y Calderón." <u>Quaderni Ibero-Americani</u>, No. 25 (1960), 26-27.

Garoslav Vrchlicky, Czech poet.

Hardy, Swana L. <u>Goethe, Calderón und die romantische Theorie des Dramas</u>. Heidelberg, Carl Winter Universitätsverlag, 1965. Pp. 200. (Heidelberger Forschungen, 10.) Rev: Martin Franzbach, <u>Germanisch-romanische Monatsschrift</u>, 16 (1966), 437-38; Peter Pfaff, <u>Ruperto-Carola</u> (Heidelberg), No. 40 (1966), 462; R. Ayrault, <u>Etudes Germaniques</u>, 22 (1967), 287-88; Juan María Díez Taboada, <u>Segismundo</u>, 3 (1967), 417-18; Horst Steinmetz, <u>Neophilologus</u>, 51 (1967), 308-09.

A careful and detailed study, whose six chapters deal with the development of the interest in Calderón in Germany, his appeal to the Romantics, especially to A. W. Schlegel, and finally the accumulative effect on the work of Goethe, especially in <u>Pandora</u> and the second part of <u>Faust</u>.

Hatzantonis, Emmanuel Stamatios. <u>Circe nelle letterature classiche, medioevali e romanze: Omero a Calderón</u>. Unpub. doct. diss., Univ. of California, 1958.

Hatzfeld, Helmut. "The Situation in the Field of Hispanic Style Studies." In <u>Estudios hispánicos. Homenaje a Archer M. Huntington</u>, Wellesley, Mass., Spanish Dept., Wellesley College, 1952, pp. 235-52.

Mentioned in this critical review of recent Spanish and Portuguese style studies, intended to continue the Hispanic sector of Hatzfeld's earlier bibliographies in Romance stylistic studies, are Calderonian studies by Max Kommerell, Ernst Robert Curtius, and Everett W. Hesse.

- "Poetas españoles de resonancia universal." <u>Hisp</u>, 40 (1957), 261-69.

For Hatzfeld, there are six poets whose "figura sobresale aun hoy o que han vuelto a descubrirse en nuestros días, poetas que presentan al hombre moderno algo único, algo que lleva el sello del espíritu español." The six are San Juan de la Cruz, Cervantes, Góngora, Lope de Vega, Quevedo, and Calderón. For our dramatist, the conclusion is that "sin Calderón, no tendríamos un criterio para comprender la circunstancialidad literaria, las excelencias y las limitaciones de un dramaturgo teólogo y católico."

- <u>Estudios sobre el barroco</u>. Madrid, Gredos, 1964. Pp. 487. (Bib. Románica Hispánica, II. Estudios y Ensayos.) Rev: Alan S. Trueblood, "The Baroque Premises and Problems: A Review Article," <u>HR</u>, 35 (1967), 355-63 ("Calderón presents a particular problem. Now he is seen as baroque and on the basis of the two plays <u>La vida es sueño</u> and <u>El alcalde de Zalamea</u> is credited with a change of taste, 'allegorical to realistic' and 'aristocratic to popular'.").

- "Spanish Criticism. Through the Renaissance." In <u>Dictionary of World Literature</u>, ed. J. T. Shipley (revised ed.), Patterson, N. J., Littlefield, Adams, 1962, pp. 385-90.

Brief mention of Calderón, with reference to the defence of his dramatic works by contemporaries and later writers and theoreticians.

Hermenegildo, Alfredo. <u>Burgos en el romancero y en el teatro de los Siglos de Oro</u>. Madrid, Publicaciones de la Fundación Universitaria Española, 1958. Pp. ix, 186. Rev: Jim P. Artman, <u>BA</u>, 33 (1959), 448; Juan de Castro y Delgado, <u>Razón y Fe</u>, 159 (1959), 541; Fr. Angel López, <u>Estudios</u>, 15 (1959), 309-10; Maxime Chevalier, <u>BH</u>, 62 (1960), 459-60; Norma Pérez Martín, <u>RUBA</u>, 5 (1960), 138-39; Stephen Reckert, <u>BHS</u>, 37 (1960), 64.

The publication of Hermenegildo's "Tesis de Licenciatura en la Universidad de Madrid," presented June 21, 1957. Calderón is represented by one play only: <u>Origen, pérdida y restauración de la Virgen del Sagrario</u>, in a very short reference to the "jura de Santa Gadea" made by King Alfonso VI.

Herrero García, Miguel. <u>Madrid en el teatro</u>. Madrid, CSIC, 1963. Pp. viii, 450.

Frequent references to and quotations from Calderón's plays.

Heselhaus, Clemens. "Calderón und Hofmannsthal. Sinn und Form des theologischen Dramas." <u>Archiv</u>, 191, Nos. 1-2 (1954), 3-30.

Hess, Rainer. <u>Das romanische geistliche Schauspiel als profane und religiöse Komödie ... 15. und 16. Jahrhundert</u>. Munich, 1965. Rev: M. Nerlich, <u>RF</u>, 78 (1966), 582-86.

Hesse, Everett W. "Calderón y Velázquez." <u>Clav</u>, 2, No. 10 (1951), 1-10.

The stated purpose of this interesting study is to show the similarity of certain aspects of theme, style, technique, and attitudes in the works of Calderón and Velázquez. Pointing out that Velázquez was born just one year before Calderón and noting further parallels in the noble lineage of both and in the advantages which accrued to both with the advent of the Buen Retiro palace, Hesse goes on to suggest convincing comparisons of the works of these Golden Age contemporaries. He analyses what he considers perhaps the best example of a parallel, <u>The Surrender of Breda</u> (1635) and the play, <u>El sitio de Bredá</u> (1625) and, after noting similarities, suggests that lines of Calderón's play may even have influenced Velázquez in certain details of his painting. Satire is mentioned as an aspect of the art of the two, as well as the duality known as the baroque split. The close parallels drawn by Hesse are provocative and convincing.

- "Calderón and Velázquez." <u>Hisp</u>, 35 (1952), 74-82.

The English version of the preceding article (without the six reproductions of Velázquez's paintings).

- "La dialéctica y el casuismo en Calderón." <u>Estudios</u>, 9 (1953), 517-31.

- "Calderón's Popularity in the Spanish Indies." <u>HR</u>, 23 (1955), 12-27.

Covers performances in the Spanish colonies as estabished by available records, indicating Calderón's supremacy in the colonial theatre.

- <u>Calderón de la Barca</u>. New York, Twayne, 1967. Pp. 192.
Rev: Sidney F. Wexler, <u>Hisp</u>, 51 (1968), 922 (Favourable. The reviewer considers the study of <u>El médico de su honra</u> to be particularly fine. "The author approaches the drama as poetry, with deep understanding of its imagery and techniques."); Margaret Wilson, <u>BHS</u>, 46 (1969), 163-64.

This "life and works" is intended for the general reader, and, in succeeding in that purpose, it also achieves a success as a scholarly monograph. Professor Hesse is to be congratulated on one more tribute to Calderón.

- <u>Análisis e interpretación de la Comedia</u>. Madrid, Castalia, 1968. Pp. 115.
Rev: Ramón Esquer Torres, <u>Arbor</u>, 72 (1969), 126-27; Sidney F. Wexler, <u>Hisp</u>, 52 (1969), 959.

"El motivo de este volumen es reunir una serie de estudios míos que han aparecido en diversos lugares. Los he revisado, agregando ideas nuevas, y cambiando el punto de vista." There is a careful and detailed exegesis of <u>Eco y Narciso</u>, and an examination of the plot, theme, symbols and characters of <u>La vida es sueño</u>. Also included is an essay "La reeducación de Segismundo y Basilio," which treats the factors that lead to the transformation of Basilio and Segismundo, and a bibliography.

Hilborn, Harry W. "The Calderonian <u>gracioso</u> and Marriage." <u>BCom</u>, 3, No. 2 (1951), 2-3.

In cases in which the <u>gracioso</u> parodies the action of the <u>galán</u> through the matrimonial solution of the dénouement in

the comedias of Lope and Calderón, Hilborn points out and
documents the following distinguishing characteristics:
Whereas Lope's gracioso generally seeks and accepts with
gratitude the final mating, "when the Calderonian gracioso
is given an opportunity to share in the final marriages, his
attitude, unlike that of Lope's gracioso, is one of aversion
or resignation."

- "Comparative culto vocabulary in Calderón and Lope." HR, 26
(1958), 223-33.

"Calderón has generally been regarded as especially prone to
the use of culto vocabulary ..., while Lope ... has been
credited with offering a resolute resistance to the movement"
(i.e., Gongorism). After comparing the culto vocabulary of
Lope and Calderón in dated comedias of the period 1623-29,
Hilborn concludes that "Lope's mockery of the culto style
has served to divert attention from his own practice. Calderón
undertook no bold venture in his use of culto vocabulary in
his comedias, he merely carried a little further a movement
in which Lope also was participating, and both dramatists
accepted only a minor portion of the vocabulary censured as
culto by their contemporaries." Hilborn's appendix lists all
culto words and indicates the comedias where they occur.

Hofer, S. "La huella de España en la cultura austríaca." Arbor,
43 (1959), 406-20.

Especially the influence of Lope de Vega and Calderón.

Hogan, Floriana T. "Notes on Thirty-one English Plays and Their
Spanish Sources." Restoration and 18th Century Theatre
Research, 6 (1967), 56-59.

Restoration and 18th century English and 17th century
Spanish plays.

Honig, Edwin. "The Seizures of Honor in Calderón." Kenyon Review,
23 (1961), 426-47.

After an introduction dealing with the nature of honour in
Spanish society of the 17th century, the author discusses

four of Calderón's plays which illustrate his diversified treatment of the honour theme and his originality as a thinking dramatist. The four are: <u>A secreto agravio, secreta venganza</u>, <u>La devoción de la Cruz</u>, <u>El alcalde de Zalamea</u>, and <u>La dama duende</u>.

- "The Concept of Honor in the Dramas of Calderón." <u>New Mexico Quarterly</u>, 35 (1965), 105-17.

"... the strangeness behind the strangeness in his use of honor is that he thereby establishes a dramatic way of pointing toward the difficult ascension of the human, the discovery of what it means to be a human being."

Horst, K. A. "Calderóns geistige Welt." <u>Deutsche Beiträge</u> (Munich), 1954, pp. 44-58.

Hunter, William A. "The Seventeenth-century Nahuatl <u>entremés</u> In Ilamatzin Ihuan in Piltontli," KFLQ, 5 (1958), 26-34.

This is an <u>entremés</u> bound between two plays, the first of these being the <u>auto sacramental</u>, <u>El gran teatro del mundo</u> (See under Editions, above.). Of the <u>auto</u> Professor Hunter writes: "No satisfactory explanation for the appearance in Mexico of a translation of a Spanish play thirteen years before its publication in Madrid has yet been offered." (See also Olmedilla, Studies — General.)

Iglesias de Souza, L. "Dos autos marianos de Calderón." <u>Atlántida</u> (La Coruña), No. 1 (1954).

Iriarte, Joaquín. "Calderón o la temática moderna." In <u>Pensaães e historiadores: I. Casa de Austria (1500-1700)</u>, Madrid, Edit. Razón y Fe, 1960, pp. 401-63. (Bib. de Filosofía y Pedagogía.)

A great deal of attention is paid to the nineteenth-century Germans and Calderón, with stress on <u>La vida es sueño</u>.

- "Schopenhauer, admirador de Gracián y de Calderón." <u>Razón y Fe</u>, 162 (1960), 405-18.

Isar, Erbert E. "La cuestión del llamado senequismo español."
Hispanó, No. 2 (1958), 11-30.

Nothing of importance on Calderón. It is to be remembered that
Valbuena Briones, in reviewing Hesse's edition of El mayor
monstruo los celos, considers the ending of the play to be of
"un típico senequismo español."

Jarrett-Kerr, Martin. "Calderón and the Imperialism of Belief."
In Studies in Literature and Belief, London, Rockliff, 1954,
pp. 38-63.
Rev: TLS, Dec. 3, 1954, 782.

Discusses the extent to which Christian belief is compatible
with the creation of great tragedy. "... the final weakness
of even his (Calderón's) greatest work is that he has not
understood the genuine independence and validity of creature-
hood. Faith has tended to eliminate sympathy, and instead of
illuminating unbelief it has had the effect of erasing it."

Jones, C. A. The Code of Honour in the Spanish Golden Age Drama,
with Special Reference to Calderón. Unpub. doct. diss.,
Oxford Univ., 1955.

- "Honor in Spanish Golden-Age Drama: Its Relation to Real Life
and to Morals." BHS, 35 (1958), 199-210.

The major part of the article is devoted to Calderón's honour
plays. The author quotes Américo Castro's article "Algunas
observaciones acerca del concepto del honor en los siglos
XVI y XVII" (RFE, 3, 1916), and refutes some of its conten-
tions. Jones speaks of Calderón's attitude toward honour
evolving during his career, but fails to prove this evolution;
and he contends that "Calderón used the motive of honour ...
simply because it was part of the Lopean heritage, which
success had recommended." In general, the article lacks
depth, although parts of it are valuable.

- "Spanish Honour as Historical Phenomenon, Convention and
Artistic Motive." HR, 33 (1965), 32-39.

Frequent reference is made to Calderón.

- "Brecht y el drama del Siglo de Oro." <u>Segismundo</u>, 3 (1967), 39-55.

Brecht developed two elements which he found in the Golden Age drama: didacticism and alienation. References are made to Calderón.

Kaczewska-Markiewicz, Zofia. "Wyspianski a teatr baroku hispanskiego." <u>Przeglad Humanistyczny</u>, 13, No. 6 (1969), 59-62.

Stanislaw Wyspianski and the Spanish Baroque Theatre. References to Calderón.

Keller, John E. "A Tentative Classification for Themes in the <u>Comedia</u>." <u>BCom</u>, 5, No. 2 (1953), 17-23.

Takes up, among other Golden Age plays, <u>La vida es sueño</u>.

Kern, Hanspeter. "Ludwig Tiecks Calderonismus." <u>Gesammelte Aufsätze zur Kulturgeschichte Spaniens</u>, 23 (1967), 189-356.

Contains, among other sections, "Tiecks Calderonismus in der Forschung," "Die Reseption Calderóns," "Calderón als Vorbild," and "Der Calderonismus in Tiecks Werk."

- "Calderón und Tiecks Weltbild." <u>Gesammelte...</u>, 24 (1968), 337-96.

Köhler, Rudolf. <u>Der Einfluss Gil Vicentes auf das spanische Theater des "Goldenen Zeitalters</u>." Göttingen, Georg-August-Universität zu Göttingen, 1968. Pp. v, 312.

A doctoral dissertation, which devotes considerable space to Calderón (pp. 177-95, etc.).

Körner, Karl-Hermann. <u>Die "Aktionsgemeinschaft finites Verb + Infinitiv" im spanischen Formensystem, Vorstudie zu einer Untersuchung der Sprache Pedro Calderóns de la Barca</u>. Hamburg, Kommissionsverlag Cram, de Gruyter und Co., 1968.

Pp. 149. (Hamburger Romanistische Studien. B, Ibero-
Amerikanische Reihe, 30.)
Rev: Ann L. Mackenzie, BHS, 46 (1969), 274-75; José Joaquín
Montes Giraldo, Thesaurus, 24 (1969), 312-13; Peter Wunderli,
RF, 81 (1969), 480-85.

Includes a bibliography, pp. 131-42.

Krauss, Werner. "Calderón: Dichter des spanischen Volkes." In
Studien und Aufsätze, Berlin, 1959, pp. 139-54.

Labarta de Chaves, Teresa. "Forma cerrada y forma abierta en
el teatro del espacio y del tiempo en el teatro español de
los siglos XVI y XVII." Hispanó, No. 34 (1968), 27-45.

The author explores the opposition of the "closed" and "open"
forms studied in Darnell H. Roaten and F. Sánchez y Escribano,
Wölfflin's Principles in Spanish Drama: 1500-1700 (1952).
Using La dama duende as a primary example, she studies this
dramatic technique with relation to time and space.

Lacosta, Francisco C. "Los autos sacramentales de Pedro Calderón
de la Barca." Archivo Hispalense, 42 (1965), 9-26.

After an historical sketch of the auto in general, and a
definition of the genre as practised by Calderón, the author
lists Calderón's chief sources (Saints such as Augustine,
Thomas Aquinas, Gregorio Nacianceno) and Calderón's own
qualifications to write with a genius that even his few
adverse critics do not deny him. This "católico y autor
sublime" combined dogma, logic, art, and 17th-century customs
in an almost miraculous way.

Laplane, Gabriel. "Calderón et l'Espagne." Revue de Paris, No.
5 (1957), 98-109.

This enjoyable essay, which has no scholarly pretensions nor
is obviously intended for Calderonian scholars, is well
organized and gives a general view of the highlights of all
Calderonian plays, with the exception of his mythological
comedias and fiestas cantadas. Some reference is made to the
present state of the dramatist in his own country; and with

sadness Laplane points out that, when in recent times directors
and producers stage Calderón, there is no response among the
Spanish public. And, when staged, there are so many changes
in the plays that if these changes were perpetrated with the
French classics, "nous paraîtraient sacrilèges s'il s'agissait
de Racine ou de Molière." Laplane points out, among other
things, the rhythm and musicality of Calderón verse (impossible to translate) and many characteristics of Calderón's
dramatic technique.

La Prade, John H. Golden Age Authors as Characters on the
Nineteenth-Century Spanish Stage. Unpub. doct. diss., Univ.
of North Carolina, 1963. (DA, 24, 1964, 3750.)

One aspect of the Romantic interest in the national past was
the large number of plays in which literary figures were
characters. Most attention was paid to Golden Age authors,
including Calderón.

Leavitt, Sturgis E. "The Gracioso Takes the Audience into His
Confidence." BCom, 7, No. 2 (1955), 27-29.

Reference made to Calderón's use of this form of humour in
seven different plays, the best effort being found in Hado y
divisa de Leonido y Marfisa, Calderón's last comedia.

- "Humor in the Autos of Calderón." Hisp, 39 (1956), 137-44.

Concludes that Calderón in his autos surpasses all other
writers of autos in humour and in the creation of humorous
allegorical characters.

- "Strip-Tease in Golden Age Drama." In Homenaje a Rodríguez-
Moñino, I, Madrid, Castalia, 1966, pp. 305-10.

Contains references to Calderón, but, as Professor Leavitt
says, they are not particularly interesting cases.

- "Scenes of Horror in Golden Age Drama." RomN, 10 (1968),
114-18.

There are references to several comedias, including El alcalde de Zalamea ("Abren una puerta, y aparece dado garrote en una silla el Capitán") and Las tres justicias en una ("Abre la puerta ... y se ve a don Lope, dado garrote").

Lebois, A. "Créations, pourvoirs et révolte des personnages. Sources étrangères du pirandellisme." Annales de la Faculté des Lettres de Toulouse, 9 (1960), 81-111.

Cervantes, Calderón, Unamuno.

Lelièvre, Renée. "Le Théâtre des variétés étrangères (1806-1807)." Rev. d'Hist. du Théâtre, 12 (1960), 193-309.

Part II, Chapt. 2, pp. 232-34: "Le théâtre espagnol: Calderón, Antonio de Solís."

Ley, Charles David. El gracioso en el teatro de la Península (Siglos XVI-XVII). Madrid, Rev. de Occidente, 1954. Pp. 263. Rev: C. Bravo-Villasante, Clav, 6, No. 31 (1955), 73; A. Zamora Vicente, Insula, 10 (1955), 6-7; Margaret Wilson, BHS, 33 (1956), 171-72 (Calls this an "antología del gracioso," with no notes, classifications or general conclusions.); N. E. Zingoni, Rev. de Educación (Buenos Aires), 1 (1956), 226-28.

Ley studies antecedents of the gracioso in the classical theatre and shows how this figure became a fundamental element in the Spanish drama of the Golden Age. The Calderonian gracioso is referred to as grotesque, conventional, and without human interest. The Wilson review criticizes the book for being superficial, and states that "a full study of the development of the gracioso remains to be written." (The volume was a doct. diss., Univ. of Madrid, 1950.)

Lionetti, Harold. "La preocupación del 'más allá'." Hisp, 41 (1958), 26-29.

Lionetti deals with the problem in general terms and goes from the Middle Ages to Machado and Unamuno. Incidentally he deals with Calderón, whom he calls "más teólogo que Lope," and who, as a "representante de las viejas usanzas medioevales, medita sobre el más allá y los castigos ultraterrenos." The Calderonian examples are drawn from El purgatorio de San Patricio and La vida es sueño.

Lorenz, Erika. "Calderón und die Astrologie." RJ, 12 (1961), 265-77.

After giving an historical background of astrology, the author explores what seems to be contradictions in Calderón's attitude to astrology, showing that in reality he follows closely the attitude of Thomas Aquinas. In conclusion she states that Calderón considered that the stars had a real, though somewhat limited, influence on the actions of men. Consequently astrological allusions are not to be considered only bare metaphors in Calderón's plays.

Löwenthal, Leo. Literature and the Image of Man. Sociological Studies of the European Drama and Novel 1600-1900. Boston, Beacon Press, 1953. Pp. 242. (2nd printing, 1963. Trans. Tobias and Helga Rülcker, as Das Bild des Menschen in der Literatur, Neuwied, Luchterland, 1966. Pp. 305.)
Rev: Gustav Konrad, Welt und Wort, 22 (1967), 166.

The volume contains references to Lope de Vega and Calderón: "The Spanish Writers" (pp. 11-19).

Lund, Harry. Pedro Calderón de la Barca: A Biography. Edinburg (Texas), Privately Printed (Andrés Noriega Press), 1963. Pp. 128.
Rev: C. A. Jones, BHS, 42 (1965), 131-32; H. W. Hilborn, Hisp, 48 (1965), 937-38.

A carelessly and poorly written (and printed) account of Calderón and his times. The author brings together much information concerning Calderón and his family, but digresses to tell about the "Felipes" and other not entirely relevant matters. There is little critical comment concerning his work. The whole is rather disorganized, and the style is almost repelling.

(M.) "Una página inédita de Calderón." Correo Erudito, 5, Nos. 35-36 (1953), 200.

Deals with Calderón's opinion of the office of the "ensayador de la moneda."

Malkiel, Yakov. "Bibliographic Notes: Nuggets of Linguistic Information in Critical Editions of Siglo de Oro Texts." RPh, 18 (1964-65), 137-42.

Comments briefly on Ebersole's edition of Calderón's La desdicha de la voz (not very favourably), and Černý's edition of El gran duque de Gandía (favourably).

Mancini, Guido. "Nota per lo studio della scenografia spagnola nel sec. XVII." Studi Mediolatini e Volgari, 2 (1954), 39-48.

Mentions Lope and Calderón, among others, for their descriptions of the theatrical spectacles of their periods. For Calderón, see Muñoz Morillejo, Escenografía española, Madrid, 1923.

- (ed.). Calderón in Italia. Studi e ricerche. Pisa, Goliardica, 1955. Pp. 165. (Studi di Letteratura Spagnola. Facoltà di Magistero dell'Università di Roma. Quaderno, 4.)

Contains: "Introduzione," by Guido Mancini, pp. 5-25; "Note sull'interpretazione di Calderón nel Seicento," by Guido Mancini, pp. 27-44; "Motivi calderoniani nella letteratura settecentesca," by Inoria Pepe, pp. 45-61; "Giudizi di Romantici italiani su Calderón," by Rinaldo Froldi, pp. 63-84; "Calderón nella critica italiana del Novecento," by Carmelo Samonà, pp. 85-165.

Manson, William R. Attitudes Toward Authority as Expressed in Typical Spanish Plays of the Golden Age. Unpub. doct. diss., Univ. of North Carolina, 1963. (DA, 25, 1965, 4703.)

Quotes from the plays of a number of Golden Age dramatists, including Calderón (at least 15 plays), to show the attitude toward parental, ecclesiastical and temporal authority. One of his conclusions is that Calderón is best in portraying attitudes of disrespect for the authority of minor governmental officials. Calderón possesses no such disrespect himself, but was merely presenting the customs of the time.

On the whole, Calderón was the least interested of dramatists in matters of government.

Maravall, José Antonio. "Una interpretación histórico-social del teatro barroco." <u>CHA</u>, 78 (1969), 621-49; 79 (1969), 74-108.

Marcos Rodríguez, Florencio. "Un pleito de don Pedro Calderón de la Barca, estudiante de Salamanca." <u>Rev. de Archivos, Bibliotecas y Museos</u>, 67 (1959), 717-31.

Author publishes the record of a lawsuit which shows that Calderón was sued for non-payment of rent while he was a student at Salamanca.

Martín Acosta, Sister María I. <u>The Mythological "autos" of Calderón de la Barca</u>. Unpub. doct. diss., Columbia Univ., 1969.

Martín Andrés, Ana María. "Ensayo bibliográfico sobre las ediciones, traducciones y estudios de Calderón de la Barca en Francia." <u>RL</u>, 17 (1960), 53-100.

Also thesis, Univ. de Madrid, 1960.

May, T. E. "Extremo-término." <u>BHS</u>, 31 (1954), 37-38.

"Extremo" as used in classical Spanish works; with examples from Calderón, etc.

Mazur, Oleh. "Various Impacts upon the <u>Salvaje</u> in the Spanish <u>Comedia</u>." <u>HR</u>, 36 (1968), 207-35.

Mentions <u>El mayor encanto amor</u>, <u>Céfalo y Pocris</u>, and <u>El castillo de Lindabridis</u>.

McCready, Warren T. "A Volume of Rare <u>Sueltas</u>." <u>BCom</u>, 6, No 1 (1954), 4-8.

Contains, attributed to Calderón, _Los riesgos que tiene un coche_, _La más hidalga hermosura_, _La vanda y la flor_, _Muchos indicios sin culpa_.

- _La heráldica en las obras de Lope de Vega y sus contemporáneos_. Toronto, A costa del autor, 1962. Pp. xii, 470.

Calderón, pp. 303-18, passim. As the reviews have indicated (cf. Arnold G. Reichenberger, _HR_, 32, 1964, 366-68), "These are the results of Dr. McCready's patient and painstaking investigation." The monograph "establishes a descending frequency of heraldic matter from Lope to Calderón, thus confirming again the division of the two 'schools' and the change of taste." The study is one of highest importance, and Calderón is given his due place in this significant research.

- _Bibliografía temática de estudios sobre el teatro español antiguo (1850-1950)_. Toronto, Univ. of Toronto Press, 1966. Pp. 445.
Rev: Carlos Ortigoza, _HAHR_, 48 (1968), 688-89; Rafael Osuna, _Thesaurus_, 23 (1968), 587-90; Richard W. Tyler, _MP_, 45 (1968), 246-47 ("Professor McCready's Bibliography has been most properly done; and it is indeed a tremendous job..."); Walter Poesse, _HR_, 37 (1969), 414-17 ("This is a tremendous achievement, some 18 years in the making... Professor McCready can take great and justifiable pride in his contribution to Hispanic scholarship..."); N. D. Shergold, _BHS_, 46 (1969), 86-87.

The Bibliography (final date, 1950) which ours supplements for Calderón.

McKnight, William A., and Mabel Barrett Jones. _A Catalogue of Comedias Sueltas in the Library of the University of North Carolina_. Chapel Hill, Univ. of North Carolina Library, 1965. Pp. vii, 240.

Lists a large number of Calderón items.

Meregalli, Franco. "L'ispanismo tedesco dal 1945." _Quaderni Ibero-Americani_, No. 16 (1954), 524-27, and No. 18 (1956), 103-09.

References to studies on Calderón, among others.

Merlino, Mario. "Lo medieval en Calderón y la función soterio-
lógica del sueño." In Cvitanovic (ed.), El sueño..., 1969,
pp. 106-22.

See Studies — General.

Metford, J. C. J. "The Enemies of the Theatre in the Golden
Age." BHS, 28 (1951), 76-92.

Although the seemingly exhaustive study of Cotarelo y Mori
(Bibliografía de las controversias sobre la licitud del teatro
en España, Madrid, 1904) left little to be done with regard
to the discovery of bibliographic manifestations of the
controversy, there still remained the task of analysing and
correlating the evidence with the history of the Spanish
stage in particular epochs. Metford cites the study in which
I. L. McClelland accomplished this for the eighteenth century,
and he here provides a "similar examination with reference to
the Golden Age and, more particularly, to the periods of the
flourishing and of the decline of the Spanish Comedia, from
the advent of Lope de Vaga to the death of Calderón." Tracing
the opposition of the Christian church from the degenerate
tastes of the Roman theatre in its decline to the days of the
decline of the Spanish Comedia, Metford observes that the
theatre was not seriously curbed by its opponents, the continued persistence of whose attacks indicates the practical
impunity enjoyed by the theatre. There is only incidental
mention of Calderón on two occasions.

Mitchell, Margarete Koch. Die christliche Thematik im Drama Hugo
von Hofmannsthals in Lichte Calderón de la Barca. Unpub. doct.
diss., Indiana Univ., 1965. (DA, 26, 3345-46.)

Hofmannsthal progressed from "worldly" to "Christian" poetry,
tending first toward Calderón, then away from him again. El
gran teatro del mundo and La vida es sueño (both auto and
comedia) are chiefly involved. Das kleine Welttheater (1897)
has nothing specifically Christian, while the unfinished Das
Leben ein Traum (c. 1904) seems a conscious effort to contra-
dict Calderón. Das Salzburger Grosse Welttheater (1922),
though lacking Calderón's basis in Catholic dogma, is

Hofmannsthal's nearest approach to Calderón's Catholic Christian world. From the first Die Turm (1925) to the second (1927), Hofmannsthal keeps going farther from Calderón.

(Modern Humanities Research Association.) The Year's Work in Modern Language Studies.

Our period is covered by this excellent, running bibliographical-critical commentary, published in Cambridge, England.

(Modern Language Association of America.) "Annual Bibliography." In PMLA, 72, No. 2 (Apr., 1957) on.

The annual "American Bibliography" (begun in 1919) ceased in Vol. 71, No. 2 (Apr., 1956), and since 1957 (material of 1956), the coverage has been international. Calderón is well treated. No book reviews.

Moir, Duncan. "The Classical Tradition in Spanish Dramatic Theory and Practice in the Seventeenth Century." In Classical Drama and its Influence. Essays Presented to H. D. F. Kitto, London, Methuen, 1965, pp. 193-228.

Moldenhauer, G. Reflejos clásicos en el actual teatro alemán. Rosario (Argentina), Univ. Nac. del Litoral, 1953. Pp. 28. Rev: J. Boyer, RLC, 29 (1955), 424-25.

Studies, among other influences, the influence of Calderón.

Molinaro, J. A., J. H. Parker, and Evelyn Rugg. A Bibliography of Comedias Sueltas in the University of Toronto Library. Toronto, Univ. of Toronto Press, 1959. Pp. 150. Rev: A. E. Sloman, BHS, 38 (1961), 312-13.

Lists forty sueltas by Calderón.

Moll, Jaime. Catálogo de Comedias sueltas conservadas en la Biblioteca de la Real Academia Española. Madrid, RAE, 1966.

Includes Calderón items. Previously pub. in BRAE, 44 (1964), 113-68, 309-60, 541-56; 45 (1965), 203-35; 46 (1966), 125-40.

Monge, Félix. "Culteranismo y conceptismo a la luz de Gracián." In Homenaje. Estudios para celebrar el tercer lustro del Instituto de Estudios Hispánicos, Portugueses e Iberoamericanos de la Universidad Estatal de Utrecht, The Hague, 1966, pp. 355-81.

Monleón, José. "Dos autos sacramentales en El Escorial: La cena del rey Baltasar y El gran teatro del mundo." Primer Acto, No. 44 (1963), 58-60.

The reviewer is more concerned with the autos than with the performances and has a marked preference for El gran teatro over La cena, which he calls "hermetic and confused." To him El gran teatro "says precisely what the author wanted to say" and "gives us all the answers"; it expresses clearly "the ideological synthesis which determines several centuries of Spanish history, in its maximum extent."

Montaner, Joaquín. La colección teatral de don Arturo Sedó. Barcelona, Seix y Barral, 1951. Pp. 353.

Contains Calderón items.

Montoliu, Manuel de. Manual de historia de la literatura castellana. 6th ed. Barcelona, Cervantes, 1957. (Two new chapters by Luis Moya Plana.)

This well-known manual devotes Chapter VII to the theatre of the Golden Age. Twenty-six pages are assigned to Calderón. This book has proved through the years to be a very good reference book at the undergraduate level. What pertains to Calderón remains unchanged in this new edition.

Morgan, Gerald. "Conrad, Madach et Calderón." Etudes Slaves et Est-Européennes, 6 (1962), 196-209.

Part one of this article consists of an analysis of Conrad's "baroque existentialism," in which attention is paid to Calderón's influence on Conrad's philosophy. Calderón's words, "el mayor delito del hombre es haber nacido," provide the point of departure for the study.

Morrison, Robert R. Sainthood in the Golden Age Drama of Spain. Unpub. doct. diss., Univ. of Florida, 1963. (DA, 25, 481.)

Morteo, Gian Renzo. "Vita e fortuna di Pedro Calderón de la Barca." Quaderni del Teatro Stabile della Città di Torino, No. 9 (1967), 41-56.

Moussinac, Léon. Le Théâtre des origines à nos jours. Paris, Amiot-Dumont, 1957. Pp. 438.

Calderón is often mentioned in this book. His autos are called moralités (p. 91). Mentioned are four of Calderón's plays and one of his autos in which Moussinac considers that "le génie y atteint souvent à la grandeur."

Muñoz, Matilde. Historia del teatro dramático en España. Madrid, Edit. Tesoro, 1953. Pp. 338. (Previously pub., 1948.)

Due to the general character of the work, the author limits herself to a brief and superficial treatment of Calderón and that mostly biographical.

Newels, Margarete. Die dramatischen Gattungen in den Poetiken des Siglo de Oro. Ein einletende Studie zum Thema der Dramentheorie in goldenen Zeitalter. Wiesbaden, Steiner Verlag, 1959. Pp. 192.
Rev: Alan Soons, NRFH, 17 (1963-64), 386-88.

References to Calderón.

Newman, Richard William. Calderón and Aquinas. Unpub. doct. diss., Boston Univ., 1956. (Boston Univ. Abstracts, 1956.)

Ochse, Horst. Studien zur Metaphorik Calderóns. Munich, Wilhelm Fink Verlag, 1967. Pp. 127. (Freiburger Schriften zur romanischen Philologie, I.)
Rev: Edward Glaser, RF, 80 (1968), 606-10 ("Ochse brings to bear on his research a solid knowledge of both the classical and the Christian heritage upon which Calderón drew. The German scholar's analytical method is sound; moreover, he

reveals admirable sagacity in probing isolated passages as
well as in relating them to the totality of Calderón's
Gedankenwelt."); Stefanie Jauernick, Die neueren Sprachen,
67 (1968), 413-14.

Ochse previously studied this subject as a thesis for the
University of Freiburg (1959); and in his monograph he has
made an important contribution to Calderón scholarship. He
pays a great deal of attention to Semíramis of La hija del
aire.

Olmedilla, Carlos. "Lope y Calderón en México: 1641." Historia
   Mexicana, 7 (1957), 237-38.

This brief note refers mainly to W. A. Hunter's article, "The
Alva manuscripts in the Bancroft Library," KFLQ, 3 (1956),
76-81, in which he deals with a Nahuatl translation of El
gran teatro del mundo and with the Aztec translations of El
animal profeta y dichoso and La madre de la mejor.

Oppenheimer, Max, Jr. "A Spurious Edition of the Segunda Parte
   of the Vera Tassis Edition of Calderón's Comedias." HR, 19
   (1951), 346-52.

The author's purpose is to clarify the bibliographical data,
such as chronological order, filiation, and authenticity, of
the various printings of Volume II of the nine-volume Vera
Tassis edition of Calderón's comedias. La Barrera had listed
a 1682 edition; but Oppenheimer, siding with Buchanan, assumes
that La Barrera erred in this matter and eliminates the 1682
edition from his bibliographical consideration of Volume II.
Oppenheimer concludes that the spurious 1683 collection of
sueltas was made up between the years 1686 and 1763 and,
on the basis of spelling variants, advances 1720 as a "highly
plausible" date for the spurious Segunda Parte.

Orozco Díaz, Emilio. El teatro y la teatralidad del Barroco
   (Ensayo de introducción al tema). Barcelona, Edit. Planeta,
   1969. Pp. 245.

Above all on "el sentido teatral que se impone en las artes
y, en general, en todas las manifestaciones de la vida de la
época." The author continues in his Introduction to speak of

"La obra barroca con el dinamismo impetuoso del movimiento
de sus formas y figuras, con sus hirientes efectos de luces
y colores, con todas sus riquezas sensoriales, con sus
arrebatadoras perspectivas, lo que está luchando por expresar,
tras la visión de ese mundo seductor que nos lanza hacia un
espacio continuo e infinito, es el fluir incesante del paso
del tiempo;..."; and concludes the Introduction by declaring
that "Lo que late, pues, en el fondo de la gran obra barroca
es la gran verdad de la fugacidad de la vida."

Ortigoza Vieyra, Carlos. Los móviles de la Comedia en Lope,
Alarcón, Tirso, Moreto, Rojas, Calderón. Mexico, Universidad
Nacional, 1954. Pp. 340.
Rev: A. G. Reichenberger, HR, 25 (1957), 138-41 (Feels that
the author has not succeeded in showing the complexity and
originality of the characters of the comedia through an
analysis of their motivation. Insists that the comedia should
be studied according to its own laws, which centre around
honour and faith. "Although he (Ortigoza) modestly states
that he is not writing for the specialist, he is actually the
first investigator who was bold enough to present the comedia
as a whole by studying the móviles operative in its characters,
situations and actions. While we gladly certify that he has
succeeded in "esbozar la diferente intensidad, y la variedad
de matices en los seis dramaturgos," we would be lacking in
candor if we did not state that the stability of the comedia
pattern emerges from his study at least as impressively as
its "variedad."); Thora Sorenson, Hisp, 40 (1957), 248-49
(Points out that "an emphasis is laid on the psychological
complexity of the characters in the plays; a close adhesion
to universal human emotions and reactions is noted at the
same time that proofs are presented of the dynamic and
generally ignored complexity of the works." Notes that close
to sixty Calderón comedias are referred to.); J. H. Parker,
CMLR, 14, No. 3 (1958), 55.

Pabst, Walter von. "Gaspar Buesso de Arnal, Glossator Góngoras
und Korrektor Calderóns." RJ, 13 (1962), 292-312.

Paglialunga de Tuma, Mercedes. "Séneca y Filón de Alejandría
en la temática calderoniana." In Cvitanovic (ed.), El sueño...,
1969, pp. 90-105. See Studies — General.

Palacín Iglesias, Gregorio B. <u>Historia de la literatura española</u>.
2nd ed. Mexico, Author, 1958. Pp. 564.

Calderón is briefly studied. The author repeats most of the
valid judgments as well as the errors found in many literary
histories. Space is given to plots.

Papini, Giovanni. <u>Retratos</u> (<u>Cervantes, Don Quijote, Calderón,
Unamuno</u>). Trans. José Miguel Velloso. Barcelona, Caralt,
1962. Pp. 200.

Páramo Pomareda, Jorge. "Consideraciones sobre los 'autos
mitológicos' de Calderón de la Barca." <u>Thesaurus</u>, 12 (1957),
51-80.

One of the most valuable and solid contributions in the field.
There stands out his redressing of Valbuena Prat's misguided
readings of St. Augustine (in his <u>Calderón: su personalidad,
su arte dramático, su estilo y sus obras</u>, Barcelona, 1941).

Pardo Canalís, Enrique. "Calderón de la Barca, selección y
notas." <u>RIE</u>, 19 (1961), 145-72.

A selection of prose passages as well as excerpts from plays,
for the purpose of illustrating Calderón's views on poetry,
music, the <u>comedia</u>, sculpture, painting, etc. Of particular
interest are the two prose passages in defence of poetry and
painting.

Parker, Alexander A. <u>Valor actual del humanismo español</u>. Madrid,
Ateneo, 1952. Pp. 37. (Col. "O crece o muere.")

Part IV: "La posición de Calderón."

- "Reflections on a New Definition of Baroque Drama." <u>BHS</u>, 30
(1953), 142-51.

This is an important review article on the Roaten-Sánchez y
Escribano <u>Wölfflin's Principles</u> (1952). Parker rejects the
validity of the application made by the two authors of
Wölfflin's principles of Baroque art to Baroque drama. He

concludes that Wölfflin's principles are of no aid to drama since "drama, because it deals with human acts, manipulates moral values and judgments, thus possessing a dimension in which Wölfflin's principles of plastic art cannot move and to the understanding of which they can offer no clue."

- The Approach to the Spanish Drama of the Golden Age. London, The Hispanic and Luso-Brazilian Councils, 1957. Pp. 27. (Col. Diamante, 6.) (Reprinted in TDR, 4, 1959, 42-59.)

This extremely valuable seminal study formulates five principles of dramatic construction which prove highly effective keys for analysing Calderón as well as other Golden Age playwrights. El médico de su honra, La devoción de la Cruz, La vida es sueño, and El mágico prodigioso are dealt with. "The Spanish drama of the Golden Age — concludes Professor Parker — speaks a language of its own which we must first learn before we can properly understand what it says."

- The Theology of the Devil in the Drama of Calderón. London, Blackfriars, 1958. Pp. 20. (In translation: "La teología sobre el demonio en el drama calderoniano," Estudios Escénicos, Barcelona, No. 4, 1959, 7-48. Also pub. in Wardropper, Critical Essays, New York, 1965, pp. 3-23.)

"A paper read to the Aquinas Society of London in 1957," this excellent essay was written as a reaction to the book Satan published originally in French (1948) and later in English (1951). Parker points out that it seems clear that "the compilers and editors (of the book, which does not mention Calderón) were unaware of the fact that this great seventeenth-century Spanish dramatist wrote a large number of plays whose themes require the appearance of the Devil, and that nowhere else in world literature can we find as remarkable a presentation of him as a dramatic character."

- The Allegorical Drama of Calderón. An Introduction to the Autos Sacramentales. Oxford, Dolphin, 1962. Pp. 232. (1st ed., London, 1943.) (Reprinted, 1968.)

The outstanding monograph on the subject.

- "Towards a Definition of Calderonian Tragedy." BHS, 39 (1962), 222-37.

  The author considers various modern theories of tragedy, and agrees with those who say that Spanish Golden Age drama does not conform to the established definitions. However, his main purpose is to suggest that "in the drama of Calderón it is possible to detect an original, significant and valid conception of tragedy which has hitherto been overlooked." We must look for Calderón's originality in the structure of the plot, where we find illustrated a "conception of diffused responsibility, of the impossibility of confining the guilt of wrong-doing to any one individual (which) lies at the heart of the Calderonian sense of tragedy."

- "Metáfora y símbolo en la interpretación de Calderón." In Actas del Primer Congreso Internacional de Hispanistas (celebrado del 6 al 11 de septiembre de 1962), ed. Frank Pierce and Cyril A. Jones, Oxford, 1964, pp. 141-60.

  The author discusses the use of metaphor in La cisma de Inglaterra and in El médico de su honra, and the use of the symbols of the prison and the sun, the former in such plays as La hija del aire and Eco y Narciso, and the latter in Apolo y Climene. He believes that the use of symbolism culminates in the mythological comedias and concludes that symbols are an important key in an interpretation of Calderón.

- "The Father-Son Conflict in the Drama of Calderón." FMLS, 2 (1966), 99-113.

  The idea of "diffused responsibility," where one person's wrong-doing may produce another's, even after many years, was almost an obsession with Calderón, especially, of course, in La vida es sueño, but also in such works as La devoción de la Cruz and Las tres justicias en una. The obvious, "Oedipus complex" explanation of Segismundo will not fit the other two plays, or the circumstances of Calderón's own life with a tyrannical father who sought to control his sons even after his death, via his will. This weakens the stereotype of Calderón as a remote, detached playwright, tending toward abstractions.

- "The Chronology of Calderón's <u>Autos Sacramentales</u> from 1647."
<u>HR</u>, 37 (1969), 164-88.

As well as establishing dates from documentary sources, Parker
determines dates of composition by studying Calderón's technical and structural development. A very useful chronological
table of the <u>autos</u> from 1647 sums up the conclusions.

Parker, J. H. <u>Breve historia del teatro español</u>. Mexico, De
Andrea, 1957. Pp. 213. (Manuales Studium, 6.)
Rev: Almela y Vives, <u>Arbor</u>, 43 (1958), 337-38 ("...como manual
de iniciación. Y en este sentido merece sinceros elogios tanto
por el plan previamente fijado como por el desarrollo del
mismo."); C. Alvajar, <u>CCLC</u>, No. 33 (1958), 109-10 (A highly
favourable review, which characterizes the work as "concisa,
bien documentada y de indudable utilidad didáctica," even
though objections are raised concerning certain minor features
of the book.); H. W. Hilborn, <u>CMLR</u>, 14 (1958), 54 ("Everywhere
shows evidence of painstaking research and careful composition"; laments the slight treatment of the <u>gracioso</u> and the
lack of distinction between critiques and studies in the
bibliography.); W. K. Jones, <u>BA</u>, 32 (1958), 308 (An outstanding work; a trustworthy guide to authors, works, periods and
bibliography.); Carlos Ortigoza, <u>Hisp</u>, 41 (1958), 539 (Favourable, but the reviewer does not agree with the statement that
in <u>La vida es sueño</u> "se incluye una innecesaria intriga
secundaria de amor," and argues in favour of the unity of
theme with the support of recent studies by British scholars:
A. A. Parker, E. M. Wilson and A. E. Sloman. Otherwise the
reviewer considers very highly Professor Parker's contribution
among the works of similar scope because "trata de evitar la
repetición de errores que otras 'historias' han perpetuado
como herencia de una crítica trasnochada, procurando presentar
algunos puntos de vista de la crítica moderna... Las biblio-
grafías que completan cada capítulo, sin olvidar las
objecciones mencionadas, resultan útiles y al día. En fin,
resulta un auxiliar práctico y valioso por el gran acopio de
datos que contiene."); Helena Percas, <u>RHM</u>, 24 (1958), 230
(Valuable reference work, broad basis of documentation,
succinct critical studies, bibliography.); E. R. Storni,
<u>Universidad</u> (Univ. Nac. del Litoral, Santa Fe, Argentina),
No. 37 (1958), 266-67 ("Escrito con sentido didáctico, este
libro tiende a satisfacer la inquietud de quien pretenda
asomarse a la dramática española con afán de estudio." The
review is vague, and does not single out anything in

particular.); M. S. Carrasco Urgoiti, The Americas, 15 (1958-59), 412-14 (Favourable, but bibliographical treatment of fertile authors like Calderón is considered scanty.); Charles V. Aubrun, BH, 61 (1959), 460-61 (Praises, with certain reservations, the clarity, objectivity, compactness and accuracy of this guide.); Albert E. Sloman, BHS, 36 (1959), 241 ("The account is straightforward and objective ... and the great merit of this volume is that the facts are well arranged and correct." The reviewer points out that some "items of criticism have been overlooked," singling out Calderón, where Wilson's important article on La vida es sueño, is not included. "But, on the whole, the documentation is excellent."); Ramon Rozzell, HR, 28 (1960), 92 (This "handy source of accurately compiled historical data and bibliography" is highly commended, the reviewer regretting only that the "over modest author" has not relied more on his own judgment rather than on those he quotes.).

Calderón, Chapter VIII, pp. 73-80. See opinions expressed in reviews above. The author has long ago repented of having spoken of "una innecesaria intriga secundaria de amor" in La vida es sueño (having seen the unity of the play and the importance of Rosaura's rôle) and has repented of his insistence on including even outdated monographs, in bibliography, with the omission of important articles which represent an important critical reevaluation of Calderón's dramatic art.

Pavia, Mario N. Drama of the Siglo de Oro: A Study of Magic, Witchcraft and other Occult Beliefs. New York, Hispanic Institute, 1959. Pp. 166. (Doct. diss., Univ. of Chicago, 1947.)
Rev: A. Irvine Watson, BHS, 37 (1960), 260 (Unfavourable.).

Calderón is treated extensively.

Pedro, Valentín de. América en las letras españolas del Siglo de Oro. Buenos Aires, Edit. Sudamericana, 1954. Pp. 370.

While Lope de Vega and other authors of the Golden Age concentrated on greed as the main motivation in the conquest of the New World, Calderón stresses evangelization as the chief factor which inspired the conquistadores. Pp. 156-68 discuss Calderón's La aurora en Copacabana.

Pfandl, Ludwig. Historia de la literatura nacional española en la Edad de Oro. Trans. from the German by Jorge Rubió Balaguer. 2nd ed. Barcelona, Gili, 1952. Pp. xv, 740. (First Spanish edition, 1933. German edition, Freiburg, 1929.)

Calderón, comedias, pp. 449-57; discussion of the auto sacramental, pp. 467-87.

Pietschmann, Kurt R. "Recepción e influencia de Calderón en el teatro alemán del siglo XIX." Clav, 6, No. 35 (1955), 15-25.

Indicates Calderonian influence upon Schiller and Wagner, among others.

– "Calderón auf der deutschen Bühne von Goethe bis Immermann." Maske und Kothurn, 3 (1957), 317-39.

This interesting article, dealing with the German staging of Calderón's dramas from Goethe to Immermann, is divided into eight parts: "The performance of Calderón at Weimar under Goethe"; "The Calderón performances in Berlin"; "The Calderón performances by E. T. A. Hoffmanns in Bamberg"; "The Calderón performances by Ernst August Fr. Klingemanns in Braunschweig"; "Schreyvogel's adaptations of Calderón and his Calderón performances in Vienna"; "Further stage adaptations of Calderón's works"; "Calderón's works on the German stage from 1816 to 1834"; and "Immermann's exemplary productions of Calderón's plays (at Düsseldorf from 1833 to 1838)."

Pitt-Rivers, Julian. "Honour and Social Status." In Honour and Shame: The Values of Mediterranean Society, ed. J. G. Peristiany, Chicago, Univ. of Chicago Press, 1966, pp. 19-77.

References to Calderón.

Podol, Peter. The Evolution of the Honor Theme in Modern Spanish Literature. Unpub. doct. diss., Univ. of Pennsylvania, 1968. Pp. 279.

Part I treats the honour code during the Golden Age. Chapter 10 deals specifically with the non-conventional treatment of the honour theme in that period. Several plays by Calderón are studied.

Pollin, Alice M. "Puns and Word Plays in Calderón's Autos Sacramentales." Names, 16 (1968), 423-30.

A study of Calderón's use of names and their relation to his style, structure and objectives in the autos.

Porqueras-Mayo, Alberto. El prólogo como género literario. Su estudio en el Siglo de Oro español. Madrid, CSIC, 1957. Pp. 199. (RL, Anejo 14.)

Calderón is mentioned incidentally on very few occasions.

- "Herrera y Calderón a través de un olvidado escritor del siglo XVIII." RomN, 7 (1965), 36-39.

Román Hernández, in his El no sé qué / por no sé quién (1794), renders a typical eighteenth-century judgment by denying Calderón any artistic merit, although he does praise his ingenio. However, he is also pre-Romantic enough to admire Calderón's "bellezas originales," "pasajes que arrebatan," "fecunda imaginación," and "invención ... abundante."

- El prólogo en el Renacimiento español. Madrid, CSIC, 1965. Pp. ix, 244. (RL, Anejo 24.)

- El prólogo en el Manierismo y Barroco españoles. Madrid, CSIC, 1968. Pp. xii, 297. (RL, Anejo 27.)
Rev (of the two volumes above): Edward Sarmiento, MLN, 84 (1969), 352-53.

Pörtl, Klaus. "El mundo español en el teatro alemán." Nuestro Tiempo, 31 (1969), 432-53.

"Goethe y Calderón," pp. 432-35; "Un Calderón austríaco," pp. 445-48 (Hofmannsthal).

Poyán Díaz, Daniel. Âme et esprit du théâtre espagnol. Lausanne, 1956. Pp. 28.
Rev: José Montero Padilla, RL, 11 (1957), 231-32.

A general study of Spanish drama, in which the Spanish comedia
is characterized as "un conflit entre le devoir et la passion."

Rehm, Walther. "Schiller und das Barockdrama." In Götterstille
und Göttertrauer. Aufsätze zur deutsch-antiken Begegnung,
Bern, A. Francke, 1951.
Rev: E. Lohner, CL, 5 (1953), 364-68.

Calderón's influence is discussed.

Reichenberger, Arnold G. "About Themes, Motifs and an Index."
BCom, 6, No. 1 (1954), 9.

Comment on the motif index plan proposed by John E. Keller,
BCom, 5, No. 2 (1953), 17-23.

- "The Uniqueness of the Comedia." HR, 27 (1959), 303-16.

An excellent analysis.

- "La comedia clásica española y el hombre del siglo XX." FMod,
No. 4 (1961), 21-43.

The purpose of this article is to show "los rasgos principales
que permiten comprender el teatro español del siglo XVII."

Rivas Xerif, Cipriano. "Calderón de la Barca." Libros Selectos
(Mexico), 7, No. 27 (1965), 3-8.

Intended as an introduction to a volume containing several
Calderón works, this is a general discussion of the dramatist's life and writing, stressing his probable preference
for autos over comedias. The author also recalls his own
experience in directing Calderón productions in Spain and
Mexico.

Roaten, Darnell H. An Explanation of the Forms of Three Serious
Spanish Baroque Dramas According to Wölfflin's "Principles of
Art History." Unpub. doct. diss., Univ. of Michigan, 1951.
(Microfilm Abstracts, 11, 687-88.)

See the item following.

Roaten, Darnell H., and F. Sánchez y Escribano. <u>Wölfflin's
Principles in Spanish Drama</u>: <u>1500-1700</u>. New York, Hispanic
Inst. in the United States, 1952. Pp. 200.
Rev: J. E. Gillet, <u>HR</u>, 21 (1953), 350-51; E. W. Hesse, <u>Hisp</u>,
36 (1953), 126-27; A. A. Parker, <u>BHS</u>, 30 (1953), 142-51 (See
above, under Parker.).

<u>La vida es sueño</u> (pp. 160-190) is one of the three plays
analysed in Chapter VI: "Wölfflin's Principles Applied to
the Spanish Baroque Theater." Four plots are found by the
authors: "Segismundo-Basilio," "Rosaura-Clotaldo," "Rosaura-
Astolfo," and "Astolfo-Estrella." To demonstrate the baroque
nature of the play, they analyse its thematic structure within
the framework of the five categories formulated by Wölfflin
to study the plastic arts of the Baroque: "Painterly,"
"Recession," "Open Form," "Absolute Unity," and "Relative
Unclearness."

Roig Gironella, J. "La angustia existencial por el no ser del
ser y el teatro de Calderón." <u>Gran Mundo</u> (Madrid), 7 (1953),
555-80.

Rossi, Giuseppe Carlo. "Calderón nella polemica settecentesca
sugli <u>autos sacramentales</u>." <u>Studi Mediolatini e Volgari</u>, 1
(1953), 197-224. (Repub. in Spanish translation by Jesús
López Pacheco as "Calderón en la polémica del XVIII sobre los
autos sacramentales," in G. C. Rossi, <u>Estudios sobre las
letras en el siglo XVIII</u>, Madrid, Gredos, 1967, pp. 9-40.)

Most of the polemic centred on Calderón as the most famous of
the authors of <u>autos</u>. While the charges went from immorality
in the performance to poor artistic quality (reflecting the
Neoclassics' attitude towards the Spanish Golden Age), the
defenders declared the <u>autos</u> to be just the opposite, pointing
out the extreme ability required to weave the dramatic
elements of the Christian doctrine. The royal decree against
the <u>autos</u> in 1765 was a victory for their enemies; but
Nicolas Böhl de Faber, early in the nineteenth century, would
be instrumental in their rehabilitation.

- "Calderón nella critica spagnola del settecento." FiR, 2 (1955), 20-66. (Repub. as "Calderón en la crítica española del XVIII," in G. C. Rossi, Estudios..., 1967, pp. 41-96.)

Roux, Lucette. "Quelques aperçus sur la mise en scène de la 'comedia de santos' dans la première moitié du XVIIe siècle." In Le Lieu Théâtral à la Renaissance, ed. Jean Jacquot, Paris, Centre National de la Recherche Scientifique, 1964, pp. 235-52.

- "Un exemple d'aménagement de lieu théâtral à la occasion d'une canonisation." In Le Lieu Théâtral à la Renaissance, Paris, 1964, pp. 253-58.

Rozas, Juan Manuel. "Sobre unos textos calderonistas de Menéndez Pelayo y Valera." Segismundo, 2 (1966), 125-31.

In essays on Calderón in general and especially on the autos, Valera largely copied Menéndez Pelayo's 1881 lectures. The discussion of the autos, save for the omission of paragraphs on the allegorical drama of other countries, is almost literally Menéndez Pelayo's third lecture. The other essay is a well-done summary of the lectures, with some of Valera's opinions added. Since the two men were close friends, plagiarism does not seem to be involved.

Rubio Latorre, Rafael. "Mariología en los autos sacramentales de Calderón." Segismundo, 3 (1967), 75-113.

Ruffner, Sidney J. The American Theme in Selected Dramas of the Golden Age. Unpub. doct. diss., Univ. of Southern California, 1953.

Ruiz Lagos, Manuel. "Las alegorías inanimadas como técnica escenográfica en el teatro simbólico de Calderón." Archivum (Univ. de Oviedo), 15 (1965), 256-74.

- "Algunas relaciones pictóricas y literarias en el teatro alegórico de Calderón. Notas de escenografía barroca." In Cuadernos de Arte y Literatura, Granada, 1965, pp. 21-71.

This study, says Angel Valbuena Prat, in <u>El teatro español en su Siglo de Oro,</u> Barcelona, 1969, p. 352, note 86, "prueba la base importante del influjo de enigmas y emblemas de la época sobre los personajes, el simbolismo de acción y las metáforas."

- "Una técnica dramática de Calderón: La pintura y el centro escénico." <u>Segismundo,</u> 2 (1966), 91-104.

The frequent mention of pictures in Calderón, especially in the <u>autos,</u> is no accident. A picture within the stage <u>décor</u> goes with the baroque idea of varied effects, of unfolding images on a double plane. The stage is a great window, and the spectator's attention centres on the picture. Baroque man seems to need this link with reality, especially via portraits. Thus, a painting is a centre of scenic stability, "en la retención del ser de los humanos, en ese tránsito que para Calderón es el gran teatro del mundo, en contrapartida del absurdo de la vida."

Ruiz Ramón, Francisco. <u>Historia del teatro español (desde sus orígenes hasta mil novecientos).</u> Madrid, Alianza Editorial, 1967. Pp. 503.
Rev: Juan Emilio Aragonés, <u>Estafeta Literaria,</u> No. 373 (1967), 24-25; Amos Segala, <u>Il Dramma,</u> 45, No. 11 (1969), 11.

Calderón, pp. 284-343. A very solid treatment of the dramatist, done in a comparative method.

Sagardia, Angel. <u>La zarzuela y sus compositores.</u> Bilbao, Ediciones Conferencias y Ensayos, 1958. Pp. 48.

Sage, Jack W. "Calderón y la música teatral." <u>BH,</u> 58 (1956), 275-300.

An important article on an important aspect of Calderón.

Sainz de Robles, Federico Carlos. <u>Los antiguos teatros de Madrid.</u> Madrid, Inst. de Estudios Madrileños, 1952. Pp. 47. Plates.

Includes reference to seventeenth-century productions.

Salinas, Pedro. "The Acceptance of Reality: Jorge Manrique and
Calderón de la Barca." In Reality and the Poet in Spanish
Poetry, Baltimore, Johns Hopkins Univ. Press, 1966, pp. 33-63.
(Originally pub. in 1940.)

Pp. 52-63 concern Calderón. The Renaissance, intervening
between Manrique and Calderón, had heightened the idea of a
man-vs.-world conflict, and complicated the view of life in
general. Segismundo's plea for liberty is remarkable, in one
of the most authoritarian societies of all time. Back in
prison after the visit to court, he decides to re-test reality,
but by striving toward consciousness, not with blind daring.
He will always wonder about reality, but must not renounce it:
"obrar bien es lo que importa." He alone can control this, and
"live for the good of the conscience."

Salvador y Conde, J. "Interpretación poética del arte." RIE,
26 (1968), 207-45.

References to Calderón.

Samonà, Carmelo. Calderón nella critica italiana. Milan,
Feltrinelli, 1960. Pp. 115. (Univ. degli Studi di Pisa,
Studi di Filologia Moderna, 5.)
Rev: Juana de José Prades, RL, 21 (1962), 197; L.T., GSLI,
139 (1962), 309; William M. Whitby, HR, 32 (1964), 270-73
(Considers the chapter on Croce as a critic of Calderón
disappointing, but agrees in general with the author's opinion
of Casella, although defending Casella in that the dramatic
concept of "space without time" was Calderón's idea, not just
Casella's. The reviewer calls the book a conscientious study
"of more immediate interest to Italian hispanists, but of
value to the Hispanist in general.").

Deals with 20th century criticism as an indication of the
increased interest in Spain shown by Italian scholars.

- (ed.). Studi di letteratura spagnola. Rome, 1964. Pp. 300.
Rev: Alan Soons, ZRP, 82 (1966), 610-15.

Contains: Carmelo Samonà, "L'esperienza cultista nel teatro
dell'età di Lope. Appunti ed esempi" (pp. 99-168). The
reference is to the years 1610-30, preceding the mature
production of Calderón.

128

Sánchez, Alberto. "Reminiscencias cervantinas en el teatro de
   Calderón." <u>Anales Cervantinos</u>, 6 (1957), 262-70.

   An "ovillejo" is quoted from Calderón's <u>La fiera, el rayo y</u>
   <u>la piedra</u>, and from the <u>auto</u> <u>Tu prójimo como a ti</u>. Reference
   is made to the most important "de los Quijotes calderonianos,"
   Don Mendo of <u>El alcalde de Zalamea</u>, although it is pointed
   out that this character "está más bien emparentado con el
   escudero toledano del <u>Lazarillo de Tormes</u>." A third chapter
   speaks of plays connected with "Aventuras y caballerías," and
   a fourth the idea of the world as a theatre (inspiration for
   Calderón from Cervantes).

- "Conexiones temáticas de la comedia cervantina <u>El rufián</u>
   <u>dichoso</u>." In <u>Filología y crítica hispánica: Homenaje al Prof.</u>
   <u>Federico Sánchez Escribano</u>, ed. Alberto Porqueras-Mayo and
   Carlos Rojas, Madrid-Atlanta, Ediciones Alcalá-Emory Univ.,
   1969, pp. 121-41.

   The article studies "Cervantes y Calderón," and deals at some
   length with <u>La devoción de la Cruz</u>.

Sánchez Escribano, Federico, and Alberto Porqueras-Mayo.
   <u>Preceptiva dramática española del Renacimiento y el Barroco</u>.
   Madrid, Gredos, 1965. Pp. 258.
   Rev: Jean Caravaggio, <u>BH</u>, 68 (1966), 407-08; E. C. Riley, <u>HR</u>,
   36 (1968), 276-79.

   Some references to Calderón.

Sarrailh, Jean. <u>Mélanges à la Mémoire de Jean Sarrailh</u>. 2 vols.
   Paris, Centre de Recherches de l'Institut d'Etudes Hispaniques,
   1966-67. Pp. 474, 469.
   Rev: Alberto Gil Novales, <u>CHA</u>, 71 (1967), 212-17.

   Contains some Calderón material. See Individual Works — <u>La</u>
   <u>devoción de la Cruz</u> — Serrano Plaja (1967).

Sauvage, Micheline. <u>Calderón dramaturge</u>. Paris, L'Arche, 1959.
   Pp. 159.
   Rev: N. Solomon, <u>BH</u>, 62 (1960), 460 (Considers the book to
   be a valuable contribution in the reevaluation of the

Calderonian theatre from the sociological point of view.)

A useful manual for general information on the dramatist.

Schajowicz, Ludwig. "Orfeo y Anfión. La imagen del protoartista en la poesía moderna." Torre, 2, No. 5 (1954), 31-53.

References to Calderón.

Schier, Donald. "Voltaire's Criticism of Calderón." CL, 11 (1959), 340-46.

Reference to En esta vida todo es verdad y todo mentira and La devoción de la misa.

Schilling, Hildburg. Teatro profano en la Nueva España (Fines del siglo XVI a mediados del XVIII). Mexico, Imprenta Universitaria, 1958. Pp. 290.
Rev: J. E. Etcheverry, Rev. Iberoamericana de Literatura (Montevideo), 1 (1959), 114.

Results of research about the corrales in Veracruz, Puebla and Mexico City reveal almost an absence of performances of plays by Calderón. Performances of plays by minor dramatists are most frequently mentioned.

Scholberg, Kenneth R. "Las obras cortas de Calderón." Clav, 5, No. 25 (1954), 13-19.

Gives a brief account of thirteen of Calderón's shorter comic pieces.

Scholz, W. von. "Erneuerter Calderón." Welt und Wort, 9 (1954), 113-15.

Schrader, Ludwig. Sinne und Sinnesverknüpfungen. Studien und Materialen zur Vorgeschichte der Synästhesie und zur Bewertung der Sinne in der italienischen, spanischen und französischen Literatur. Heidelberg, Carl Winter Universitätsverlag, 1969. Pp. 293. (Beiträge zur neueren Literaturgeschichte. Dritte Folge, Bd. 9.)

130

Rev: Wolfram Krömer, <u>RF</u>, 81 (1969), 522-25.

Contains references to the <u>autos sacramentales</u>.

Schwarz, Egon. <u>Hofmannsthal und Calderón</u>. The Hague, Mouton;
Cambridge, Harvard Univ. Press; 1962. Pp. 120. (Harvard
Germanic Studies, 3.)
Rev: Elisabeth Teichmann, <u>RLC</u>, 38 (1964), 472-73 (A short,
but favourable, review, concerned mainly with Hofmannsthal,
but noting that in the chapter "Von <u>La vida es sueño</u> zum
<u>Turm</u>," the analysis in favour of Calderón is missing, research
being limited to isolated assertions.); Juan María Díez
Taboada, <u>Segismundo</u>, 1 (1965), 452-54.

Meant to complement and continue studies by Grete, Curtius,
Schraeder, etc., the book compares the imperial cultures of
Spain and Austria, and the two writers' lives. The two are
well contrasted: "El momento de serenidad que representa la
ideología calderoniana y el momento crítico y pesimista que
vive Hofmannsthal...." Among Calderón's works, Hofmannsthal
was concerned mainly with <u>El gran teatro del mundo</u>, <u>La dama</u>
<u>duende</u>, and <u>La vida es sueño</u>.

Sebba, Gregor. "Baroque and Mannerism: A Retrospect." In
<u>Filología y crítica hispánica</u>: <u>Homenaje al Prof. Federico</u>
<u>Sánchez Escribano</u>, ed. Alberto Porqueras-Mayo and Carlos
Rojas, Madrid-Atlanta, Ediciones Alcalá-Emory Univ., 1969,
pp. 145-63.

Seidler, Herbert. "Prunkreden in Grillparzers Dramen." In
<u>Oesterreichische Akademie der Wissenschaften</u>, Philosophisch-
Historische Klasse Sitzunberichte, 244, Band 4, Vienna, 1964.

In discussing "pompous speech" in Grillparzer's work, the
author mentions Calderón in passing, referring to pompous
speech in <u>El príncipe constante</u>, <u>La vida es sueño</u>, and others.
He mentions Grillparzer's interest in Spanish and then points
out that the pompous speech of Calderón is incorporated into
the action, an essential difference from Grillparzer. The
author's concern is quite incidental.

Selig, Karl-Ludwig. "Some Remarks on the <u>Comedia</u> and the New
Criticism." <u>BCom</u>, 12, No. 1 (1960), 12-13.

Admits the possibility of the New Criticism for the comedia, suggesting that there must be a compromise between the two schools; the common ground being that the historical background and setting of a literary text should be analysed only when it is relevant.

Serís, Homero. "La ortoepía." Symposium, 8 (1954), 76-81.

Peculiarities of various authors, including Calderón, are pointed out.

Serrano Poncela, Segundo. "Amor y apetito en el teatro clásico español." Asomante, 9, No. 4 (1953), 46-62.

A study of love seen as equivalent to physical desire. The theatre reflects a morally lax society of the 17th century, hidden partly by a thin layer of hypocrisy. The real protagonist behind all love scenes is always "el apetito sexual propio de una sociedad demasiado reprimida en sus tendencias naturales." Calderón's El mágico prodigioso, on the other hand, attempts to provide a platonic definition of love.

- "Unamuno y los clásicos." Torre, 9, Nos. 35-36 (1961), 505-35.

Reflects Unamuno's essentially anti-Calderonian viewpoint. Unamuno also compared Calderón to Shakespeare, to the detriment of the Spanish dramatist.

Shergold, N. D. The Staging of Secular Drama in Spain, 1550-1700. Unpub. doct. diss., Cambridge Univ., 1954.

- "Calderón and Vera Tassis." HR, 23 (1955), 212-18.

In spite of the arbitrary alterations of Calderón's texts, Shergold concludes that Vera Tassis' stage-directions may give a clearer idea of the dramatist's ultimate intentions than those found in the Partes.

- A History of the Spanish Stage from Medieval Times until the End of the Seventeenth Century. Oxford, Clarendon Press, 1967. Pp. xxx, 624. Plates.

Rev: C. A. Jones, <u>MLR</u>, 64 (1969), 685-86 ("This valuable work provides an enormous amount of reference material for amplifying study of the drama along accepted lines and stimulating new or neglected approaches."); A. A. Parker, <u>BHS</u>, 46 (1969), 57-60 (An "authoritative and indispensable work ... that constitutes a landmark in Spanish studies and that will surely remain the standard authority on this subject for a long time to come.").

A monograph of highest significance. Devotes a good deal of space to Calderón.

Shergold, N. D., and J. E. Varey. "Documentos sobre los autos sacramentales en Madrid hasta 1636." <u>Rev. de la Bib., Archivo y Museo</u> (Madrid), 24 (1955), 203-313.

- "Un documento nuevo sobre D. Pedro Calderón de la Barca." <u>BH</u>, 62 (1960), 432-37.

The record of a debate in the Ayuntamiento of Madrid, 1648, regarding the payment of a gratuity to the dramatist for coming to the Capital to write <u>autos</u>. The document is reproduced.

- <u>Los autos sacramentales en Madrid en la época de Calderón, 1637-1681: Estudios y documentos</u>. Madrid, Ed. de Historia, Geografía y Arte, 1961. Pp. xxxii, 380.
Rev: C. A. Jones, <u>MLR</u>, 57 (1962), 618-19 ("Supplements rather than replaces or completes the information already contained in the works of other scholars who have published documents concerning the <u>autos</u> and Calderón"; a book "which students of the Golden Age cannot afford to neglect."); A. G. Reichenberger, <u>HR</u>, 30 (1962), 337-39 ("The book gives the impression of absolute reliability ... only the highest praise for this first-rate piece of scholarship."); E. M. Wilson, <u>BHS</u>, 39 (1962), 248-50 ("This book is monumental and definitive.").

A continuation of the above-mentioned "Documentos ... hasta 1636." Valuable documented information concerning the production of <u>autos</u>. Plates show contemporary sketches. Practical details concerning budget and the contemporary bureaucracy.

- "Some Early Calderón Dates." BHS, 38 (1961), 274-86.

More accurate dating of some 22 of Calderón's plays, mostly between 1622 and 1637, on the basis of information in contemporary royal documents. Information in the lists of Cruzada Villaamil and Rennert has been corrected where necessary. The first known printed editions of each play has been noted.

- "Some Palace Performances of Seventeenth-Century Plays." BHS, 40 (1963), 212-44.

The article is intended "to correct the inaccuracies of Villaamil and Rennert and to present the additional information from legajo 6.764 which they failed to publish" with regard to the chronology of Spanish drama. A number of Calderonian titles are given and reference is made to the complete bibliographical details in BHS, 38, 1961, 274-86 (see above).

- "A Problem in the Staging of Autos Sacramentales in Madrid, 1647-1648." HR, 32 (1964), 12-35.

The authors show that the change in the number of autos from four to two and in the number of carts used from two to four occurred in 1647, a date which aids Calderonian chronology, since the poet left descriptions and directions with regard to the scenery that he wanted built for the carts.

Shervill, Robert Newton. The Old Testament Drama of the Siglo de Oro. Unpub. doct. diss., Univ. of North Carolina, 1958. (DA, 19, 1959, 2093b.)

Shervill states that "So far as can be determined, the Golden Age Old Testament theater consists of some twenty-seven full-length comedias, two of which are no longer extant." Calderón is among the dramatists studied. Shervill notes that "La sibila del oriente is basically the work of Calderón with additions to plot and characterization provided by an anonymous author." (This dissertation was directed by Professor Sturgis E. Leavitt.)

Shtein, A. "Problema 'bezobraznogo' v iskusstve ispanskogo barokko." Voprosy Literatury, 13, No. 8 (1969), 136-47.

134

The problem of ugliness, or the grotesque, in Spanish Baroque art. References to Calderón.

Simón Díaz, José. "Textos dispersos de clásicos españoles. XIII: Acuña, Hernando de; XIV: Belmonte Bermúdez; XV: Bonilla, Alonso de; XVI: Calderón de la Barca." RL, 22 (1962), 99-121.

Several sonnets and aprobaciones by Calderón are published in this article, as a continuation of the "textos dispersos" published in earlier numbers of this journal.

- "Los clásicos españoles en la prensa diaria de Madrid (1830-1900)." RL, 23 (1963), 209-40.

Mention of performances and reviews of performances of Calderón's plays, publication of his works, and other references to him which include the 200th anniversary of his death, 1881. (See especially pp. 212-24 of the article.)

- Bibliografía de la literatura hispánica. Tomo VII: Literatura castellana de los Siglos de Oro. Autores (continuación). (Caballar — Cervantes.) Madrid, CSIC, 1967. Pp. xiii, 959. Rev: Hensley C. Woodbridge, Hisp, 52 (1969), 161 (Notes the almost 3000 entries, which include the faithful listing of all important books; sees a lack of reference to some U.S.A. studies, on the side of doctoral dissertations, articles, and book reviews.).

Calderón, Nos. 524-3427, pp. 59-317. Includes: Bibliografía, Códices, Ediciones, Traducciones, Estudios.

Sloman, Albert E. "Calderón and Falconry: A Note on Dramatic Language." RPh, 6 (1953), 299-304.

The author shows, from Calderón's use of the image of falconry, how he gradually restrained his lyrical impulses to increase the dramatic effect.

- The Dramatic Craftsmanship of Calderón: His Use of Earlier Plays. Oxford, Dolphin, 1958. Pp. 327.
Rev: E. S. Ch., CCLC, No. 38 (1959), 111-12 (The reviewer

gives an excellent summary of the contents of the book and its
purpose. He concludes by stating that "El libro del profesor
Sloman, con su adecuada erudición y su sereno y agudo juicio,
nos permite apreciar muy bien el cálculo continuo y la mucha
escrupulosidad estética con que Calderón llevaba adelante su
grande arte."); Everett W. Hesse, Hisp, 42 (1959), 287-88
("Professor Sloman's book is an important contribution to the
field of Calderón studies."); Ronald Hilton, Hispanic American
Report, 12 (1959), 63-64; Raymond R. MacCurdy, Symposium, 13
(1959), 350-53; Luis J. MacLennan, Arbor, 43 (1959), 478-79;
Alexander A. Parker, BHS, 36 (1959), 182-84; Noël Salomon,
BH, 41 (1959), 452-54; Joseph H. Silverman, BA, 33 (1959),
354; Alice M. Pollin, RHM, 26 (1960), 135; R. D. Pring-Mill,
RJ, 10 (1960), 383-86; William M. Whitby, RR, 51 (1960), 281-
83; Edward M. Wilson, MLR, 55 (1960), 124-25 (Professor Wilson
hopes that it will "bring new readers to see the dramatic
excellence of La niña de Gómez Arias and Las armas de la
hermosura. The treatment of La vida es sueño is less interesting."); A. Zamora Vicente, ZRP, 76 (1960), 169-71; Pablo
Cabañas, RFE, 44 (1961), 451-54 ("Contribuye, no sólo al
conocimiento de Calderón, sino del teatro del Siglo de Oro en
general, emerge del libro un Calderón de la Barca de meticulosa
y sutil técnica dramática que, en sus mejores momentos, es
impecable; un poeta dramático de profunda significación
humana."); Pierre Groult, LR, 15 (1961), 177-80 (Highly
praised. Reaches valid, sensible conclusions about each of
the eight plays analysed, and synthesizes his findings into
a final chapter which provides solid new insights into
Calderón's theatre.); Arnold G. Reichenberger, HR, 29 (1961),
254-56 ("Professor Sloman has given us a thorough and detailed
study of Calderón's dramatic art.... Calderón emerges as a
religious moralist of firm and unwavering convictions and a
dramatic poet in full possession of structural and stylistic
craftsmanship."); Juana de José Prades, RL, 21, Nos. 41-42
(1962), 194-95 ("Agudo análisis de ocho importantes obras de
Calderón.").

Albert E. Sloman makes a detailed comparison of eight plays
by Calderón, five of which were based upon plays of his
predecessors, and another three upon earlier comedias by
Calderón in collaboration with others. In each case, after a
careful analysis of the Calderón play and its source, the
author concludes that "Calderón used what he borrowed to write
plays that are new." An "Introduction" and a "Conclusion"
comprise the first and the tenth chapters, and the other eight
are devoted to each of the plays. The Calderón plays are

studied in the following order: El médico de su honra, Las armas de la hermosura, Los cabellos de Absalón, El mayor encanto amor, La niña de Gómez Arias, El príncipe constante, El alcalde de Zalamea, and La vida es sueño. Comedia after comedia, Professor Sloman shows how Calderón's craftsmanship built upon a known source-play a new and original drama. In the chapter "Conclusion," the author states that "Calderón's source-plays differ considerably from each other, and the procedure he adopted in recasting them varied accordingly. But one point is common to all these recastings: an unswerving and persistent quest for unity." Related to this last fundamental observation, Sloman points out that the main plot and the sub-plot or the background action are thematically united: "What emerges, however, from our studies is the thematic link between the characters of the main action and those of the subsidiary action." Stating further: "The plays studied in these pages are seen to be the development and elaboration of a basic theme or set of ideas. An episode or character of a source-play which detracted from, or failed to contribute to, the theme underlying the main plot was rejected. And when, by rearranging the action of the source-play, or by rejecting source material, Calderón had room for other characters which could contribute something new to the theme, he added them." Among the valuable observations given as conclusion for all the previous chapters are the following: "The key for the understanding of Calderón's plays ... is not the plot itself, much less the separate episodes of the plot, but the characters and beyond them the theme which binds them together." Because of Calderón's view of the moral responsibility of man, this "imposed a strict causal sequence upon the different incidents." "Every action in Calderón's plays is motivated." Although the source-dramatists of Calderón's plays anticipated the play's dénouement from the start, "Calderón both extended and refined it, and resorted to a wide range of devices to give it effect." Yet other valuable observations are that the Calderón plays are more concentrated than the sources "both in respect to time and place," the shifting of a scene "which moves with the action from one place to another without noticeable breaks," and with respect to the characters themselves, the fact that Calderón seems to be consistent with their number and their distribution, that the gracioso, in addition to being funny and contrasting the behaviour of his master, "makes a serious and quite distinctive contribution to the dramatic exposition to the play's theme." And with regard to the protagonist, the fact that Calderón gives him greater prominence by subordinating the other dramatis personae of importance, and as a result he "towers above the other characters who are conceived to throw him into relief." Finally, Professor Sloman refers to Calderón's use of imagery, casuistry, monologues, stanza-forms, staging, music, and songs. An outstanding monograph.

Smieja, Florian. "Nowe przeklady z hiszpańskiego," Kultura (Paris), Nos. 117-18 (1957), 194-211.

The article refers to translations made of Spanish Golden Age works into Polish, 1948-56. It included El alcalde de Zalamea and La vida es sueño.

Sofer, Johann. "Idee und Gestaltung des Welttheaters." Österreich in Geschichte und Literatur, 7 (1963), 472-89.

The author summarizes definitions of the idea of the "world as a theatre" from a number of studies, and traces the idea to ancient times. But, although the idea was common in the time of Calderón, his great merit was to have shaped it for the first time to a spiritual drama. The article continues with Hofmannsthal's Das Salzburger Grosse Welttheater and its relationship with Calderón's play. This is a good summation of the work that has been done on the theme.

Soons, Alan. Ficción y comedia en el Siglo de Oro. Madrid, Estudios de Literatura Española, 1967. Pp. v, 166. Rev: Enrique Ruiz Fornells, Hisp, 51 (1968), 574; H. Th. Oostendorp, Neophilologus, 53 (1969), 221.

Twenty-one essays, mainly reprints; including interpretation of plays by Calderón: El alcalde de Zalamea, El médico de su honra, El pintor de su deshonra, and A secreto agravio, secreta venganza.

Soria, Andrés. "Nota sobre la métrica en el teatro de Lope y Calderón." Molino de Papel (Granada), No. 2 (1954), 4-5.

Stafford, Lorna Lavery. "Historia y crítica y dramática de La prudencia en la mujer." In Estudios hispánicos. Homenaje a Archer M. Huntington, Wellesley, Mass., 1952, pp. 575-84.

Includes a discussion of Calderón's popularity in the 17th century as compared to Tirso's.

Strzalkowa, Maria. "La Pologne et les Polonais dans le théâtre du XVIIe et XVIIIe siècles espagnols." In <u>Comparative Literature. Proceedings of the Second Congress of the International Comparative Literature Association</u>, ed. Werner P. Friederich, Chapel Hill, Univ. of North Carolina Press, 2, 1959, pp. 635-49.

- <u>Studia polsko-hispańskie</u>. Cracow, P.W.N., 1960. Pp. 185. Rev: J. M. Díez Taboada, <u>RL</u>, 22 (1962), 272; B. Jereczek, <u>BH</u>, 64 (1962), 102-06.

Includes a study of the fortunes of Calderón in Poland, and a chapter on <u>La vida es sueño</u>.

<u>Studies in Philology</u>. "Recent Literature of the Renaissance. A Bibliography and Index." In <u>SP</u>, 36, No. 2, part 2 (1939) to 66, No. 3 (1969).

Earlier volumes had contained "Continental Influences: Selected Studies of Renaissance Literature in Foreign Countries" as part of "English Renaissance Bibliography." In the number for Apr., 1939, an annual bibliography (material for 1938) for Spanish was begun and continued until the Spring, 1969 (material for 1968). Regrettably the Bibliography ceased at that time. The last bibliographer for Spanish was Peter B. Bell.

Sturcken, H. Tracy. "An <u>Aparte</u> to the <u>Querella Calderoniana</u>." <u>BCom</u>, 11, No. 1 (1959), 14-15.

Excerpts from two letters by Turgenev to Pauline Viardot (Paris, Dec. 19 and 25, 1847), which speak enthusiastically of Calderón.

Subirá, José. "Repertorio teatral madrileño y resplendor transitorio de la zarzuela (años 1763 a 1771)." <u>BRAE</u>, 39, No. 158 (1959), 429-62.

Deals mainly with 17th century <u>comedias</u>; and points to the continuing popularity of Calderón.

- <u>El gremio de representantes españoles y la Cofradía de Nuestra Señora de la Novena</u>. Madrid, CSIC, 1960. Pp. 269.
Rev: R. Benítez Claros, <u>RL</u>, Nos. 33-34 (1960), 172-73; José Montero Padilla, <u>Arbor</u>, Nos. 177-78 (1960), 158-61; J. E. Varey, <u>BHS</u>, 37 (1960), 190-91.

Includes reference to Calderón's <u>autos</u>.

- "Músicos al servicio de Calderón y de Comella." <u>Anuario Musical</u>, 22 (1967; pub. 1969), 197-208.

- "Lo histórico y lo estético en la zarzuela." <u>RIE</u>, 27 (1969), 103-25.

References to Calderón.

Szarota, Elida Maria. <u>Künstler, Grübler und Rebellen. Studien zum europäischen Märtyrerdrama des 17. Jahrhunderts</u>. Bern, Francke, 1967. Pp. 396.
Rev: Irmgard Böttcher, <u>Deutsche Literaturzeitung</u>, 90 (1969), cols. 203-06; Zdenka Ratajová-Svobodová, <u>Philologica Pragensia</u>, 12 (1969), 49-50; Peter Skrine, <u>MLR</u>, 64 (1969), 621-23; Ferdinand van Ingen, <u>Neophilologus</u>, 53 (1969), 329-30.

Includes chapters on Calderón's <u>El mágico prodigioso</u>, <u>Los dos amantes del cielo</u>, and <u>El príncipe constante</u>.

Taylor, Darrel. "Los autos sacramentales de don Pedro Calderón de la Barca." <u>Universidad de San Carlos</u> (Guatemala), 40 (1957), 209-38.

This article is of a general nature, and its scope would be likened to a series of superficial remarks about the genre.

<u>La Tijera Literaria</u> (Colección). Enciclopedia histórico-antológica de las más famosas obras en lengua castellana. Cuaderno 6: <u>Vida y obras de Calderón de la Barca</u>. Madrid, Edit. Siglo Ilustrado (Distrib. Correo del Libro), 1969.

Torner, Eduardo M. Lírica hispánica: Relaciones entre lo popular y lo culto. Madrid, Castalia, 1966. Pp. 460. (La lupa y el escalpelo, 5.)

Contains the odd reference to lines in Calderón's plays.

Torre, Guillermo de. Del 98 al barroco. Madrid, Gredos, 1969. Pp. 451.

Contains revised essays written "hace más de veinte años." "Sentido y vigencia del barroco español" (pp. 398-427) includes "Calderón a la luz del psicoanálisis" (pp. 421-24).

Trend, J. B. Lorca and the Spanish Poetic Tradition. Oxford, Blackwell, 1956. Pp. 178.

Contains an interesting chapter on Calderón and his powers of dramatic presentation.

Trifilo, S. Samuel. "Influencias calderonianas en el drama de Zamora y de Cañizares." Hispanó, No. 11 (1961), 39-46.

Although officially neo-classical, 18th century Spain looked to Golden Age drama as a model. This is evident in the plays of Zamora and Cañizares, who, lacking the talent of Lope, Tirso or Calderón, produced imitations and "reworkings" of classical comedias, which met with more success than any other type of play in Madrid theatres of the 18th century.

Tudela Aranda, Amelia. Los elementos educativos en los autos sacramentales de don Pedro Calderón de la Barca. Unpub. diss., Univ. de Madrid, 1959.

Turkevich, Ludmilla B. "Status of Spanish Studies in the Soviet Union." Hisp, 41 (1958), 485-90.

Professor Turkevich regrets that the death of Vladimir Samoilovich Uzin (May 30, 1957) "leaves the tiny Spanish circle further bereft." Uzin was a Russian scholar who specialized in Golden Age literature and who "also assembled and edited a four volume set entitled The Spanish Theatre of the XVIIth Century," which included Calderón's La dama duende.

- *Spanish Literature in Russia and in the Soviet Union, 1735-1964*. Metuchen, New Jersey, The Scarecrow Press, 1967. Pp. xi, 273.

Ulsamer, Federico. "Hans Schlegel y la difusión del teatro español en Alemania." *Estudios Escénicos* (Barcelona), 1 (1957), 79-85.

Valbuena Briones, Angel. *Ensayo sobre la obra de Calderón*. Madrid, Ateneo, 1958. Pp. 53. (Col. "O crece o muere.")

The four parts of the booklet are: "La palabra," "El último estilo de Calderón," "Calderón, el demonio y las estrellas," and "Los espacios reducidos."

- "El concepto del hado en el teatro de Calderón." BH, 63 (1961), 48-53.

An exploration of the rôle of Fate in Calderón's theatre, and its relation to Christian doctrine. Fate (an excellent dramatic device, certain to appeal to the 17th century audience) could influence man's will (leading him towards catastrophe) but could not force it. When reason opposed Fate, man might then govern the course of his actions. Astrology, also a topic of great contemporary interest, was closely allied to the concept of Fate.

- "El simbolismo en el teatro de Calderón: La caída del caballo." RF, 74 (1962), 60-76.

The author traces the symbol of the horse and rider through various literary works of other writers, and explains its significance in the plays of Calderón. The horse represents passion, the rider reason. When the horse with its rider falls, instinct is dragging reason down to destruction. "En Calderón el motivo obtiene una simbología fija para expresar poéticamente el conflicto primordial de su teatro."

- "El senequismo en el teatro de Calderón." PSA, 31 (1963), 249-70.

The author maintains that Calderón resorted frequently to
Seneca for his inspiration and that he could not have formulated his theatre without his support. He shows the use of
Fortuna by the two writers, the idea of tempus fugit, the
reference to the same mythological figures and the introduction of similar symbols (cárcel, for example).

- Perspectiva crítica de los dramas de Calderón. Madrid, Rialp,
  1965. Pp. 425.
  Rev: Emiliano Aguado, La Estafeta Literaria, No. 341 (1966),
  15 (Offers a rich store of ideas. The conclusion is that
  "Angel Valbuena Prat (in many previous studies) y Angel
  Valbuena Briones han pagado bien su tributo a la obra de
  Calderón."); Juan Manuel Rozas, Segismundo, 2 (1966), 221-22
  (The reviewer considers Part I the most valuable, but finds
  considerable, if uneven, merit throughout the book.); Herman
  Iventosch, MP, 66 (1968), 75-77 ("For reasons heavily, if not
  entirely, nationalistic and Roman Catholic, the author sets
  about explaining and defending the master Catholic dramatist
  of Spain. The exegeses read well, in general; the author has
  spent many years in consideration of the Baroque master and
  has original and interesting things to say concerning his
  thought, mostly, style, a great deal, and form. In general,
  the studies may be classed in a sort of 'semi-learned essay'
  category, a genre far indeed above literary journalism and
  yet a bit removed from what we are wont to call objective
  scholarship."); A. Vermeylen, LR, 23 (1969), 379-80.

  Part I, "Cuatro incursiones en el pensamiento de Calderón,"
  contains three essays previously published. The fourth, "La
  palabra sol en los textos calderonianos," was read at the
  Second International Congress of Hispanists in Nijmegen, 1965.
  Part II is an "Itinerario crítico a través de 39 dramas de
  Calderón," and Part III is called "Calderón y los mitos."

- "La palabra sol en los textos calderonianos." In Actas de la
  Asociación Internacional de Hispanistas (2º Congreso),
  Nijmegen, 1967, pp. 667-77. (See above.)

Valbuena Prat, Angel. "Un calderonista en Madison: Everett W.
  Hesse." Clav, 2, No. 7 (1951), 79.

  Praise of Hesse's work after a general comment on the

"floración de un nuevo calderonismo en los Estados Unidos."
Valbuena Prat speaks of Hesse's critical work on Calderón,
published and in preparation.

- "En torno al hispanismo en Norteamérica." <u>Clav</u>, 2, No. 12
(1951), 38-40.

In an enthusiastic report on the quantity and quality of
"hispanismo" which he found in several North American cities
and universities, Valbuena Prat specifically mentions contributions to Calderón studies made by Everett Hesse, Bruce
Wardropper and Max Oppenheimer (adding the names of Wilson,
Parker, Entwistle, and, most recently, Sloman, "máximos
exponentes en Inglaterra").

- "Los autos calderonianos en el ambiente teológico español."
<u>Clav</u>, 3, No. 15 (1952), 33-35.

Possible doctrinal sources for Calderón's <u>autos</u> are suggested;
such as the <u>Discursos para los Evangelios en la Cuaresma</u>, by
the Augustinian friar Basilio Ponce de León (Salamanca, 1608),
the <u>Theología mystica, sciencia y sabiduría de Dios, misterios,
oscura y levantada para muchos</u>, by Fray Agustín de San
Ildefonso (1644), and <u>Comentarios y disputas acerca de la
Tercera Parte de Santo Tomás</u>, by Francisco Suárez.

- "A los veinticinco años de la vuelta a Calderón." <u>Revista</u>
(Barcelona), 3, No. 96 (1954), 7.

- <u>Historia del teatro español</u>. Barcelona, Noguer, 1956. Pp. 708.
Rev: J. L. Cano, <u>Arbor</u>, 35, No. 132 (1956), 531-32; M. Muñoz
Cortés, <u>Clav</u>, 8 (1957), 70-74 (Not a "manual," but rather a
study which presents "muchas perspectivas, ... agrupaciones
por épocas y ciclos, estudios temáticos, consideraciones
caracterizadoras de autores, análisis de obras aisladas, etc."
The reviewer does not hesitate to praise very highly the total
contents of this <u>Historia</u>, which starts with the medieval
theatre and ends with the contemporary dramatists.); R. R.
MacCurdy, <u>Symposium</u>, 12 (1958), 206-11; E. González López,
<u>RHM</u>, 25 (1959), 241-42; Ramon Rozzell, <u>NRFH</u>, 13 (1959),
376-80.

This important volume studies Calderón in various aspects.

- _Historia de la literatura española_. 5th ed., revised. 3 vols. Barcelona, 1957.

Reprints the fourth edition, and there are no changes in what Professor Valbuena Prat has previously said in his chapters on Calderón in the second volume. For general information, it is one of the best treatments of all Calderón's works we have in an easily available form. Chapter XLVI, "El pensamiento y el estilo barroco de Calderón," deals with Calderón's biography, his style, his philosophical thought, and his _autos sacramentales_. Chapter XLVII deals with Calderón's honour plays, the _comedias de capa y espada_, which Valbuena Prat calls "el segundo estilo de Calderón," and the philosophical and religious drama of Calderón, plus other items of general information. Among the histories of Spanish literature, this is one which presents a comprehensive and understanding approach to Calderón's works.

- _Estudios de literatura religiosa española. Epoca medieval y Edad de Oro_. Madrid, Afrodisio Aguado, 1964. Pp. 282.

This collection of _estudios_ includes the following devoted to Calderón: "Calderón, el dramático teológico y cortesano," "Calderón y la apoteosis del catolicismo," "Calderón y el Año Santo de 1650," "Los autos calderonianos en el ambiente teológico español," and "Los motivos del drama católico nacional." The selections are in part from _El sentido católico y la literatura española_ (1940), with some details brought up to date. The "Año Santo" is of 1950, and the others a little later. Part also appeared in French after World War II in _Europa_.

- _El teatro español en su Siglo de Oro_. Barcelona, Edit. Planeta, 1969. Pp. 402.

"Calderón y su personalidad en el siglo XVII," pp. 245-355, makes reference to recent Calderonian scholarship and currently discussed problems. There are several sub-headings to this section, such as "La estructura dramática calderoniana," "Del drama a la comedia 'de capa y espada'," "Los dramas de honor," "Dramas religiosos," "El mito teatral, desde la historia a la fábula," "El auto sacramental," etc. Another section, pp. 357-402, studies "La escuela de Calderón." Professor Angel Valbuena Prat is to be congratulated once again on his continuing studies of the Golden Age and of Calderón in particular.

Varey, J. E. "La mise en scène de l'auto sacramental à Madrid au XVIe et XVIIe siècles." In Le Lieu Théâtral à la Renaissance, Paris, 1964, pp. 217-25.

Mentions Calderón's part in setting specifications of stage machinery, discusses his La cena de Baltasar and its production, then that of Sueños hay que verdad son.

- "Calderón, Cosme Lotti, Velázquez, and the Madrid Festivities of 1636-1637." Renaissance Drama, n.s., 1 (1968), 253-82.

Varey, J. E., and A. M. Salazar. "Calderón and the Royal Entry of 1649." HR, 34 (1966), 1-26.

Vera Tassis claims that Calderón was ordered to Madrid to write the Noticia del recibimiento i entrada de la Reyna nuestra Señora doña María-Ana de Austria en la muy noble i leal coronada Villa de Madrid (1650), and that he designed and described the triumphal arches built for the occasion. The authors reject both attributions, and mention a Juan Alonso Calderón, who figured prominently in the festivities, and doubtless influenced the Noticia, though he did not write it, either.

Verhesen, Fernand. Etude sur les autos sacramentales de Calderón de la Barca, et spécialement sur "La cura y la enfermedad." Paris, Centre de Documentation Universitaire, 1953. Pp. 91.

Vetter, Ewald M. "Der verlorene Sohn und die Sünder im Jahrhundert des Konzils von Trient." Spanische Forschungen der Görresgesellschaft, 15 (1960), 175-218.

Reference to Calderón, among others.

Vian, C. "Calderón de la Barca." In Enciclopedia dello Spettacolo, Vol. II, Rome, 1954, pp. 1500-1508.

Viqueira, José Maria. "Temas clásicos en Calderón de la Barca." Euphrosyne, 2 (1959), 107-37.

This is a very valuable article which analyses Calderón's technique of adaptation within Christian norms of works of pagan mythology. For example: the legend of the Argonauts is made into an exploratory mission for Truth and Life in El divino Jasón and Los tres mayores prodigios; Cupid and Psyche is made into the eternal problem of Faith in Ni amor se libra de amor; and the story of Ulysses and Circe is adapted into the psychological struggle of man with his passions in Los encantos de la culpa and El mayor encanto amor.

- "Portugal en el teatro de Calderón." In Miscelânea de Estudos a Joaquim de Carvalho, ed. Manuel Montezuma de Carvalho, Figueira da Foz, 1959-60, pp. 276-89.

Von Richthofen, Erich. "Der gegensätzliche Parallelismus westromanischer Dramentecknik." In Estudios dedicados a Menéndez Pidal, IV, Madrid, CSIC, 1953, pp. 509-34.

Includes references to Calderón.

Wade, Gerald E. "The Interpretation of the Comedia." BCom, 11, No. 1 (1959), 1-6.

Professor Wade expresses the idea that the twentieth century critic will never be able to interpret with finality just what an entire play meant for the Golden Age dramatist, insofar as that play "sums up a concept or a battery of concepts to explain any substantial part of the totality of Spain's Golden Age." What we can agree on at least is "the major meaning of the concept for us in our age."

Wais, K. "Calderón und Deutschland: Max Kommerell." In An den Grenzen der Nationalliteraturen, Berlin, De Gruyter, 1958, pp. 267-70.

Wardropper, Bruce W. Introducción al teatro religioso del Siglo de Oro (La evolución del auto sacramental: 1500-1648). Madrid, Rev. de Occidente, 1953. Pp. 330. (Reprinted, Salamanca, Anaya,

1967, pp. 339; with a few corrections and an updated bibliography.)(Cf. doct. diss., The Growth of the "Auto Sacramental"
before Calderón, Univ. of Pennsylvania, 1949.)
Rev: J. Caso González, Archivum, 3 (1953), 443-47; Marcel
Bataillon, BH, 56 (1954), 431-35; Courtney Bruerton, NRFH, 8
(1954), 328-30 ("Por su cuidadosa disposición de gran número
de detalles significativos, por sus breves citas y resúmenes
de los argumentos, por la sensatez de sus juicios, ... es un
modelo de proporción y claridad de exposición, y su lectura
es muy amena."); R. de G., Insula, 9, Nos. 100-101 (1954),
10; Jerónimo Mallo, Hisp, 37 (1954), 384-85; J. Montero
Padilla, RL, 5 (1954), 416-18; Salvador Dinamarca, RHM, 21
(1955), 346-47 (Commends Wardropper's "objetividad y mesura,"
mentions the excellent treatment of Valdivielso, and says
that the author has continued in an admirable manner the
"trayectoria iniciada por Alexander A. Parker."); H. Lausberg,
Archiv, 192 (1955), 248; José Montero Padilla, RFE, 39 (1955),
365-68; A. A. Parker, BHS, 32 (1955), 49-51; Beatrice P. Patt,
HR, 23 (1955), 68-73; Edward Sarmiento, MLR, 50 (1955), 223-24.

The Wardropper monograph has been praised highly (very
rightly), and is a complete introduction to the auto (although
A. A. Parker maintains that "the history of the auto as an
attempt to portray in drama the nature and scope of religious
experience still remains to be written"). Wardropper considers
Calderón to be the most intellectual of all auto writers; and
he points to the close relationship between the developing
autos and Christmas and other plays. He reaffirms Bataillon's
idea that the auto is a phenomenon of the Catholic Reformation
and not of the Counter-reformation. The book stresses the
origins of the auto leading up to Calderón.

- "On the Fourth Centenary of the Birth of Lope de Vega." Drama
Survey, 2 (1962), 117-29.

A successful attempt to characterize and compare the dramatic
art of Lope de Vega and Calderón.

- (ed.). Critical Essays on the Theatre of Calderón. New York,
New York Univ. Press, 1965. Pp. xvi, 239.
Rev: TLS, Nov. 11, 1965; Victor Dixon, MLR, 62 (1967), 543;
Rodrigo A. Molina, Quaderni Ibero-Americani, 9, No. 34 (1967),
109-10; J. H. Parker, HR, 35 (1967), 392-93; J. E. Varey,
BHS, 44 (1967), 131-34.

A collection of eleven articles, previously published elsewhere, and presented in four sections: "Calderón's Art and
Thought" (2 articles); "La vida es sueño" (4); "El príncipe
constante" (2); "Other Plays" (3). (Reference to these
articles will be found in each case elsewhere in this Bibliography.) The preface contains general statements on Lope and
Calderón, stressing the latter's changing critical fortunes.
A biographical sketch of Calderón precedes the articles, and
the book ends with "Notes on the Contributors." The essays
chosen by Wardropper are outstanding and by leading contemporary scholars.

- "Menéndez Pelayo on Calderón." Criticism, 7 (1965), 363-72.

Menéndez Pelayo's inept Calderón criticism of 1881 is to
blame for much of the present-day lack of regard for Calderón
in Spain, though Menéndez Pelayo later virtually repudiated
the lectures given in 1881. His admiration for 18th-century
goût made him accuse Calderón and the Baroque period of bad
taste, which he would not define. He also overrated sponta-
neity and originality, and was distressed by anachronisms
that bothered Calderón not at all. His eclecticism led him
into contradictions, based on measuring all art by "Nature,"
whose meanings vary. Menéndez Pelayo also overemphasized
simplicity: a disaster in dealing with a complex writer like
Calderón. (It might be noted that Dámaso Alonso, in Menéndez
Pelayo crítico literario, Madrid, Gredos, 1956, p. 99, spoke
of a "nueva benevolencia para Calderón" and "una mayor
generosidad y comprensión" on the part of Menéndez Pelayo,
as he wrote the prologue to Blanca de los Ríos' Del Siglo de
Oro in 1910.)

- "El problema de la responsabilidad en la comedia de capa y
espada." In Actas del Segundo Congreso de la Asociación
Internacional de Hispanistas, Nijmegen, 1967, pp. 689-94.

- "Spanish Literature." In Modern Literature, Vol. II: Italian,
Spanish, German, Russian and Oriental Literature, ed. Victor
Lange, Englewood Cliffs, New Jersey, Prentice-Hall, 1968, pp.
67-119.
Rev. article: Elias L. Rivers, "Wardropper and American
Hispanism," MLN, 84 (1969), 335-36.

Contains references to American scholarship and Calderón.

Weiner, Jack. The Spanish Golden Age Theater in Tsarist Russia:
1672-1917. Unpub. doct. diss., Indiana Univ., 1968. Pp. 286.
(DA, 29, 3162A.)

Treats the rôle of Spain's Golden Age theatre in Russia and
the part it played in the development of the Russian realistic
and symbolist theatres. There is mention, among others, of
Calderón's El alcaide de sí mismo, El alcalde de Zalamea, and
Amar después de la muerte.

- "The Introduction of Spain's Golden Age Theater into Russia
(1672-1800)." Annali dell'Istituto Universitario Orientale
(Naples), Sezione Romanza, 11 (1969), 193-223.

Refers, among other plays, to Calderón's El alcaide de sí
mismo and El escondido y la tapada.

Weise, G. "Manierismo e letteratura. III: La tradizione
letteraria delle contrapposizioni concettose nella poesia
spagnola dal tardo Medioevo al Seicento." RLMC, 21 (1968),
85-127.

Pp. 122-26 deal with Tirso and Calderón.

Whitby, William M. Structural Symbolism in Two Plays of Pedro
Calderón de la Barca. Unpub. doct. diss., Yale Univ., 1954.
Pp. 206.

El príncipe constante and La vida es sueño. Whitby's study
of El príncipe constante, BCom, 8, No. 1 (1956), 1-4, is
based on part of this thesis, as is the article on La vida
es sueño, HR, 28 (1960), 16-27 (reprinted in Wardropper's
Essays).

Whiting, Frank M. "Spain: The Golden Age." In An Introduction
to the Theatre, New York, Harper, 1954, pp. 31-35. (Revised
ed., 1961.)

Lope de Vega and Calderón are discussed.

Wilhelm, Julius. "La crítica calderoniana en los siglos XIX y

XX en Alemania." CHA, No. 73 (1956), 47-56. (Reprinted in
Beiträge zur romanischen Literaturwissenschaft, Tübingen,
1957, pp. 288-98.)

Wilhelm presents a bird's eye view of the "ups and downs" of
Calderón's esteem in Germany and incidentally in Austria. He
starts with the last half of the 18th century (Bertuch,
Lessing, and Herder), and continues with the early years of
the 19th century (A. W. Schlegel and his brother F. Schlegel,
Schelling, Rosenkranz, Goethe) and the second half of the
last century (Eichendorff, Grillparzer, Tieck, Schack, Keil,
Schmidt, Lemeke, Günthner, and Krenkel). For the 20th century,
Wilhelm mentions the contributions of Pfandl, H. Hatzfeld,
Weisser, Vossler, Curtius, and Kommerell. The author concludes
his article by dividing into four phases the Calderonian
criticism in Germany: "Contacto," "Apoteosis romántica,"
"Exploración positivista," and "Revaloración comprensiva."
Although the article presents well-known facts, its main
value is the diffusion of these facts among the general
public.

Wilson, Edward M. "Gerald Brenan's Calderón." BCom, 4, No. 1
    (1952), 6-8.

Discusses Brenan's treatment of Calderón in his The Literature
of the Spanish People (1951).

- "Some Calderonian Pliegos Sueltos." In 1930-1955, Homenaje a
J. A. van Praag, Amsterdam, Librería Española "Plus Ultra,"
1956, pp. 140-44.
Rev (of the volume): Gustavo Correa, HR, 26 (1958), 296-99.

Some "Relaciones," from Calderón plays, published in the
eighteenth century as "pliegos sueltos."

- "On the Pando Editions of Calderón's Autos." HR, 27 (1959),
324-44.

An important bibliographical discovery by Wilson showing that
there was a second edition of the Pando y Mier collection of
the autos of Calderón. Individual copies of the two editions
are examined in detail. One of the two editions of the Primera
Parte of 1640 is shown to be falsely dated and printed later
in the century, with possible changes by Calderón himself.

- "The Two Editions of Calderón's _Primera Parte_ of 1640." _The Library_, Fifth Series, 14 (1959), 175-91.

- "Calderón's _Primera Parte de Autos Sacramentales_ and Don Pedro de Pando y Mier." _BHS_, 37 (1960), 16-28.

    After examining the relative textual reliability of the volume of _Autos_ published in 1677, the reprint of 1690, and the Pando edition of 1717, Wilson decides in favour of the first.

- "Las 'dudas curiosas' a la aprobación del maestro fray Manuel de Guerra y Ribera." _Estudios Escénicos_ (Barcelona), No. 6 (1960), 47-63.

    Wilson publishes the text of a satire provoked by the Guerra y Ribera _aprobación_ of 1682.

- "Notas sobre algunos manuscritos calderonianos en Madrid y en Toledo." _Rev. de Archivos, Bibliotecas y Museos_, 68 (1960), 477-87.

- "Textos impresos y apenas utilizados para la biografía de Calderón." _Hispanó_, No. 9 (1960), 1-14.

    The article publishes a collection of some contemporary printed references to Calderón.

- "Calderón and the Stage-Censor in the Seventeenth Century. A Provisional Study." _Symposium_, 15 (1961), 165-84.

    Examples are given of various changes made in Calderón's works by contemporary censors who from time to time objected to allusions which seemed profane or irreverent, immoral, scandalous, or heretical.

- "An Early List of Calderón's _Comedias_." _MP_, 60 (1962), 95-102.

    An 18th century copy of a list compiled by Calderón himself and presented to Carlos II by Don Francisco Marañón. Wilson

makes a comparison of this manuscript (in the Biblioteca
Nacional) with the 1680 list submitted by Calderón to the
Duque de Veragua, and with the Vera Tassis list (1682). It
bears a close relation to the former, and is probably older.
The Vera Tassis is the least reliable of the three, and not
likely based on the two previous lists.

- "¿Escribió Calderón el romance Curiosísima señora?" Anuario
  de Letras (Mexico), 2 (1962), 99-118.

  Professor Wilson presents the results of his research on this
  "romance," concluding that "todas estas circunstancias hacen
  pensar que Cepeda escribió el romance Curiosísima señora, y
  que Calderón, aun en el caso de que llegara a conocer el
  romance, no hizo sino admitir tácitamente la atribución que
  de él se le hacía."

- "Further Notes on the Pando Edition of Calderón's Autos." HR,
  30 (1962), 296-303.

  Wilson provides important additional information, found
  during a visit to the Biblioteca Nacional, after he had
  published the article "On the Pando Editions...," HR, 27
  (1959). (See above.)

- "On the Tercera Parte of Calderón: 1664." Studies in Bibliography (Virginia), 15 (1962), 223-30.

  An examination of the two distinct editions of the Tercera
  Parte of Calderón, dated 1664, and a discussion of problems
  occasioned by them.

- "Miguel de Barrios and Spanish Religious Poetry." BHS, 40
  (1963), 176-80.

  Includes references to Calderón.

- "Seven aprobaciones by Pedro Calderón de la Barca." In Studia
  Philologica, Homenaje ofrecido a Dámaso Alonso, III, Madrid,
  Gredos, 1963, pp. 605-18.

The author points out how Calderón, in seven <u>aprobaciones</u> (in
a postscript he adds an eighth) which he wrote, reveals his
own aims and intentions. From them we learn that Calderón
watched plays other than his own, that he sought to imitate
Tirso in the moral, exemplary and religious aspects of his
plays, and that he considered his own plays, including <u>capa
y espada</u>, to have a moral purpose. Wilson also concludes that
Calderón was not a figure isolated from his contemporaries,
and that he was a good prose writer as well as poet.

- "Calderón's Enemy: Don Antonio Sigler de Huerta." <u>MLN</u>, 81
  (1966), 225-31.

After returning from Rome, where he praised Pope Gregory XV
in a Latin oration and helped to plan a monument for Felipe
III, Sigler seems to have been largely a hack writer. In a
sonnet, probably antedating Calderón's service in Cataluña
in 1640, he attacks Calderón as a debt-ridden womanizer. This
may have been revenge for a vigorous satire in Rojas Zorrilla's
<u>Vejamen</u> of 1637. Calderón replied in kind; little is to be
said for either, but the poems "throw a little light on the
human reactions of a great Spanish dramatist at an unguarded
moment."

- "Nuevos documentos sobre las controversias teatrales: 1650-
  1681." In <u>Actas del Segundo Congreso de la Asociación
  Internacional de Hispanistas</u>, Nijmegen, 1967, pp. 155-70.

- <u>Some Aspects of Spanish Literary History</u>. Oxford, Clarendon
  Press, 1967. Pp. 47. (The Taylorian Lecture, May 18, 1966.)
  Rev: <u>TLS</u>, Nov. 30, 1967, p. 1174; Frank Pierce, <u>MLR</u>, 63 (1968),
  496-97 ("The text is followed by illuminating notes and by
  two interesting appendices, one describing English and Spanish
  chapbooks, the other reproducing a medieval tale from a
  seventeenth-century collection which may have been used by
  Calderón for one of his great plays. Professor Wilson is to
  be congratulated on a fascinating account of a facet of
  Spanish literary culture which is only now beginning to
  receive the attention it deserves."); Arthur Terry, <u>BHS</u>, 46
  (1969), 51-52.

Broadsides and chapbooks as a reflection of the popular esteem
for works of earlier periods. Includes a note on the source of
<u>El médico de su honra</u>.

- "La poesía dramática de don Pedro Calderón de la Barca." In Hans Flasche, <u>Litterae hispanae et lusitanae</u>, Munich, 1968, pp. 487-500. (See Flasche, 1968, Studies — General.)

A detailed analysis of Calderón's use of poetry in his drama.

- "Calderón y Fuenterrabia: El panegírico al Almirante de Castilla." <u>BRAE</u>, 49 (1969), 253-78.

Wilson, Edward M., and Jack Sage. <u>Poesías líricas en las obras dramáticas: Citas y glosas</u>. London, Tamesis, 1964. Pp. xix, 165.
Rev: Eunice Joiner Gates, <u>HR</u>, 34 (1966), 173-74 (176 items appear, well cross-referenced, with Góngora cited most often. Some of the poems were used before their publication, since MS poems used to circulate widely. The authors hope to have paved the way for further studies.); Duncan Moir, <u>BHS</u>, 43 (1966), 225-27 (In a sense, this book parallels and supports Sloman's <u>Dramatic Craftsmanship</u>, by showing Calderón as a <u>refundidor</u>. We see how ideas change, from the Middle Ages to Carlos II, and are led to refute the stereotype, "Lope, poeta popular; Calderón, poeta culto."); R. D. F. Pring-Mill, <u>RJ</u>, 17 (1966), 367-69 (While regretting the lack of space for the editors to quote extensively, the reviewer recognizes that it is now others' turn to study the uses of the poems in greater detail, but hopes that the compilers themselves will give their own interpretations of some of the data.); Enrique Rull, <u>Segismundo</u>, 2 (1966), 222-24 (The compilation shows Calderón's works as a sort of "gran depositario del Barroco," but also reflects his predecessors: Fray Luis, the <u>Romancero</u>, medieval literature, Lope, <u>et al</u>.); A. Valbuena Briones, <u>MP</u>, 63 (1966), 268-69 (Useful in locating new ballad lines not italicized in Hartzenbusch or in Schmidt (<u>Die Schauspiele Calderóns</u>), showing that Calderón often had these lines in mind. <u>Céfalo y Pocris</u> has the most data, yet Wilson has called it doubtfully Calderón's.); A. B., <u>Brotéria</u>, 84 (1967), 397; C. A. Jones, <u>MLR</u>, 63 (1968), 726-27 (Favourable. The reviewer considers this a useful reference book for Calderón scholars. "One can be sure that the authors of this scholarly and useful work would be the first to acknowledge further information which might amplify what is already a remarkable tour de force of erudition, bibliographical skill, and meticulous care in which they have been well served by their publishers."); J. A. van Praag, <u>Neophilologus</u>, 52 (1968), 90; Sidney F. Wexler, <u>Hisp</u>,

51 (1968), 196 (Favourable. The reviewer considers the book
to be a carefully constructed piece of scholarship with
several useful indexes, although it is neither wholly
original nor truly exhaustive.).

A collection of more than 175 citations of verses found in the
plays of Calderón which already existed in one form or another
in other poetry of the time and which Calderón has utilized
in his works, with references to the originals and where they
may be found.

Wilson, Margaret. Spanish Drama of the Golden Age. Oxford,
Pergamon Press, 1969. Pp. xi, 221.
Rev: (Anon.), Modern Languages, 50 (1969), 175 (The book
traces the history of Spanish drama from its earliest beginning to the death of Calderón. Numerous quotations are given,
each with a translation. Comparisons are made with Shakespeare
and his contemporaries.); G. St. Andrews, CMLR, 26, No. 1
(1969), 79.

Calderón, pp. 149-76.

Ynduráin, Francisco. Relección de clásicos. Madrid, Edit. Prensa
Española, 1969. Pp. 335.
Rev: Raúl Chavarri, Estafeta Literaria, No. 430 (1969), 203;
Carlos Murciano, Poesía Española, No. 203 (1969), 4-6.

Reprints of earlier materials, with some reference to the
Golden Age theatre, including Calderón.

Zudaire, Eulogio. "Un escrito anónimo de Calderón de la Barca."
Hispania (Madrid), 13 (1953), 268-93.

Zudaire publishes an anonymous tract on the Catalan revolt of
1640 which appears to be by Calderón.

S T U D I E S

INDIVIDUAL WORKS

A Dios por razón de estado

Fiore, Robert Louis. Neo-Scholasticism... (1967). See Studies —
General.

A secreto agravio, secreta venganza

Brenan, Gerald. The Literature... (1951). See Studies — General.

Wilson, Edward M. "La discreción de don Lope de Almeida." Clav,
2, No. 9 (1951), 1-10.

An interesting study of the four major characters of A secreto
agravio, secreta venganza, in which emphasis is placed on the
adaptation of don Lope's discretion and prudence to the code
of honour. Wilson ends with the provocative suggestion that
this play could well be considered "una especie de disfrazada
comedia de santos," in which Calderón presents the development
of a secular code as manifested in the lives of the four main
characters. In line with this theory, the four main characters
are described as follows: Don Lope: "Su fe en el honor controla sus sentimientos; su discreción controla su juicio y
sus acciones; es como un místico del honor"; Don Juan: "cree
en el honor, pero su discreción es menor, no puede protegerlo
completamente"; Doña Leonor: "una pecadora del honor"; and
Don Luis: "un apóstata del honor." Wilson's conclusion, that
vengeance is to be followed by the death of the vengador, is
part of his revision of the traditional interpretation of the
secret-vengeance plays, discussed also in his article on
"Gerald Brenan's Calderón," BCom, 4, No. 1 (1952), 6-8.

- "Notes on the Text of <u>A secreto agravio, secreta venganza</u>."
<u>BHS</u>, 35 (1958), 72-82.

This valuable article of Professor Wilson's lays the foundations for what could be a critical and almost definitive
edition of this play. Wilson corrects an error in the above
study on "Discreción," when he wrote that the Astrana Marín
edition (Madrid, 1945), from which he was quoting, was "una
transcripción del manuscrito autógrafo que se conserva en la
Biblioteca Nacional de Madrid." Since then he has obtained
the necessary photostats, and, prompted by the Valbuena
Briones edition of the same play (Madrid, 1956, Clás Cast.),
he has produced this article. Discussing 17th century printings, Wilson speaks of two of 1637, Q (for María de Quiñones,
the printer) and QC (for María de Quiñones and Pedro Coello,
<u>mercader de libros</u>); and accepts the priority of QC over Q
(theories advanced by Cotarelo and Heaton). Wilson warns
future editors of the play that it "will be unwise if they
disregard QC and follow only Q; both Astrana and Valbuena
Briones seem to have done this." To the question once asked
by Toro y Gisbert "¿Conocemos el texto verdadero de las
comedias de Calderón?" (<u>BRAE</u>, 5, 1916, 413-21), he gives a
negative answer, and leaves a rather bitter taste in the
mouth of the seriously interested scholar of Calderón when
he states that with the exception of five Calderón plays
which have had critical editions, "we can be sure of very
few."

Honig, Edwin. "The Seizures of Honor..." (1961). See Studies —
General.

May, T. E. "The Folly and Wit of Secret Vengeance: Calderón's
<u>A secreto agravio, secreta venganza</u>." <u>FMLS</u>, 2 (1966), 114-22.

The author finds none of the Christian message hinted at by
<u>La vida es sueño</u>. <u>A secreto agravio,...</u> seems rather to bear
out his comment that a play beginning with a happy marriage
will not contain revenge; and that a wife's murder means that
in some way "she was never properly a wife at all." "El qué
dirán" is an important influence: the false report of D.
Luis's death causes Leonor to marry D. Lope, and "report"
also sends King Sebastian and his men to seek fame at
Alcazarquivir.

Soons, Alan. Ficción y comedia... (1967). See Studies — General.

El alcaide de sí mismo

Weiner, Jack. The Spanish Golden Age Theater... (1968). See Studies — General.

- "The Introduction..." (1969). See Studies — General.

El alcalde de Zalamea

Brenan, Gerald. The Literature... (1951). See Studies — General.

Petriconi, H. "El tema de Lucrecia y Virginia." Clav, 2, No. 8 (1951), 1-5.

El burlador de Sevilla and El alcalde de Zalamea are rather unconvincingly presented as manifestations of a theme in which "se usa de una seducción o violación para justificar preferentemente una revolución política." The source-play, El alcalde de Zalamea, considered by Petriconi to be by Lope de Vega, is discussed much more than is Calderón's play.

Sloman, Albert E. "Scene Division in Calderón's El alcalde de Zalamea." HR, 19 (1951), 66-71.

Hartzenbusch is taken to task for having been the first editor of El alcalde de Zalamea to have instituted scene division. "Before Hartzenbusch, editors had reproduced the directions found in the earliest extant edition of the play: El garrote más bien dado, in El mejor de los mejores libros que han salido de comedias nuevas (Alcalá, 1651), and had made no attempt to break up the action into individual scenes, with stage directions.... Recent editors, with the exception of Krenkel, have followed blindly the directions of H.; the edition of Maccoll shows two minor variations, but Menéndez y Pelayo, Geddes, Miss Farnell, and Astrana Marín reproduce his indications to the letter." "Calderón in El alcalde de Zalamea has allowed his scene to follow the centre of interest;

when the action is fixed his scene too is fixed, when it moves
his scene moves with it. If the exact location of the action
is essential to his purpose, it is made abundantly clear from
the dialogue. Recent editors who take pains to clear the stage
in order to divide up the play into independent scenes break
up and detach what the dramatist has deliberately welded
together, and provide a text misleading to the modern reader
and contrary to the author's purpose."

Pérez Máiquez, Fernando. "En torno a Pedro Crespo. El más fino
matiz de la tragedia." Alcántara (Cáceres), 8 (1952), 81-84.

Buchynskyj, D. "Ivan Frankó y la literatura española." RL, 3
(1953), 55-77.

An Ukrainian adapter of the Quijote and El alcalde de Zalamea.

Ducay, Eduardo. "Entre la espada y la pared." Insula, 9, No. 98
(1954), 11.

El alcalde de Zalamea in the cinema.

Küchler, Walther. "Calderóns comedia El alcalde de Zalamea als
Drama der Persönlichkeit." Archiv, 190, No. 4 (1954), 306-13.

Küchler sees the play as a drama of personalities, with
Crespo, the man, at least as important as Crespo, the alcalde.

Anderson Imbert, Enrique. "Azorín." Sur, No. 232 (1955), 42-45.

In a conversation, Azorín condemns El alcalde de Zalamea as
an absurd anti-militaristic drama.

Jones, C. A. "Honor in El alcalde de Zalamea." MLR, 50 (1955),
444-49. (Also pub. in Wardropper, 1965, pp. 193-202. See
Studies — General.)

Jones shows that in this play Calderón uses the idea of true
honour and contrasts it with the conventional honour of Lope
and some of his own earlier plays, which had not altogether
satisfied him.

Leavitt, Sturgis E. "Pedro Crespo and the Captain in Calderón's El alcalde de Zalamea." Hisp, 38 (1955), 430-31.

Calderón is lauded as a practical dramatist, sacrificing a magnificent character "in order to be certain that the sympathy of the audience went to the right candidate."

Reyes, Alfonso. "Las representaciones de clásicos." In Obras completas, Vol. IV, Mexico, 1956, pp. 410-11.

Sánchez, Alberto. "Reminiscencias cervantinas..." (1957). See Studies — General.

Smieja, Florian. "Nowe przeklady..." (1957). See Studies — General.

Sloman, Albert E. The Dramatic Craftsmanship... (1958). See Studies — General.

Carrasquer, F. "El alcalde de Zalamea en La Haya." PSA, 12 (1959), lxii-lxiv.

Performance of a translation by Dolf Verspoor.

Elizondo, Sergio D. "Dr. Sturgis E. Leavitt, a Modern Pedro Crespo." BCom, 11, No. 2 (1959), 5-6.

At year-end ceremonies, Professor Leavitt was honoured by his past and present students for his dedication to the study of Calderón, and especially for his work on El alcalde de Zalamea. In recognition of this, the mayor of Zalamea named Professor Leavitt Honorary Alcalde of Zalamea for life.

Dunn, Peter N. "Honour and the Christian Background..." (1960). See Studies — General.

Soons, C. A. "Caracteres y imágenes en El alcalde de Zalamea." RF, 72 (1960), 104-07.

Bayon, D. C. "Zalamea en Aviñón." CCLC, No. 55 (1961), 84-85.

Pillement, Georges. "Calderón et l'Alcalde de Zalamea. La
    justice militaire et la Justice." Bref (Paris), No. 47 (1961),
    2-3.

Dunn, Peter N. "Patrimonio del alma." BHS, 41 (1964), 78-85.

The article seeks to show the interrelation between divine
and human law, referring to lines 873-76 of the play, and
goes on to discuss how Roman legalistic terms and concepts
were adopted by the Church. "Thus we see that the use of a
phrase which is simultaneously juristic and theological,
though unique in its wording (the only use of such a word in
El alcalde de Zalamea), is not isolated ideologically within
the play..." There is a "continuum" of ideal human society,
Nature and Divine Law, and human nature persistently disrupts
it.

Hatzfeld, Helmut. Estudios... (1964). See Studies — General.

Reynolds, H. R. "Mayor of Zalamea at the Nottingham Playhouse."
    In The New Vida Hispánica, 12, London, 1964, pp. 19-20.

A review of a performance of an English version which took
many liberties with the original text, omitting and introducing lines and changing the time to the Napoleonic era. It was
well staged, with an economy of settings. "This was the play's
best aspect; its worst, one could say, is that it was not
Calderón."

Abrams, Fred. "Imaginería y aspectos temáticos del Quijote en
    El alcalde de Zalamea." Duquesne Hispanic Review, 5 (1966),
    27-34.

The two works offer several parallels, notably between Pedro
Crespo's advice to his son, Juan, as the latter prepares to
leave with Don Lope de Figueroa's troops, and Don Quijote's
remarks to Sancho on seeing him off to govern his "ínsula."

Honig, Edwin. "Calderón's Mayor: Honor Humanized." TDR, 10 (1966), 134-55.

Pedro Crespo's handling of his honour problem gives the rigid code an unaccustomed flexibility, and leaves his own personality intact, while the pastoral ethic triumphs over both the military viewpoint and the usual honour code. The Captain's overconfidence is his undoing; he misjudges both Isabel and her father. The latter surprises even Isabel when he has her sign a complaint, thus making the dishonour a matter of record and therefore worse, as usually understood.

Leavitt, Sturgis E. "Cracks in the Structure of Calderón's El alcalde de Zalamea." In Hispanic Studies in Honor of Nicholson B. Adams, Chapel Hill, North Carolina, 1966, pp. 93-96.

D. Mendo and Nuño are expendable, and were added probably because someone wanted a comic part included. Act I ends with no conflict, unless the Captain persists, which we don't learn about until Act II. His friendliness with Rebolledo is implausible, after Rebolledo exposed his scheme in Act I. Pedro Crespo's completely forgetting the election is unlikely, as is his belief that the Captain might marry Isabel. Her speech in Act III is much too long, probably to please some demanding actress.

Soons, Alan. Ficción y comedia... (1967). See Studies — General.

Casanova, Wilfredo O. "Honor, patrimonio del alma y opinión social, patrimonio de casta en El alcalde de Zalamea de Calderón." Hispanó, 11, No. 33 (1968), 17-33.

A detailed study of the significance of the lines:
>   Al Rey la hacienda y la vida
>   se ha de dar; pero el honor
>   es patrimonio del alma,
>   y el alma sólo es de Dios.

Castelli, Eugenio. Análisis de "El alcalde de Zalamea." Buenos Aires, Centro Editor de América Latina, 1968. Pp. 54.

Leavitt, S. E. "Scenes of Horror..." (1968). See Studies —
General.

Marañón, Gregorio. "Mas no el honor." In Obras completas, ed.
Alfredo Juderías, IV, Madrid, Espasa-Calpe, 1968, pp. 883-86.

Reference to a performance of El alcalde de Zalamea.

Smieja, Florian. "The Lord Mayor of Poznán: An Eighteenth-
Century Polish Version of El alcalde de Zalamea." MLR, 63
(1968), 869-71.

Weiner, Jack. The Spanish Golden Age Theater... (1968). See
Studies — General.

Amar después de la muerte

Fredén, G. Tres ensayos cervantinos. Madrid, Insula, 1964.

In the third essay, the author makes a comparison with
Calderón's Amar después de la muerte.

Weiner, Jack. The Spanish Golden Age Theater... (1968). See
Studies — General.

Amor, honor y poder

Valbuena Briones, Angel. "Consideraciones en torno a la fuente
de Amor, honor y poder." BCom, 8, No. 2 (1956), 1-4.

The author believes the immediate source of the play to be
Agreda y Vargas' "novelita" entitled Eduardo Rey de Inglaterra,
published in 1620.

Andrómeda y Perseo (auto)

Flasche, Hans. "Antiker Mythos..." (1965). See Studies — General;

and <u>Los encantos de la culpa</u>, Flasche, 1968. (See <u>Las fortunas de Andrómeda y Perseo</u>.)

Apolo y Climene

Gallego Morell, Antonio. "El mito..." (1956). See Studies — General.

Parker, Alexander A. "Metáfora y símbolo..." (1964). See Studies — General.

Las armas de la hermosura

Sloman, Albert E. "One of Calderón's 'minor' characters: Lelio in Calderón's <u>Las armas de la hermosura</u>." <u>Atlante</u>, 1, No. 3 (1953), 130-35.

The dramatic significance of Lelio in the play.

- <u>The Dramatic Craftsmanship...</u> (1958). See Studies — General.

Parker, Alexander A. "History and Poetry: The Coriolanus Theme in Calderón." In <u>Hispanic Studies in Honour of I. González Llubera</u>, Oxford, 1959, pp. 211-24.

El astrólogo fingido

Oppenheimer, Max, Jr. "Two Stones and One Bird; A Bird Lore Allusion in Calderón." <u>MLN</u>, 67 (1952), 253-54.

Oppenheimer discusses Calderón's use, in this play, of the image of a bird carrying a stone in his claw, the better to penetrate the wind, and another in his beak, to show that he is maintaining vigilance and preserving a faithful silence. Two passages in Pliny's <u>Natural History</u> are cited as possible sources, but Oppenheimer feels that "the true and complete source" for Calderón's lines is to be found in two passages

of Plutarch's <u>Moralia</u>, the sole change effected by Calderón
being the fusing into one bird of Plutarch's geese which carry
great stones in their mouths, and his cranes whose night vigil
entails holding a stone in the claw of one foot.

<u>La aurora en Copacabana</u>

Pedro, Valentín de. <u>América en las letras españolas...</u> (1954).
See Studies — General.

Pagés Larraya, Antonio. "El Nuevo Mundo en una obra de Calderón."
<u>Atenea</u>, 33, No. 371 (1956), 108-29.

<u>La aurora en Copacabana</u>.

López Cabo, María. <u>La aurora en Copacabana</u>. Diss., Univ. de
Madrid, 1959.

Pagés Larraya, Antonio. "El Nuevo Mundo en una obra de Calderón."
<u>Atenea</u>, 39, No. 396 (1962), 70-92.

- "El Nuevo Mundo en una obra de Calderón." <u>La Palabra y el
Hombre</u> (Xalapa), No. 21 (1962), 49-70.

- "El Nuevo Mundo en una obra de Calderón." <u>CHA</u>, 57 (1964),
299-319.

A detailed analysis of Calderón's <u>La aurora en Copacabana</u>,
which the author admires, and which he considers a religious
drama, a presentation of evangelization. The work has many
of the conventions of the <u>comedia de capa y espada</u>. Some of
the names are from the <u>Araucana</u>. The author also points out
historical inaccuracies.

- "El Perú de la conquista en un drama de Calderón." <u>La Torre</u>,
17 (1969), 69-96.

<u>Los cabellos de Absalón</u>

Sloman, Albert E. <u>The Dramatic Craftsmanship...</u> (1958). See
Studies — General.

Rank, Otto. "The Incest of Amnon and Tamar." <u>TDR</u>, 7 (1962),
38-43.

Treatment by Lope de Vega, Calderón and Cervantes of the
incest theme. Calderón's <u>Los cabellos de Absalón</u> is considered
briefly. The author notes that the entire second act is almost
a verbatim copy of the third act of <u>La venganza de Tamar</u> by
Tirso de Molina, and he discusses the reasons for this.

Giacoman, Helmy F. "En torno a <u>Los cabellos de Absalón</u> de Pedro
Calderón de la Barca." <u>RF</u>, 80 (1968), 340-53.

A study of the play, comparing it with Tirso's <u>La venganza de
Tamar.</u>

<u>Casa con dos puertas mala es de guardar</u>

Glaser, Edward. "Referencias antisemitas en la literatura
peninsular de la Edad de Oro." <u>NRFH</u>, 8 (1954), 39-62.

Reference to <u>Casa con dos puertas....</u>

Hodoušek, Eduard. "J. K. Tyl jako první český překladatel
Calderóna." <u>Časopis pro Moderní Filologii</u> (Prague), 39 (1957),
1-7.

During the romantic period, the Calderón cult from Germany
spread to other parts of Europe. In Bohemia, Calderón's plays
were known through German translations. The first Czech
translation appeared in 1841, and was made by Josef Kajetan
Tyl. The author of this illuminating article compares the
original Calderonian text with the German translation of <u>Casa
con dos puertas...</u> made itself from a French translation by
Alexander Cosmar, a bookseller from Berlin. The Tyl translation was made from the Cosmar version, which adapts the

characters to German middle class environment, leaving out
servants and episodes, and gives the characters German names.
Tyl changed the names to Czech, but did not change the play.
Although Tyl's version is conventional, artificial and not a
good one, he is actually the first translator of a Calderón
play into the Czech language, as the title of the article
indicates. Tyl translated Casa con dos puertas... in 1838, and
it was first printed in 1841.

Wardropper, Bruce W. "Calderón's Comedy and his Serious Sense
  of Life." In Hispanic Studies in Honor of Nicholson B. Adams,
  Chapel Hill, North Carolina, 1966, pp. 179-93.

Calderón's comedies, as exemplified by Casa con dos puertas...,
seem strange in one so serious, but actually are about the
same thing as his other works: the world's "confusing reality,
the disastrous effects of human frailty and sinfulness, problems of cognition and identification, the deceptive appearance
of truth and falsehood." There are honour problems, but no
gory revenge, for these people are unmarried, not "one flesh"
that might need an amputation. Even so, the swords are kept
sharpened, and "As we watch Calderón's fun-making, our heart
is in our mouth. Those we watch fear, and we who watch fear
for them."

El castillo de Lindabridis

Mazur, Oleh. "Various Impacts..." (1968). See Studies — General.

Céfalo y Pocris

Martin, H. M. "Notes on the Cephalus-Pocris Myth as Dramatized
  by Lope de Vega and Calderón." MLN, 66 (1951), 238-41. (See
  below.)

Wilson and Sage. Poesías líricas... (1964). See Studies —
  General.

Devoto, Daniel. "Un cantar aludido por Calderón." BH, 70 (1968),
  85-88.

Deals with a cantar from Act II of the play.

Mazur, Oleh. "Various Impacts..." (1968). See Studies — General.

Celos aun del aire matan

Martin, Henry M. "Notes on the Cephalus-Pocris Myth as Dramatized by Lope de Vega and Calderón." MLN, 66 (1951), 238-41.

Lope's La bella aurora and Calderón's Celos aun del aire matan
are discussed as dramatizations of the myth. Ovid's Metamorphoses and Ars Amatoria are cited as the direct sources of
both dramatists, although Martin also detects the influence
of certain elements of other sources such as Hyginus, romances
and books of chivalry, and Boccaccio. There is very brief
mention of some of the modifications in the classical myth
which are effected by Lope and Calderón.

Subirá, José. "Calderón de la Barca, libretista de ópera.
Consideraciones literario-musicales." Anuario Musical
(Barcelona), 20 (1965), 59-73.

Lope's La selva sin amor and Calderón's La púrpura de la rosa
(music lost, in both cases) have been considered early Spanish
operas; but Calderón's fiesta cantada, Celos aun del aire
matan, was not so regarded until two fortunate discoveries
gave the music, samples of which are reproduced in the article.
Given the popularity of the Céfalo-Pocris-Aurora tradition,
one may wonder why Celos... was not performed after its
première before the Royal Family at the Coliseo in the Buen
Retiro (1660). Answers: the needed array of fine voices could
not easily be assembled often; and such theatres as the Cruz
or Príncipe lacked the money, personnel, and technical
resources of the Coliseo.

La cena del rey Baltasar

Fucilla, Joseph G. Relaciones... (1953-54). See Studies —
General.

Monleón, José. "Dos autos..." (1963). See Studies — General.

Varey, J. E. "La mise en scène..." (1964). See Studies — General.

La cisma de Inglaterra

Parker, Alexander A. "Metáfora y símbolo..." (1964). See
Studies — General.

Herbold, Anthony. "Shakespeare, Calderón, and Henry the Eighth."
East-West Review, 2 (1965), 17-32.

While conceding that Henry VIII offers enough parallels to
look like Calderón's source, the author doubts that Calderón
knew of Shakespeare; if indeed Shakespeare wrote Henry VIII
at all. Instead, Calderón used a 1605 Historia... by Pedro de
Rivadeneira, and adapted it freely. He makes Enrique a tragic
hero, much more central to the plot than in the English play.
While neither dramatist let himself be imprisoned by historical fact, Calderón seems to have had somewhat the freer hand,
given the repressive secrecy of Elizabeth I's England, which
in many ways resembled a contemporary "iron curtain" country.
As a result, Calderón's play is "even better theater" than
Henry VIII, which Herbold calls "episodic, loose, shifting."

Cabantous, M. "Le Schisme d'Angleterre vu par Calderón." Les
Langues Néo-Latines, 62 (1968), 43-58.

El conde Lucanor

Fradejas Lebrero, José. "Un cuento de don Juan Manuel y dos
comedias del Siglo de Oro." RL, 7, No. 15 (1955), 67-80.

One of the comedias is Calderón's El conde Lucanor.

La cura y la enfermedad

Verhesen, Fernand. Etude... (1953). See Studies — General.

La dama duende

Dalbor, John B. "La dama duende, de Calderón, y The Parson's Wedding, de Killigrew." Hispanó, No. 2 (1958), 41-50.

After reviewing scores of critics who have contended that the source of Killigrew's play of pre-restoration drama was La dama duende and also presenting the views of A. Harbage and M. Summers who reject such contention, Dalborg compares the texts and situations of both plays. The author's observations are that: "Después de analizar los puntos culminantes de ambas comedias, no se puede negar que hay ciertas semejanzas." However, after presenting the resemblances, he points out that there are "grandes diferencias." Dalbor's final paragraph seems somewhat ambiguous, because he states that "De ninguna manera es correcto afirmar que 'the two plays have absolutely nothing in common'" (quotation from M. Summers, Restoration Comedies), and then seems to converge with this view in his closing sentence: "No hay bastante prueba concluyente en los dos textos, pues, para afirmar, como han hecho tantos, que Killigrew fue influido por La dama duende, ya sea en cuanto a la comedia entera, al argumento, a los temas o a una situación individual."

Turkevich, Ludmilla B. "Status..." (1958). See Studies — General.

Honig, Edwin. "The Seizures of Honor..." (1961). See Studies — General.

- "Flickers of Incest on the Face of Honor: Calderón's Phantom Lady." TDR, 6 (1962), 69-105.

A detailed analysis of themes in La dama duende. When the play ends, we feel that the irrational, in the double form of phantom lady and imaginary devil, has been given its due. The incest threat flickering across the anxious face of honour has been put down, and for once in Calderón, the rites of love have superseded the black honour formula with its insult-vengeance complex.

Schwarz, Egon. Hofmannsthal und Calderón (1962). See Studies —
General.

Gättke, Walter. "Zu Calderóns Komödie Dame Kobold." Die
Volksbühne (Hamburg), 14 (1963), 47-48.

A brief article outlining Calderón's La dama duende, praising
its construction and the wealth of its main rôles, pointing
out that this form (comedia de capa y espada) of the Baroque
theatre calls for musical treatment, and mentioning a draft
of an opera based on this play by Felix von Weingartner.

Acerete, Julio C. "Calderón de la Barca." Primer Acto, No. 78
(1966), 64.

A review of José Luis Alonso's performance (1966), at the
Teatro Español, of La dama duende, a play that the critic
considers of value only if well staged, and "insoportable"
if not. He also feels that Calderón wrote it at Royal urging,
for a court audience, the only suitable one for a play so "de
espaldas a toda realidad de la época..." While Alonso's
version may not have been the most appropriate, it "tuvo
calidad," as did the actors' performance, effectively supporting the director's intentions.

Aragonés, Juan Emilio. "La dama duende y el otro Calderón." La
Estafeta Literaria, No. 342 (Apr. 23, 1966), 12-13.

The play recalls Valbuena Prat's description of Calderón as
the great perfector, "el final sintético de una espléndida
carrera de dramaturgos." It also parodies the honour code
usually associated with Calderón. José Luis Alonso's faithful
reproduction and attention to detail are praised, as are the
actors' performances, especially those of María Fernanda
d'Ocón (Angela) and Antonio Ferrandis (Cosme, the gracioso).

Quinto, José María de. "La dama duende o el verso encontrado."
Insula, 21, No. 234 (May, 1966), 14.

In "Crónica de Teatro," another triumph for José Luis Alonso
is noted, although the tone may be somewhat too "playful" for
what is no doubt a satire of Spanish women's situation in the

17th century. The director's skill is especially visible in the actors' performances, which enabled the audience to be completely identified with the action, without feeling that they were at a performance or being uncomfortably aware of the verse. This could pave the way for a more general return to "los clásicos."

Santaló, José Luis. "La dama duende, en el Español." Arbor, 64, No. 245 (1966), 89-90.

After commenting on the surprising "agelessness" of the classical theatre in general (English and French, as well as Spanish) Sr. Santaló praises the Teatro Español version of La dama duende, especially the work of María Fernanda d'Ocón in the title rôle, and approvingly mentioning several others. The sets and the direction come in for their share of praise, as does the facsimile of the 1691 edition of Calderón's works, on the printed programme. These comments (by Acerete, Aragonés, Quinto, and Santaló) were all inspired by the 1966 performances in the Teatro Español, Madrid.

Labarta de Chaves, Teresa. "Forma cerrada..." (1968). See Studies — General.

La desdicha de la voz

Malkiel, Yakov. "Bibliographic Notes..." (1964-65). See Studies — General.

La devoción de la Cruz

Bomli, P. W. La Femme... (1950). See Studies — General.

Aubrun, C. V. "Les Enfants terribles..." (1957). See Studies — General.

Parker, Alexander A. The Approach... (1957). See Studies — General.

McPheeters, D. W. "Camus' Translations of Plays by Lope and
Calderón." Symposium, 12 (1958), 52-64.

El caballero de Olmedo, La devoción de la Cruz.

Honig, Edwin. "Calderón's Strange Mercy Play." Massachusetts
Review, 3 (1961), 80-107. (Repub. in Wardropper, Critical
Essays..., 1965, pp. 167-92.)

An analysis of La devoción de la Cruz. It is pointed out that
"only when the play is read allegorically does it become
intelligible despite its strange immorality." The rôle of
allegory is discussed, especially with respect to the symbol
of the cross. The author explains that the honour theme "is
superseded and defeated (by the law of heaven, symbolized in
the cross) as a partial truth, but without being destroyed
or removed."

X - "The Seizures of Honor..." (1961). See Studies — General.

X Parker, Alexander A. "The Father-Son Conflict..." (1966). See
Studies — General.

Quaderni del Teatro Stabile della Città di Torino. No. 9 (1967).
Pp. 101.

Issued to mark the Company's production of La devozione alla
Croce, Fall, 1967, in an Italian version by Roberto Lerici,
and under the direction of Gianfranco De Bosio. This number
of Quaderni includes four reprints: Leo Spitzer, "Il barocco
spagnolo," pp. 9-27 (from Bol. del Inst. de Investigaciones
Históricas, 28, 1943-44, pp. 12-30); Micheline Sauvage, "La
Spagna di Calderón," pp. 29-40 (from her Calderón dramaturge,
1959); W. J. Entwistle, "La Devozione nella cultura spagnola,"
pp. 68-80 (from BH, 50, 1948, pp. 472-82); and Carmelo Samonà,
"Bibliografia calderoniana," pp. 83-90 (from his Calderón
nella critica italiana, Milan, 1960). It also includes the
original articles of De Bosio, Doglio, and Samonà, as listed
below in this section; and Morteo's "Vita e fortuna..."
(1967) — See Studies — General.

De Bosio, Gianfranco. "Per una lettura fonico-visiva della
Devozione alla Croce." Quaderni...Torino (1967), 12 pages,
between pp. 82-83.

De Bosio, Gianfranco, and Roberto Lerici. "La famosa commedia
della devozione alla Croce di Pedro Calderón de la Barca."
Sipario, No. 258 (1967), 39-43.

Notes by the Director and Adapter of the Italian production
of La devoción de la Cruz, including a scene from Lerici's
version.

Doglio, Federico. "Validità di una proposta." Quaderni...Torino
(1967), pp. 57-63.

Re the production of the play.

Samonà, Carmelo. "Una inimitabile lezione di stile." Quaderni...
Torino (1967), pp. 64-67.

Serrano Plaja, Arturo. "El absurdo en Camus y en Calderón de la
Barca." In Mélanges à la Mémoire de Jean Sarrailh, II, Paris,
1967, pp. 389-405; and in El arte comprometido y el compromiso
del arte y otros ensayos, Barcelona, Delos-Aymá, 1968, pp.
29-51. (See Studies — General — Sarrailh.)

Re Caligula and La devoción de la Cruz.

McKendrick, Melveena. "The Bandolera of Golden Age Drama: A
Symbol of Feminist Revolt." BHS, 46 (1969), 1-20.

Reference is made to Julia, the heroine of La devoción de la
Cruz (pp. 13-15).

Sánchez, Alberto. "Conexiones temáticas..." (1969). See
Studies — General.

La devoción de la misa

Schier, Donald. "Voltaire's Criticism..." (1959). See Studies —General.

El divino Jasón

Viqueira, José Maria. "Temas clásicos..." (1959). See Studies —
General.

El divino Orfeo

Osma, José M. de. "Apostilla al tema de la creación en el auto
El divino Orfeo de Calderón de la Barca." Hisp, 34 (1951),
165-71.

The author expounds upon the fact that, in his opinion,
Calderón has quite appropriately employed the classical myth
of Orfeo for allegory a lo divino in two different autos,
both of which bear the same title. El divino Orfeo, version
A, was printed in the Primera Parte of Calderón's Autos
(Madrid, 1677); version B was not known in published form
until it appeared as an appendix to the 1949 doctoral dissertation of Pablo Cabañas, El mito de Orfeo en la literatura
española (Madrid, CSIC, 1948). Orfeo and Eurídice are
considered by Osma as very apt figures to represent respec-
tively the Saviour and La Naturaleza Humana. Version B
simplifies and abbreviates, but also follows the source myth
more closely than does Version A.

Los dos amantes del cielo

Szarota, Elida Maria. Künstler,... (1967). See Studies — General.

Eco y Narciso

Brüggemann, Werner. "Romantisches in Calderóns 'comedia
mitológica' Eco y Narciso." In Gesammelte Aufsätze zur
Kulturgeschichte Spaniens (Spanische Forschungen der Gorres-
gesellschaft), Münster, Westfalen, Vol. 13, 1958, pp. 239-58.

The author states that one of the unresolved problems in
modern German literary history pertains to the phenomenon of
the reception of Calderón by German Romanticism. There are

abundant quotations from Goethe, A. W. Schlegel, F. Schlegel,
Malsburg, Müller, etc., and from modern writers such as
Kommerell, Curtius and Friedrich. Regarding Eco y Narciso,
Brüggemann makes a detailed summary of the plot, indicates
its sources, and discusses the adverse criticism it received
in the Spanish Neoclassic period. The author's most important
contribution is his approach to Eco y Narciso employing F.
Schlegel's definition of the "arabesque" as beautiful confu-
sion and fantasy. Furthermore, the author states that the
Spanish comedia occupies, in the view of the Romantics, that
place which the Greek drama had in the culture of antiquity,
and without hesitation he states that in the quest for poetic
universality and objectivity in the modern world of consciousness and artistic trends, Calderón appears equal to Dante,
Shakespeare, Cervantes, and Goethe, as an example and as a
model.

Hesse, Everett W. "The 'Terrible Mother' Image in Calderón's
   Eco y Narciso." RomN, I (1960), 133-36.

The author traces Narciso's self-love directly to the
unwholesome influence of the "terrible mother" who is frus-
trating his budding love for Eco. This forces Narciso to find
his emotional outlet in another love: self-love.

- "Estructura e interpretación de una comedia de Calderón: Eco
   y Narciso." Filología (Univ. de Buenos Aires), 7 (1961), 61-
   76. (Reprinted in BBMP, 39, 1963, pp. 57-72, and in Hesse's
   Análisis e interpretación de la Comedia, 1968, pp. 69-83.)

The author traces the development of the two plots:
(a) Narciso-Eco-Leríope and (b) Febo-Silvio-Eco. He shows how
they are interwoven and how Leríope, seeking to avoid the
fulfillment of a prophecy, brings it about. He interprets the
work as setting forth the abuse of the authority of parents
and the education of children and as a study of a domineering
mother.

Cros, Edmond. "Paganisme et christianisme dans Eco y Narciso
   de Calderón." RLR, 75 (1962), 39-74.

Calderón retains the essential elements of Ovid's myth, but
adds two new features: the pastoral setting (as a concession

to contemporary audiences), and a plot with three main
characters instead of two, which supports his dogmatic and
religious thought.

Groult, Pierre. "Sur Eco y Narciso de Calderón." LR, 16 (1962),
103-113.

A criticism of Aubrun's edition of the play, 1961, which
Groult maintains has been misinterpreted by Aubrun. (See
Editions — Individual Works.)

Aubrun, Charles V. "Les Débuts du drama lyrique..." (1964).
See Studies — General.

Parker, Alexander A. "Metáfora y símbolo..." (1964). See
Studies — General.

Conard, Pierre. "Du néo-platonisme dans Echo et Narcisse de
Calderón." Les Langues Néo-Latines, 59 (1965), 91-97.

The play follows Pedro Sánchez Viana's translation and
commentaries on Ovid's Metamorphoses (1589) and Marsilio
Ficino's commentaries on Plato's Convivium. Narcissus (vanity,
admiration of bodily beauty) seeks Echo (fame's immortality)
on the bases of hearing and sight; but she will never see him,
and will not accept mere hearing, preferring to seek his soul.
Calderón, wishing to do more than to delight the spectators'
vision and hearing, sought to lead them by example onto the
path of Divine Grace and the Quest for God.

Vinge, Louise. The Narcissus Theme in Western European Litera-
ture up to the Early 19th Century. Trans. Robert Dewsap,
Lisbeth Grönlund, Nigel Reeves, and Ingrid Söderberg-Reeves.
Lund, Gleerups, 1967. Pp. xv, 448.
Rev: Dietrich Briesemeister, Archiv, 205 (1968), 202-04; J.
Donovan, MLR, 63 (1968), 924-25; R. O. Jones, BHS, 45 (1968),
254-55 ("The Spanish scholar will not find much novelty,
naturally enough, but there are interesting remarks on the
plays which are worth bearing in mind, in particular Miss
Vinge's discussion of whether Calderón's is allegory.");
Erich Köhler, RF, 80 (1968), 444-48.

178

Calderón's _Eco y Narciso_, pp. 237-44.

Hesse, Everett W. _Análisis e interpretación..._ (1968). See above, and Studies — General.

Van Liew, Lucille Marie, and Karem Getty. "Del Narciso secular al divino Narciso. Sobre las obras de Calderón y Sor Juana." _Et Caetera_ (Guadalajara), 3 (1968), 41-70.

Treats Calderón's _Eco y Narciso_ and Sor Juana's _El divino Narciso_.

Los empeños de un acaso

Castañeda, James A. "_Los empeños de un acaso_ y _Los empeños de una casa_: Calderón y Sor Juana—La diferencia de un fonema." _Rev. de Estudios Hispánicos_, 1 (1967), 107-16.

En esta vida todo es verdad y todo mentira

Schier, Donald. "Voltaire's Criticism..." (1959). See Studies — General.

Los encantos de la culpa

Hatzantonis, E. S. _Circe nelle letterature..._ (1958). See Studies — General.

Viqueira, José Maria. "Temas clásicos..." (1959). See Studies — General.

Garasa, Delfín Leocadio. "Circe en la literatura española..." (1964). See Studies — General.

Flasche, Hans. _Die Struktur des Auto sacramental "Los encantos_

de la culpa" von Calderón; and <u>Antiker Mythos in christlicher</u>
<u>Umprägung</u>: <u>Andrómeda y Perseo bei Calderón</u>. Köln-Opladen,
Westdeutscher Verlag, 1968. Pp. 96. (Geisteswissenschaften der
Arbeitsgemeinschaft für Forschung des Landes Nordrhein-
Westfalen, 150.)
Rev: E. P., <u>Rev. de Portugal</u>, 39 (1969), 511-12.

Pp. 53-96 deal with <u>Andrómeda y Perseo</u>.

El escondido y la tapada

Weiner, Jack. "The Introduction..." (1969). See Studies —
General.

La estatua de Prometeo

Aubrun, Charles V. "Realismo y poesía..." (1964). See Studies —
General.

Trousson, Raymond. <u>Le Thème de Prométhée dans la littérature</u>
<u>européenne</u>. Geneva, Droz, 1964. Pp. vi, 561.
Rev: Pierre Moreau, <u>RLC</u>, 42 (1968), 291-96.

Includes: "Une synthèse tardive: <u>La estatua de Prometeo</u>,"
pp. 167-78.

La fiera, el rayo y la piedra

Sánchez, Alberto. "Reminiscencias cervantinas..." (1957). See
Studies — General.

Fieras afemina amor

Wilson, Edward M. "La edición príncipe de <u>Fieras afemina amor</u>
de don Pedro Calderón de la Barca." <u>Rev. de la Biblioteca,</u>
<u>Archivo y Museo</u>, 24 (1955), 327-48.

Describes a <u>suelta</u> of <u>Fieras afemina amor</u>, probably printed for the first performance in 1670, and thus the play's first edition.

Las fortunas de Andrómeda y Perseo (comedia)

Flasche, Hans. "Antiker Mythos..." (1965). See Studies — General; and <u>Los encantos de la culpa</u>, Flasche, 1968. (See <u>Andrómeda y Perseo</u>.)

El gran duque de Gandía

Černý, Václav. "Un drame inconnu de Calderón, nouvellement découvert en Bohême." <u>Acta Musei Nationalis Pragae</u>, VI, serie C, Historia Literarum (Prague, 1961), 75-100.

Černý discusses his important finding of the lost San Francisco de Borja play by Calderón (<u>El gran duque de Gandía</u>), in the library of the Kuenburg castle in Mladá Vožice, Czechoslovakia (among volumes owned by Maria Josepha Countess Kuenburg, née Harrach). He provides a description of the play, and examines it in relation to the others printed by Hartzenbusch which deal with this subject. The important discovery received notice in Spain (e.g., <u>Arbor</u>, 48, No. 184; <u>El libro español</u>, No. 37), in North America (e.g., <u>BCom</u>, 13, No. 1), and in Britain (e.g., <u>The London Times</u>, Jan. 8, 1964: "'Lost Play' by Calderón for Bregenz Festival").

Reynolds, John J. "Noticia de una obra inédita calderoniana." <u>BCom</u>, 13, No. 1 (1961), 11.

Reynolds gives details about the Černý discovery of the MS of Calderón's <u>El gran duque de Gandía</u> in Czechoslovakia, mentioning the study of it by Černý, and the fact that a critical edition is soon to be published in Prague.

Martino, E. "<u>El gran duque de Gandía</u>, una comedia 'nueva' de Calderón de la Barca." <u>Humanidades</u> (Colmillas), 15 (1963), 291-99.

Mainly a résumé of the play's action with the citation of a number of lines. The author does not doubt Calderón's authorship, as some have done. He laments the numerous errors in the Černý edition of Prague, 1963, asking whether they result from a misreading of the original or from the printing.

Casona, Alejandro. "Calderón ha estrenado anoche un drama, El gran duque de Gandía." Hechos y Dichos (Zaragoza), 40 (1964), 258-61.

After a brief history of the play, Casona comments on the typically Calderonian characteristics of the drama: the slow development of sanctity (in contrast to sudden conversion), the antitheses (light-shadow, jest-philosophy, greatness-wretchedness, love-death), and his lyricism. There is no reference to a specific performance.

Hornedo, Rafael M. de. "La comedia de El gran duque de Gandía." Razón y Fe, 169 (1964), 131-44.

By referring to the Días sagrados y geniales of P. Fomperosa (1672), the author establishes the date of the play, which he attributes to Calderón, and its performance, along with the loa and two sainetes of the manuscript, at the Colegio Imperial on the afternoon of August 10, 1671, in the presence of the King and his consort. He ends with a brief discussion of the historical aspects of the play. An informative addition to Černý's edition.

Mikhal'chi, D. "Neizvestnaia drama Kal'derona" (An unknown drama of Calderón). Voprosy Literatury, 8, No. 3 (March, 1964), 252-54.

The author gives a brief history of the newly-discovered (1958 at Mladá Vožice) manuscript of El gran duque de Gandía and comments on Calderón and his religious dramas. He praises the work of Černý, who made the discovery and prepared the edition.

Malkiel, Yakov. "Bibliographic Notes..." (1964-65). See Studies — General.

Černý, Václav. "Das unbekannte Weltdrama Calderóns." Maske und Kothurn, 11 (1965), 1-9.

After hailing El gran duque de Gandía as one of Calderón's best, Černý stresses the importance of antithesis in this and Calderón's other plays, reflecting an absurdly divided and contradictory world destined for better things, but fallen into weakness. El gran duque de Gandía is a "drama de santo," of holiness not "ready-made," but reached through growth and progress. It also exemplifies vanitas vanitatum and desengaño, in the baroque tradition. To the extent that Calderón's hero is a désabusé, he anticipates those of Malraux and Hemingway.

Juliá Martínez, Eduardo. "Una comedia de Calderón recuperada." RL, 27 (1965), 5-31.

This is of course El gran duque de Gandía. Recalling that the manuscript is anonymous and in five hands, Sr. Juliá discusses Calderón's authorship, which he accepts. The title is on the list sent to Veragua; and Calderón's priesthood and fear of loss of court favour may have led him not to acknowledge the play at the time. Černý credits Father Ribadeneyra as Calderón's source for the play, but Juliá prefers Father Nieremberg, who offers all the elements found in Ribadeneyra.

Siebenmann, Gustav. "El gran duque de Gandía. Ein neuentdechtes Drama von Calderón." Germanisch-romanische Monatsschrift, 15 (1965), 262-75.

Hailing the finding of the play as closing a centuries-old gap in Calderón's repertoire, Siebenmann wonders if Calderón's personal devotion, based on Jesuit training, led him to write it. In any case, it seems no routine, casual task. The work is a unique combination in Calderón, of comedia and miracle play, and hence a severe challenge for modern producers. While taking issue with Černý, the editor, on certain critical issues (e.g., the importance of antithesis in the play), Siebenmann calls the Černý edition in general a thoroughly welcome contribution.

Freund, Markéta L. Baroque Technique... (1966). See Studies — General.

Reichenberger, Arnold G. "The Counts Harrach and the Spanish

Theater." In <u>Homenaje a Rodríguez-Moñino</u>, II, Madrid, Castalia, 1966, pp. 97-103.

Includes reference to Černý's discovery of <u>El gran duque de Gandía</u>, and speaks, among others, of the Count Harrach (1637-1706) who was ambassador to Spain, and of his daughter Maria Josepha Countess Kuenburg, née Harrach. (The two volumes of the Rodríguez-Moñino <u>Homenaje</u> were reviewed by Rafael Bosch, <u>Hispanó</u>, No. 36, 1969, 47-55.)

Calvo Costa, Juan A. <u>Estudio analítico de "El gran duque de Gandía"</u>: <u>Contribución al estudio de las comedias de santos de don Pedro Calderón de la Barca</u>. Unpub. doct. diss., Michigan State Univ., 1967. Pp. 216. (DA, 38, 2202A.)

An analysis of the structure, the poetic form and the dramatic characteristics of <u>El gran duque de Gandía</u>. The author treats the baroque ambient in which the <u>comedia de santo</u> was presented and examines the historical significance of the protagonist and the other characters of the play. The religious themes, the poetic elements and the idea of <u>desengaño</u> so prevalent in Calderón's latter period are studied in detail.

- "Aportación al estudio de la métrica de <u>El gran duque de Gandía</u>." <u>BCom</u>, 21 (1969), 12-15.

<u>El gran teatro del mundo</u>

Ritter, Federica de. "<u>El gran teatro del mundo</u> (la historia de una metáfora)." <u>RNC</u>, 14 (1952), 133-53. (Repub. in <u>Panorama</u>, 2, 1953, pp. 81-98.)

A short history of the metaphorical comparison of real life to a drama in which man becomes an actor ... from Plato's image of man as a puppet of divine origin through Pirandello's (1921) and Hofmannsthal's (1922) treatments of the general theme. An introductory section documents manifestations of the metaphor in Shakespeare and Cervantes. A second section discusses <u>El gran teatro del mundo</u> in terms of its significance as the literary monument in which Calderón converts the simple metaphor into an actual drama. The third and final section comments on the nuances detected in the theme as treated in the modern era by Hofmannsthal and Pirandello.

Vázquez Zamora, Rafael. "El gran teatro del mundo en 1952." Insula, 7, No. 76 (1952), 12.

In a report on the Compañía Lope de Vega's production of El gran teatro del mundo, directed by José Tamayo, in the Teatro de la Comedia, Madrid, the author uses his favourable review as a point of departure for lamentation on the lack of public interest in, and response to, the Spanish classics. Holding the French up as a model to be imitated, Vázquez wistfully speculates: "...¿y si probásemos a perderle el miedo a lo que hasta ahora ha sido nuestro mejor teatro? ¿Y si uno, por lo menos, de los teatros oficiales, se dedicara exclusivamente, ya que están subvencionados, a presentarnos...el gran repertorio del teatro español...?"

Baquero Goyanes, Mariano. "El tema del Gran teatro del mundo en las Empresas políticas de Saavedra Fajardo." Monteagudo (Univ. de Murcia), No. 1 (1953), 4-10.

Hesse, Everett W. "La dialéctica y el casuismo en Calderón." Estudios, 9, No. 27 (1953), 517-31.

The article outlines the history of the theme of El gran teatro del mundo from Plato through Calderón and Hofmannsthal to Pirandello.

Frenk Alatorre, Margit. "El gran teatro del mundo." Univ. de México, 11, No. 8 (1957), 22-25.

"El Teatro Español de México ha presentado en el antiguo convento de Acolman El gran teatro del mundo de Calderón de la Barca." The director was Alvaro Custodio.

Jacquot, J. "Le Théâtre du monde de Shakespeare à Calderón." RLC, 31 (1957), 341-72. (See review below, 1959.)

Jacquot's article is a valuable contribution because of his research into ancient classical philosophers and Medieval writers who compared life to a stage: Democritus, Terence, Epictetus, Seneca, Plotinus, Augustine, Chrysostomus, etc. In the humanistic period, Ficino, Erasmus, and Vives repeat the same idea. However, Jacquot's article is more important for the contrasting ideas on Shakespeare and Calderón than because of its scholarship. He develops and brings together the ideas of life as a stage and life as a dream in Calderón's philosophical and theological thought. A major part of his article is aimed at the possible discovery of the sources of this idea in Elizabethan, Spanish, and French drama. However, he admits that : "Pour la période que nous avons étudiée, celle de Shakespeare, Lope, Calderón, Corneille et Rotrou, un examen plus exhaustif serait nécessaire."

Olmedilla, Carlos. "Lope y Calderón..." (1957). See Studies — General.

Sánchez, Alberto. "Reminiscencias cervantinas..." (1957). See Studies — General.

Bartina, Sebastián. "La Biblia y Calderón. Contenido bíblico en El gran teatro del mundo." Razón y Fe, 158 (1958), 337-54, and 160 (1959), 39-54. (Reprinted as a book, Barcelona, Edit. IFIBA, 1958. Pp. 36.)

This long article is divided into an Introduction, four parts, and a Conclusion. Bartina finds "en la estructura de El gran teatro del mundo varios planos que integran el conjunto." These are "teológico, filosófico, literario y artístico." After discussing these in some detail, the author takes the first 214 lines of the play, and refers to Biblical passages where similar ideas are expressed. Then he abandons the line by line method, and deals with "Pasajes bíblicos explícitamente citados," of which he finds seven. Another part of the study is devoted to "Grandes temas bíblicos," and another to "Sentencias, alusiones, y reminiscencias bíblicas." Among the valuable contributions in this article, we should point out the fact that Calderón seems to have used directly the Vulgate version of the Bible.

Hunter, William A. "The Seventeenth-Century..." (1958). See Studies — General.

Jacquot, J. "Le Théâtre du monde de Shakespeare a Calderón."
LR, 13 (1959), 90-91. (Rev. of Jacquot, 1957, by B. Debandt.)

Crumbach, F. H. "Calderón: Das grosse Welttheater." In Die
Struktur des Epischen Theaters: Dramaturgie der Kontraste,
Braunschweig, Waisenhaus, 1960, pp. 141-46.

Gascó Contell, E. "Una representación de Calderón en Alemania."
Estafeta Literaria, No. 196 (1960), 5.

Production of El gran teatro del mundo, by Wilhelm Michael
Mund, in the open-air theatre of the Industrie-Festspiele,
Wetzlar.

MacLachlan, Elaine, "Calderón's El gran teatro del mundo and
the Counter-Reformation in Spain." In Biblioteca degli
Eruditi e dei Bibliofili, Florence, 1960. Pp. 18. (Reprinted
in Scritti vari dedicati a M. Parenti, Florence, Sansoni,
1960, pp. 181-90.)

Escobar, Ignacio. "Teatro sacramental..." (1961). See Studies —
General.

Hunter, William A. "Toward a More Authentic Text of Calderón's
El gran teatro del mundo." HR, 29 (1961), 240-44.

On the basis of a manuscript adaptation of this play, in
1640-41, into Nahuatl, the language of the Aztecs, the author
states that Valbuena Prat's theory of the work's having been
written as early as 1633 is correct. This early translation
is compared to the Pando edition of 1717 and the princeps
edition of 1655. Discrepancies found are "insufficient to
justify serious doubts as to the general reliability of the
Pando edition," but they do suggest that "perhaps the edition
of 1655 is more faithful to the original composition than has
been suspected heretofore."

Lorenz, Erika. "Weltmakel und Eucharistie (Eine Bemerkung zu
Calderóns Grossen Welttheater)." RF, 73 (1961), 393-98.

Deals with the symbolism of the Eucharist in <u>El gran teatro del mundo</u>.

Rowland, A. K. "<u>El gran teatro del mundo</u> en Oxford." <u>The New Vida Hispánica</u> (London), No. 1 (1962), 25-26, 32.

Schwarz, Egon. <u>Hofmannsthal und Calderón</u> (1962). See Studies — General.

Hunter, William A. "Unas versiones aztecas de tres comedias del Siglo de Oro." <u>BH</u>, 61 (1963), 319-21.

The author discusses three manuscripts now in the Bancroft Library of the University of California of three <u>comedias</u> translated into Nahuatl, of which one is Calderón's <u>El gran teatro del mundo</u>, with dates to support a date of composition much earlier than 1649, when it was first performed.

Monleón, José. "Dos autos..." (1963). See Studies — General.

Sofer, Johann. "Idee und Gestaltung..." (1963). See Studies — General.

Mitchell, Margarete Koch. <u>Die christliche...</u> (1965). See Studies — General.

Suárez-Galbán, Eugenio. "Calderón y Pirandello." <u>Bol. de la Acad. de Artes y Ciencias de Puerto Rico</u>, 2 (1966), 907-16.

Calderón (<u>El gran teatro del mundo</u>) and Pirandello (<u>Sei personaggi in cerca d'autore</u>) combined one reality with another, presenting characters who know that they are characters, and giving them considerable freedom. On the other hand, "mientras Calderón, mediante la alegoría, afirma e ilustra, Pirandello, apoyándose en la conciencia dolorida y operante, indaga." Thus, while poles apart philosophically, both dramatists use the same technique.

Fiore, Robert Louis. <u>Neo-Scholasticism...</u> (1967). See Studies — General.

Pérez, Louis C. "Preceptiva dramática en El gran teatro del mundo." Hispanó, 10, No. 30 (1967), 1-6.

Guárdate del agua mansa

Herreras, Domiciano. Fuentes españolas de "La escuela de los maridos" de Molière. Málaga, Autor (Distributed by Gredos), 1967. Pp. 93.

Antonio Hurtado de Mendoza's El marido hace mujer y el trato muda costumbre (major); Calderón's Guárdate del agua mansa, and Lope de Vega's El mayor imposible and La discreta enamorada (minor).

Hado y divisa de Leonido y Marfisa

Leavitt, Sturgis E. "The Gracioso..." (1955). See Studies — General.

La hija del aire

Ferraro, Sergio. "Bibliografia..." (1957). See Studies — General.

Parker, Alexander A. "Metáfora y símbolo..." (1964). See Studies — General.

Edwards, Gwynne. "Calderón's La hija del aire in the Light of his Sources." BHS, 43 (1966), 177-96.

After Semíramis blended with myths of the Semitic fertility goddess, Shemiram, the Greeks left their stamp on the legend, including Diodorus Siculus' Bibliotheca Historica, one of Calderón's chief sources. Another is Marcus Antonius Coccius Sabellicus, Rapsodiae Historicae Enneadum (1498); the third is Virués' play, La gran Semíramis (pub. 1609). Calderón, however, used all this very freely, and improved on it, discarding everything irrelevant and occasionally reaching "an intensity that makes one think of the great classical plays."

Freund, Markéta L. Baroque Technique... (1966). See Studies —
General.

Edwards, Gwynne. "Calderón's La hija del aire and the Classical
Type of Tragedy." BHS, 44 (1967), 161-94.

An analysis of this two-part work by Calderón in the light of
classical tragedy. The author denies that the work can be
considered a typical tragedy, but finds classical tragic
characteristics in the Nino-Menon-Semíramis grouping. Other
features mentioned in the study fall outside of the traditional concept of what is tragedy. The author concludes that
this work is possibly "Calderón's most moving expression of
man's tragic predicament."

Ochse, Horst. Studien... (1967). See Studies — General.

Rogers, Daniel. "'¡Cielos! ¿Quién en Ninias habla?': Mother-Son
Impersonation in La hija del aire." BCom, 20, No. 1 (1968),
1-4.

A note which deals with an important detail of La hija del
aire, Part II, the return to power of Queen Semíramis through
her impersonation of her son. The dramatic possibilities of
the impersonation and its function in the play are studied.

El hijo del sol, Faetón

Gallego Morell, Antonio. "El mito..." (1956). See Studies —
General.

Aubrun, Charles V. "Les Débuts du drama lyrique..." (1964).
See Studies — General.

La humildad coronada de las plantas

Lastarria, Miguel. "La humildad coronada de las plantas de
Calderón de la Barca." Finis Terrae (Santiago de Chile), 8,
No. 32 (1961), 56-87.

A description of the plot and central themes of one of the most unusual of Calderón's <u>autos sacramentales</u>, in which most of the characters are plants and trees.

La iglesia sitiada

Wilson, Edward M. "<u>La iglesia sitiada</u>: A Calderonian Puzzle." <u>MLR</u>, 59 (1964), 583-94.

A series of observations on this <u>auto sacramental</u>, attributed to Calderón. The author believes that it was written, or revised, for Corpus Christi, 1636, and that Calderón was at least acquainted with it, but that it is probably the work of another. An appendix corrects a reading of the printed text.

El jardín de Falerina

Aubrun, Charles V. "Une anticipation de Calderón: La Télévision magique dans <u>El jardín de Falerina</u>." In <u>Estudios de Filología e Historia literaria lusohispanas e iberoamericanas publicados para celebrar el tercer lustro del Instituto de Estudios Hispánicos, Portugueses e Iberoamericanos de la Universidad Estatal de Utrecht</u>, The Hague, 1966, pp. 51-59.

An apparent reality arises among the others, as in Velázquez's self-presentation in <u>Las Meninas</u>. The audience has time and space abolished by illusion, as Falerina, with Marfisa and Lisidante in Sicily, shows them Rugero and Bradamante at Charlemagne's palace, as if on television. Then she "turns off the picture," but the ambiguity of two fictions remains.

Pollin, Alice M. "Calderón's <u>Falerina</u> and Music." <u>Music and Letters</u>, 49 (1968), 317-28.

The theme of <u>El jardín de Falerina</u> and Calderón's use of music in his drama and poetry.

El mágico prodigioso

Heaton, H. C. "Calderón and <u>El mágico prodigioso</u>." <u>HR</u>, 19

(1951), 11-36 and 93-103.

In an article, the object of which is to probe the accuracy
of various assertions made by Morel-Fatio in his 1877 edition
regarding the transmission of the text of this play, Heaton
concludes, after a close textual analysis of the two extant
versions of El mágico prodigioso (1. the "Yepes version,"
Osuna Library MS, now in the Biblioteca Nacional, Madrid;
2. the version published in Parte veinte de comedias varias...,
Madrid, 1663), that "the Osuna MS is not the autograph
original of the play," and that 1637, the date of the Yepes
version, is only a terminus ad quem for the composition of the
original play. He assumes the existence of an earlier version
of the play, which may or not have been written by Calderón,
which was adapted by Calderón for a special performance in
Yepes. Heaton cites the Yepes version as "a sample, perhaps
the best one we have, of Calderón's method of procedure in
his refundiciones." The arguments presented by Heaton in this
article are convincingly refuted by A. E. Sloman, in "El
mágico prodigioso: Calderón Defended Against the Charge of
Theft" (see next item). (Harry C. Heaton, 1885-1950, died on
Dec. 28, 1950. In a necrology, HR, 19, 1951, pp. 165-67, we
read: "Only a few hours before his death he returned the
carefully corrected galley proofs of his article on 'Calderón
and El mágico prodigioso'." Angel Valbuena Prat, "Crónicas:
Estados Unidos," Clav, 2, No. 10, 1951, p. 78, in another
necrological notice, sums up Heaton's many contributions to
Hispanic studies, adding a note of caution with regard to the
acceptance of some of his theories on Calderón's theatre, an
area in which "Heaton ha dejado una obra tan importante como
peligrosa.")

Sloman, Albert E. "El mágico prodigioso: Calderón Defended
Against the Charge of Theft." HR, 20 (1952), 212-22.

H. C. Heaton, in an article published posthumously in HR, 19
(1951), mentioned above, makes several claims with respect
to this comedia. He postulates the existence of a common
source, now lost, for the two known versions: the Yepes
manuscript and the printed version in Parte veinte de comedias
varias (1663). Heaton then argues that the manuscript version
is later than the Parte text and even claims that the authorship of the play remains to be proved. Heaton had previously
questioned Calderón's integrity in his article, "On La selva
confusa Attributed to Calderón" (PMLA, 44, 1929, pp. 243-73),

in which he thought he had given conclusive proof of
Calderón's plagiary. His approach to El mágico is influenced
by his prior study. In both instances, Heaton seems to draw
completely unwarranted conclusions from his careful collation
of a Calderón manuscript and a Parte text. Sloman easily
refutes the claims of Heaton, in many cases simply by drawing
the logical conclusions from the evidence adduced by Heaton
himself.

Atkins, S. "Goethe, Calderón and Faust: Der Tragödie Zweiter
Teil." Germanic Review, 28 (1953), 83-98.

Serrano Poncela, Segundo. "Amor y apetito..." (1953). See
Studies — General.

Rousset, Jean. La Littérature de l'âge baroque en France. Paris,
J. Corti, 1953. Pp. 312. (Later printings.)

Brief mention of El mágico prodigioso as an example of
Baroque drama outside of France.

Fucilla, Joseph G. "Un'Imitazione dell'Aminta nel Mágico
prodigioso di Calderón." Studi Tassiani, 6 (1956), 29-33.
(Reprinted in Fucilla's Superbi colli e altri saggi, Rome,
1963, pp. 181-85.)

Parker, Alexander A. The Approach... (1957). See Studies —
General.

Pageard, Robert. "Fausto y El mágico prodigioso." In Goethe en
España, Madrid, CSIC, 1958, pp. 136-66.

Gérard, Albert. "Pour une phénoménologie..." (1963). See
Studies — General.

May, T. E. "The Symbolism of El mágico prodigioso." RR, 54
(1963), 95-112.

The author argues that this play is an exact and perfect work
of art; the play must be understood as profoundly witty. He
discusses the symbolism of the pact with the devil and makes
comparisons with Marlowe's Dr. Faustus. The study continues
with an analysis of the play and points the symbolism of the
Biblical references and Christian teaching.

Franzbach, Martin. "Die 'Lustige Person' (gracioso) auf der
spanischen Bühne und ihre Funktion, dargelegt an Calderóns
El mágico prodigioso." NS, 14 (1965), 61-72.

There are fine possibilities in El mágico prodigioso: the
graciosos parody Cipriano and Justina, and overlap the
subordinate action without disturbing things, though they are
in 29 of the 60 scenes. As Cipriano seeks to define God, the
graciosos can show the transitoriness of everything worldly.
Thus they partake of the Idealism-Realism duality, so typical
of the era.

Hesse, Everett W. "The Function of the Romantic Action in El
mágico prodigioso." BCom, 17, No. 1 (1965), 5-7.

Menéndez Pelayo, not understanding this, attacked the play as
an out-of-place comedia de enredo. Truth is the connecting
link: Cipriano seeks, and gradually finds, the true God and
an idea of true love (self-sacrifice), while the Devil is
forced to reveal the truth and thus rescue Justina's reputation. The romantic action is the "plane of reality" that
Calderón uses "to clothe in dramatic form certain ideas he
expounds on the religious plane."

Szarota, Elida Maria. Künstler,... (1967). See Studies — General.

Parker, Alexander A. "The Rôle of the Graciosos in El mágico
prodigioso." In Hans Flasche, Litterae hispanae et lusitanae,
Munich, 1968, pp. 317-30. (See Flasche, 1968, Studies —
General.)

An excellent study of the graciosos in the subplot, examining
their rôle in relation to the main plot and theme.

Salvador y Conde, J. "Interpretación poética del arte." RIE,
27 (1968), 206-45.

Includes a quotation from El mágico prodigioso.

González Echevarría, Roberto. "En torno al tema de El mágico
prodigioso." Rev. de Estudios Hispánicos, 3 (1969), 207-20.

Mañanas de abril y mayo

Vernon, P. F. "Wycherley's First Comedy and its Spanish Source."
CL, 18 (1966), 132-44.

In an era when interest in Spanish drama was fashionable,
Wycherley turned to Calderón's Mañanas de abril y mayo, seeing
a chance to use its two sets of lovers in a "courtship
comedy ... fused with social satire." More than half the
English play is all new, with the graciosos' antics replaced
by satire with middle-class characters. Jealousy is deplored,
and Calderón's long speeches give way to "quick conversational
exchanges."

El mayor encanto amor

Shergold, N. D. "The First Performance of Calderón's El mayor
encanto amor." BHS, 35 (1958), 24-27.

Shergold establishes the date of the first performance of
this play as not having taken place on June 23 ("la noche de
San Juan"), in view of what is stated in a Jesuit newsletter;
"por la guerra empezada entre católicos." The performance was
postponed two days, and perhaps a fourth one, which was to be
offered "a todo el pueblo por su dinero," did not take place
"because of the uncertainties of the political situation."
There is the possibility, Shergold points out, that, since
there was "a second series of performances (which) ran from
29 July to 3 August," it was due to the fact that the play
"pleased, and was therefore repeated," or it was in order to
make up to the people for the performance which had not taken
place. There is discussion also as to whether there were two
versions of the play.

Sloman, Albert E. The Dramatic Craftsmanship... (1958). See
Studies — General.

Viqueira, José Maria. "Temas clásicos..." (1959). See Studies —
General.

Sloman, Albert E. "The Missing Lines of El mayor encanto amor."
In Studia Philologica. Homenaje ofrecido a Dámaso Alonso,
Vol. 3, Madrid, Gredos, 1963, pp. 425-30.

The author takes exception to the explanation earlier given
by H. C. Heaton concerning the difference in Quiñones and
Quiñones-Coello editions of the play. He believes that the
omission of certain verses is owing to carelessness and not
intent, nor that it was done by Calderón himself.

Aubrun, Charles V. "Les Débuts du drame lyrique..." (1964). See
Studies — General.

Garasa, Delfín Locadio. "Circe en la literatura española..."
(1964). See Studies — General.

Mazur, Oleh. "Various Impacts..." (1968). See Studies — General.

El mayor monstruo los celos (El mayor monstruo del mundo)

Hesse, Everett W. "Obsesiones en El mayor monstruo del mundo,
de Calderón." Estudios, 8 (1952), 395-409.

Citing this play as one of Calderón's four great dramas de
celos, Hesse orients his analysis to the theme of the
obsessions of its principal characters. The jealousy of
Herodes is of course the principal obsession, to which are
subordinated the obsessions of his wife, Mariene, and of the
Emperador Octaviano. Mariene's obsessive melancholy and her
fear of the puñal undoubtedly are caused by the prediction
that she will die by the hand of her husband. The obsession
of Octaviano is the love kindled in him by the retrato of a
woman of whose identity he is ignorant (although it is, of

course, a <u>retrato</u> of Mar**í**ene). The <u>puñal</u> and the <u>retrato</u> are effectively discussed both as symbols and as the coordinating elements of the obsessions upon which this drama is based.

- "El arte calderoniano en <u>El mayor monstruo los celos</u>." <u>Clav</u>, 7, No. 38 (1956), 18-30.

    Shows the elaborate and exact planning in contriving a unified plot made up of apparently independent motifs.

Isar, Erbert E. "La cuestión..." (1958). See Studies — General.

Fernández, Sergio. "El mal amor." In <u>Ensayos sobre literatura española de los siglos XVI y XVII</u>, Mexico, Univ. Nac. Autónoma de México, 1961, pp. 217-36.

Aubrun, Charles V. "Le Déterminisme naturel..." (1962). See Studies — General.

<u>El médico de su honra</u>

Amezúa y Mayo, Agustín González de. "Un dato para las fuentes de <u>El médico de su honra</u>." In <u>Opúsculos histórico-literarios</u>, I, Madrid, CSIC, 1951, pp. 3-18. (From <u>RH</u>, 21, 1909, 395-411.)

    A case of vengeance included in the <u>Libro de casos notables que han sucedido en la ciudad de Córdoba...</u> (early 17th century MS, pub. in Madrid, 1949) is proposed as the source for the blood-letting dénouement of <u>El médico de su honra</u>.

Brenan, Gerald. <u>The Literature...</u> (1951). See Studies — General.

Kossoff, A. David. "<u>El médico de su honra</u> and <u>La amiga de Bernal Francés</u>." <u>HR</u>, 24 (1956), 66-70.

    The play and the old Spanish ballad.

Parker, Alexander A. <u>The Approach...</u> (1957). See Studies — General.

Sloman, Albert E. "Calderón's El médico de su honra and La amiga de Bernal Francés." BHS, 34 (1957), 168-69.

Sloman's note is a reaction to another note by A. David Kossoff of the same title (see above). Sloman points out that Kossoff was at fault for not having read the Médico attributed to Lope de Vega, and Sloman's concluding words are "... Mr. Kossoff's main point is invalidated by the extant text of the first El médico." Sloman realizes that Kossoff was "misled by Schaeffer" (Geschichte des spanischen Nationaldramas, Leipzig, 1890, II, 7), when he assumed that the famous scene in which the jealous husband unexpectedly returns home and speaks to his wife in the darkness was not found in the Lope play. It seems obvious that Kossoff did not bother to see the latter play after he consulted the "authority" of Schaeffer (whom he quoted on his page 70, note 9), who "condemns the scene outright as a superfluous addition to the earlier play previously attributed to Lope" (Kossoff, page 70). In sum, Sloman expresses his disagreement with Kossoff's findings and views, and corrects the misconceptions which appeared in the Kossoff article.

- The Dramatic Craftsmanship... (1958). See Studies — General.

Wardropper, Bruce W. "Poetry and Drama in Calderón's El médico de su honra." RR, 49 (1958), 3-11.

Wardropper starts his article with a complaint about the critical approach to the Comedia by contemporary scholars: "Drama criticism in the Hispanic field tends to be somewhat old-fashioned. Hispanists usually regard the theatre of the seventeenth century as though it were drama in the post-Romantic sense. They judge it by its degree of realism, by its value as a social document, by its fitness as a vehicle of ideas. If they analyze it esthetically it is to the dramatic structure or characterization that they point. They seek in it drama, not poetry.... Some Hispanic critics have felt pangs of conscience about neglecting the poetry in drama. But their reaction has often been misguided: they have counted verses for non-poetic reasons; or they have, following what may well be an ironic treatise by Lope de Vega, attempted to force certain phases of the action into particular metrical molds. The poetic in drama is not reducible to such mechanics and arithmetics." Wardropper proposed his own approach to remedy the situation using as guinea pig Calderón's <u>El médico</u> <u>de su honra</u>: "I suggest that dramatic poetry might be studied in much the same way as one studies lyric poetry. And this recommendation is hardly revolutionary. Our colleagues in other literary disciplines have been doing this for years. As an illustration of what I mean I should like to examine one aspect of the poetry of <u>El médico de su honra</u>: its imagery." Wardropper sees the whole play to be "a complex extended metaphor." "Don Gutierre, the protagonist, who suspects his wife —quite wrongly, as it turns out— of having brought dishonor on his good name, regards himself as a metaphorical physician." "Gutierre not only regards himself in this poetic way, but succeeds in making other characters in the play see him in the same light."

Touchard, A. P. "Calderón on Dramatic Action: A propos of <u>The</u> <u>Surgeon of His Own Honor</u>." <u>TDR</u>, 4 (1959), 108-09.

Referring to a production of <u>El médico de su honra</u> by Charles Dullin, Touchard comments on the differences between the classical theatre and the modern theatre. The first concerned itself with an interweaving of actions, each bringing the one subject of the play into different perspectives; the modern play presents an interweaving of ideas each diverging from any potential central theme. The difference essentially lies in the fact that one is a theatre of action (not necessarily devoid of a moral subject), while the other is one of words (with little more than linear action at times).

Abel, L. "Art While Being Ruled: Abram Tertz, Brecht, and Calderón." <u>Commentary</u>, 29 (1960), 405-12.

The author compares Brecht's <u>The Measures Taken</u> with Calderón's <u>El médico de su honra</u> as products of a "totalitarian period." After underscoring the extreme cruelty of both the king and don Gutierre, Abel states that "the play breathes an almost pious devotion to the society for whose values the king and Gutierre stand."

Soons, C. A. "The Convergence of Doctrine and Symbol in <u>El</u> <u>médico de su honra</u>." <u>RF</u>, 72 (1960), 370-80.

Watson, A. Irvine. "Peter the Cruel or Peter the Just? A
Reappraisal of the Rôle Played by King Peter in Calderón's
El médico de su honra." RJ, 14 (1963), 322-46.

A detailed article in which the author seeks to show that
Pedro is really el justiciero throughout the play: in his
attitude toward his brother's fall, Leonor's complaint, the
pretendientes, Coquín, the sword-play of Gutierre and Arias,
and Gutierre's murder of his wife. He is stern, even severe,
but never cruel.

Parker, Alexander A. "Metáfora y símbolo..." (1964). See
Studies — General.

Rogers, Daniel. "'Tienen los celos pasos de ladrones': Silence
in Calderón's El médico de su honra." HR, 33 (1965), 273-89.

Much of the play is stealthy, involving spying and suspicion.
Jealousy, not honour, prevails here, and D. Gutierre must not
stoop to pedir celos of Mencía. Instead he must sentir y
callar, and be guilty of the "unworthy, underhand behavior"
that makes him speak the lines about "pasos de ladrones."
Silence also appears in many lesser connections, and is, as
the author states, "of the play's essence."

Freund, Markéta L. Baroque Technique... (1966). See Studies —
General.

Sparks, Amy. "Honor in Hartzenbusch's 'Refundición' of
Calderón's El médico de su honra." Hisp, 49 (1966), 410-13.

Hartzenbusch makes Enrique and Mencía guiltier. They flee
together, and this produces the King's approval of Gutierre's
killing Mencía, though Gutierre himself questions it, and
seeks consolation in the thought that enough such deeds would
discourage wives from yielding to temptation. Jealousy is
also emphasized more than in Calderón, and the lessening of
the love-vs.-duty conflict diminishes Gutierre's stature.

Hesse, Everett W. Calderón de la Barca (1967). See Studies —
General.

200

Soons, C. Alan. *Ficción y comedia...* (1967). See Studies —
General.

Wilson, Edward M. *Some Aspects...* (1967). See Studies — General.

Mejor está que estaba

Cordaso, Francisco. "Spanish Influence,..." (1953). See
Studies — General.

El monstruo de los jardines

Aubrun, Charles V. "Les Débuts du drame lyrique..." (1946).
See Studies — Ceneral.

Ni amor se libra de amor

Viqueira, José Maria. "Temas clásicos..." (1959). See Studies —
General.

La niña de Gómez Arias

Rozzell, Ramon. "The Song and Legend of Gómez Arias." *HR*, 20
(1952), 91-107.

Sloman, Albert E. *The Dramatic Craftsmanship...* (1958). See
Studies — General.

Rozzell, Ramon. "Estudio del tema de Gómez Arias." In Luis Vélez
de Guevara, *La niña de Gómez Arias*, ed. Ramon Rozzell, Granada,
Univ. de Granada, 1959, pp. 15-46.

Reference to Calderón.

Avalle-Arce, Juan Bautista. "El cantar de La niña de Gómez
    Arias." BHS, 44 (1967), 43-58.

An investigation of the primitive song, the origin of which
goes back to the middle of the fourteenth century (with
references to Calderón's play).

No hay más fortuna que Dios

Schmid, A. Commentary, in his translation into Rhaeto-Romanic
    of No hay más fortuna que Dios (Ventura mo en Diu). In
    Società Retorumantscha, Chur. Annalas, 71 (1958), 121-78.

Fiore, Robert Louis. Neo-Scholasticism... (1967). See Studies —
    General.

No hay burlas con el amor

Tyler, Richard W. "'Pecado nefando' y 'pecado elefante'." In
    Homenaje a Rodríguez-Moñino, II, Madrid, Castalia, 1966, pp.
    289-91.

Reference to No hay burlas con el amor, among other plays of
the period.

No hay que creer ni en la verdad

Černý, Václav. "Una nueva comedia de Calderón." Atlántida, 4
    (1966), 398-419.

No hay que creer ni en la verdad is another Calderón MS found
by Černý in the same Czechoslovakian castle as El gran duque
de Gandía. It is a typical Calderón capa y espada play, with
a highly complicated plot and several galanes and their ladies
skating on the thin ice of honour and jealousy. Černý dates
the work as 1649, and announces a forthcoming edition, the
first anejo of the theatre journal, Segismundo. (See Editions —
Individual Works.)

Siebenmann, Gustav. "Descubrimiento de una comedia de Calderón."
  Humboldt, No. 31 (1967), 96.

  A brief note announcing the discovery and forthcoming publication by Václav Černý of another play by Calderón, No hay
  que creer ni en la verdad.

No siempre lo peor es cierto

Cordaso, Francisco. "Spanish Influence..." (1953). See
  Studies — General.

Anderson, J. B. "The Spanish Source of Digby's Elvira." RLC,
  43 (1969), 108-26.

  No siempre lo peor es cierto.

Origen, pérdida y restauración de la Virgen del Sagrario

Hermenegildo, Alfredo. Burgos... (1958). See Studies — General.

Peor está que estaba

Cordaso, Francisco. "Spanish Influence..." (1953). See
  Studies — General.

Hogan, Floriana T. "Notes on Savage's Love in a Veil and
  Calderón's Peor está que estaba." Restoration and 18th
  Century Theatre Research, 8, No. 1 (1969), 23-29.

El pintor de su deshonra

Watson, A. Irvine. "El pintor de su deshonra and the Neo-
  Aristotelian Theory of Tragedy." BHS, 40 (1963), 17-34.
  (Repub. in Wardropper, Critical Essays, New York, 1965,
  pp. 203-23.)

Soons, C. A. "El problema de los juicios estéticos en Calderón: El pintor de su deshonra." RF, 76 (1964), 155-62.

The article refers to various painting terms that Calderón employs in his play. Calderón unfolds his creation in three dimensions so that one scene is reflected in three mirrors, the widest of which encompasses the other two and the smallest is but a part of what is reflected in the others. The author believes the play to be a work of art with no other pretext than the aesthetic, with no need for theological or philosophical trappings.

- Ficción y comedia... (1967). See Studies — General.

Paterson, Alan K. G. "The Comic and Tragic Melancholy of Juan Roca: A Study of Calderón's El pintor de su deshonra." FMLS, 5 (1969), 244-61.

El príncipe constante

Sloman, Albert E. The Sources of Calderón's "El príncipe constante." With a Critical Edition of its Immediate Source, "La fortuna adversa del infante don Fernando de Portugal" (A Play Attributed to Lope de Vega). Oxford, Basil Blackwell, 1950. Pp. vii, 228.
Rev: Arturo del Hoyo, Insula, 6, No. 72 (1951), 5 (A very complimentary review: "un modelo de sobriedad y de investigación literaria."); E. Allison Peers, BHS, 28 (1951), 222-23 (Lavish praise in every respect. Peers singles out for special commendation the section in the first or expository part, in which Sloman's "analytical skill and clarity of expression principally appear (as) he investigates Calderón's use of his borrowed material, as regards theme and dramatic technique." Peers cites the edition of La fortuna adversa as as a model of its kind.); Everett W. Hesse, HR, 20 (1952), 261-63 (Sloman is praised for having done a most commendable job in accomplishing his two-fold purpose: (a) to establish the sources of El príncipe constante and to make available the only extant text of its immediate source, La fortuna adversa, and (b) to study Calderón's use of borrowed material in order to shed more light on his dramatic technique. Sloman, Hesse notes, places the date of composition of the

source play between 1595 and 1604, and cautiously suggests
Francisco Agustín Tárrega as its author. He also intimates
that Tárrega's lost play, El príncipe constante, mentioned
by Gracián, may be La fortuna adversa. If this is true, then
Calderón has derived both his title and material from the
same source. Although Hesse has reservations about Sloman's
attribution of the play to Tárrega, he considers "the
essential excellence of the study" unmarred by the few
exceptions he takes, and counts the study of Calderón's use
of borrowed material and the analysis of El príncipe constante
as extremely significant contributions to our understanding
and appreciation of the play.); A. A. Parker, MLR, 47 (1952),
254-56 (Parker considers this work "a valuable contribution
to the understanding of Calderón's technique," and feels
that Sloman has made a very plausible case for identifying
La fortuna adversa with the unknown Príncipe constante of
Tárrega. Apart from a few minor corrections and suggestions
regarding the text, Parker's only criticism is directed at
Sloman's approach to the play through its connection with
the scholastic definition of Fortitude which "tends to blur
its typically Calderonian theme: the conflict not between
good and evil, but between good and good."); Angel Valbuena
Prat, Clav, 3, No. 14 (1952), 77 (A very favourable and
complimentary review in every respect: "El estudio crítico
de El príncipe constante, de Calderón, es un modelo de fina
y honda capacidad de análisis." Valbuena Prat is inclined to
be convinced by Sloman's suggested attribution of La fortuna
adversa to Tárrega.); Walther Mettmann, RF, 65 (1953), 197-
99; A. Rey, MP, 50 (1953), 278-80 (A valuable study, giving
insight into Calderón's dramatic technique; the edition of
La fortuna adversa is excellent.).

Whitby, William M. Structural Symbolism... (1954). See
Studies — General.

- "Calderón's El príncipe constante: Fénix's Rôle in the
Ransom of Fernando's Body." BCom, 8, No. 1 (1956), 1-4.

Kayser, Wolfgang. "Zur Struktur des Standhaften Prinzen von
Calderón." In Gestaltproblem der Dichtung, Bonn, Bouvier,
1957, pp. 67-82; and in Die Vortragsreise: Studien zur
Literatur, Bern, Franke Verlag, 1958, pp. 232-56.

This excellent study and analysis is divided into six parts:
1. "Zur Wirkungsgeschichte des Standhaften Prinzen"; 2."Ordo
successivorum und ordo simultaneorum"; 3. "Stufen und Rollen
im zentralen Geschehen"; 4. "Die Korrelation Fernando-Fénix";
5. "Das Typische der Struktur"; and 6. "Immermanns Deutung
des Standhaften Prinzen als tragödie." In the first part,
Kayser deals with the historical background and influence of
El príncipe constante among the German critics, stating that
since the time of A. W. Schlegel, two camps appeared with
regard to the Standhaften Prinzen. In the second part, among
other things, he makes reference to poetry, verse form, and
various other approaches of critics. Part three refers to
the levels and rôles in the main action. All of part four is
devoted to the correlation Fernando-Fénix. In part five,
Kayser states that his research on the structure of the
Standhaften Prinzen is only relevant if we look at other
Calderonian dramas and the rôle played by the feminine
figure, and so he takes several other Calderonian heroines
into account. In the last part of his study, Kayser points
out that Immermann is wrong in his interpretation because he
starts with a preconceived notion and follows it through.
Our author states that Immermann does not understand
Calderón's technique, and he ends his study by suggesting
that with Calderón's Príncipe constante a new type of
tragedy appeared.

Ortigoza Vieyra, Carlos. Los móviles de la comedia; Primera
Parte: "El príncipe constante" de Calderón de la Barca;
Segunda Parte: Investigación y estudio crítico, los móviles
del protagonista. Mexico, Robredo, 1957. Pp. 216.
Rev: John Brooks, Hisp, 41 (1958), 251-52 ("All admirers of
the Comedia should be grateful for this impassioned and
scholarly defense of its eternal values.... The book quotes
chapter and verse and takes a stand for independent analysis
and criticism and for more thoughtful and leisurely reading,
devoid of snap judgements."); Arnold G. Reichenberger, HR,
28 (1960), 70-72 ("The book's main purpose is to demonstrate
the validity of the author's teoría de los móviles by
studying 'solamente un persnaje'." "His method is to analyse
Fernando's speeches and to mark with an asterisk each
'resorte que mueve al príncipe Fernando'." Although Reichenberger states that "there are not as many móviles as there
are asterisks," he further comments: "We do not deny that
the various móviles — after eliminating the synonyms — are
there, but we can't see that they make the character of

Fernando a complex one." And he disagrees by stating in his
critical review that "The Comedia, with its view of Man
firmly rooted in la honra and la fe, is much more interested
in driving home a lesson than presenting the situation of an
individual. All variety, which is not necessarily complexity,
has to be evaluated against this common background."
Reichenberger closes his review with a paragraph which says
in part: "Much erudition and good judgement is in evidence
in some of the extended footnotes, almost excursus, in which
the author deals with questions not immediately pertinent to
his main concern.").

In the first part of the book, Ortigoza presents an historical
background of the criticism generally adverse to the Spanish
drama of the Golden Age from the XVII to the XIX centuries.
The author shows that this adverse criticism is due to the
misunderstanding of the nature of the Comedia, and repeats
the point of view expressed in his first volume (Los móviles
de la Comedia, Mexico, 1954): "The Comedia by its very nature
becomes a study of character but must rely on action for
development of character." The author answers the question
of how to appreciate and prove this development by proposing
the task of digging out the móviles or springs and forces
which cause the action of characters in situations. The
author suggests that one reason which has prevented the
observation of the Spanish drama from within is the difficulty of separating themes and dramatic impulses. The móviles,
or forces which cause the action of the characters in
situations, are mixed with the plot, and to express how they
motivate the action — without confusing them with the action
itself — is a difficult task because of the limitations of
language. In other words, the moving forces are easily
comprehended as the backbone of the action but difficult to
express as different from action: "sin ser la acción misma."
As for El príncipe constante, Ortigoza turns to prove the
wealth of motivation which develops Prince Fernando's
character "a la manera de la comedia." A great deal of
valuable information is provided about the play, including
sources, performances, editions, translations, and critical
opinions which have been expressed about the play through
the centuries. Specifically, the móviles of Fernando's
character are carefully analysed through the three acts, in
great detail. There is a final chart of the internal and
external móviles which are the mainsprings of Fernando's
action; and, in conclusion, Ortigoza lays down four principles
which sustain his theory: 1. Móviles develop the character of

the personage with great speed which produces changes;
2. Móviles impel, with varying shades, the forces of the
social, psychological, moral, philosophical and religious
order, and the action of the character in situations;
3. Móviles are dynamic causes which internally and externally
are acting in every movement of the characters; 4. Móviles
which originate impulses in the personage are part of him,
whose character shows and unrolls the action.

Sloman, Albert E. The Dramatic Craftsmanship... (1958). See
Studies — General.

Wardropper, Bruce W. "Christian and Moor in Calderón's El
príncipe constante." MLR, 53 (1958), 512-20.

The author, after recalling Entwistle's interpretation of
the play as "an imaginary auto sacramental," which Sloman
"endorsed and amplified..., introducing into it Thomistic
notions of Fortitude," and Wilson's study of the text, which
approaches the play as "I (Wilson) am moved while I am
reading the play," the author of this article proposes to
bridge the gap between the two positions. Wardropper's words
are: "Between Wilson's critical particularism and
Entwistle-Sloman's a priori schematic approach there is a
gulf which needs to be bridged." The author then proceeds to
quote the pertinent verses of both the Christian and the
Moorish characters which show their respective attitudes
towards time, death, eternal life, and other themes,
concluding that any "attempt to interpret the work either as
an allegory or as a comedia fails, it seems to me, because
it falls between these two treatments. More important, the
subject is treated poetically... (so) until, however, we
recognize that first and foremost Calderón is a dramatic
poet — rather than a dramatist who has chosen to write in
verse — we miss the nuances of his art."

Spitzer, Leo. "Die Figur der Fénix in Calderóns Standhaften
Prinzen." RJ, 10 (1959), 305-53. (Also pub. in Wardropper,
Critical Essays, New York, 1965, pp. 137-60.)

Spitzer deviates from Kayser's interpretation when he tries
to prove that the figure of Fénix is dramatically related to
that of Prince Fernando.

Gulsoy, Y., and J. H. Parker. "El príncipe constante: Drama barroco de la Contrarreforma." Hispanó, No. 9 (1960), 15-23.

The authors find that the play is one of triumphant martyrdom (not a tragedy), reflecting the Faith of a believing era.

Reichenberger, Arnold G. "Calderón's El príncipe constante: A Tragedy?" MLN, 75 (1960), 668-70. (Also pub. in Wardropper, Critical Essays, New York, 1965, pp. 161-63.)

Fernando is not a tragic hero. The suffering imposed upon him is not against his will and he does not struggle against it. He remains constant to the Faith, and wins sainthood and glory in death.

Parker, J. H. "Henry the Navigator: Hero of Peninsular Renaissance Fiction." Hisp, 44 (1961), 277-81.

Ricard, Robert. "Calderón et 'el mar de Fez'." Al-Andalus, 26 (1961), 468-70.

Calderón should not be chided too much for situating Fez by the sea. Two texts cited by Georges S. Colin, in a defence of Victor Hugo in 1945, state that ships were able to go by river from the sea to Fez. Therefore Fez could, to a certain extent, be considered a sea-port.

Wilson, Edward M. "An Early Rehash of Calderón's El príncipe constante." MLN, 76 (1961), 785-94.

A study of an early revision, in manuscript form, of El príncipe constante, which shows how easily a masterpiece could be made corrupt and debased, and illustrates the danger in accepting manuscript versions of plays as authentic, when there is no guarantee of their accuracy.

- "Fray Hortensio Paravicino's Protest Against El príncipe constante." Ibérida: Revista Filológica (Rio de Janeiro), No. 6 (1961), 245-66.

Gérard, Albert. "Pour une phénoménologie..." (1963). See Studies — General.

Seidler, Herbert. "Prunkreden..." (1964). See Studies — General.

Truman, R. W. "The Theme of Justice in Calderón's El príncipe constante." MLR, 59 (1964), 43-52.

The author shows how Fernando applies the principles of justice as set forth by St. Thomas Aquinas, Ulpian, and Cicero, in his treatment of Muley and in his attitude toward God and the Moorish king, how Muley and God also act with justice toward Fernando but that the king points up these laws in his unjust treatment of Fernando. He concludes that the theme of justice gives the play greater unity than has been claimed for it.

Shergold, N. D., and Peter Ure. "Dryden and Calderón: A New Spanish Source for The Indian Emperour." MLR, 61 (1966), 369-83.

Dryden, who had already written a version of El astrólogo fingido, this time followed El príncipe constante. Although there seems to be little in common with Montezuma, both plays concern "the clash of rival civilizations and religions." Fernando's sufferings and death are also much like Montezuma's. Dryden probably had a text and a summary of El príncipe constante at hand, but by no means imitated slavishly, in fact, he followed Calderón closely at the start, but then branched off.

Stroman, B. "Theater op het Holand festival." Die Vlaamse Gids, 50 (1966), 428-29.

The performance of the Polish version of El príncipe constante, by Juliusz Slowacki, at the Odéon, Paris, in the summer of 1966, was widely acclaimed. (See "Comedia Perform-ances," BCom, 19, No. 1, 1967, p. 23.) Playing before a select group of actors, critics, journalists, etc. (about 100 nightly), Ryszard Cieslak, as Prince Fernando, reached a peak of intensity, as prescribed by Jerzy Grotowski, director of the Wroclaw company. In this interpretation, Fernando becomes a kind of brother to Hamlet. Pictures of the production appeared in The New York Times Magazine, Sept. 11, 1966, Le Théâtre dans le Monde, 15, No. 1 (1966), 23, and Il Dramma, Nos. 359-60 (1966), 118. See also Time, Oct. 24, 1969, pp. 77-78, on this version as presented by Grotowski's Polish Laboratory Theatre.

Szarota, Elida Maria. <u>Künstler...</u> (1967). See Studies — General.

Brüggemann, Werner. "Johannes Schulzes Schrift 'Ueber den <u>Standhaften Prinzen</u> des Don Pedro Calderón de la Barca' (1811)." In <u>Gesammelte Aufsätze zur Kulturgeschichte Spaniens</u>, 24 (1968), 397-418.

Grotowski, Jerzy. "La profazione dei miti." <u>Sipario</u>, 13, No. 264 (1968), 11-13.

An interview with the director, Jerzy Grotowski, dealing with his production of <u>El príncipe constante</u>, an adaptation by the Polish writer Juliusz Slowacki. (This adaptation by Slowacki, 1809-1849, was reprinted, as <u>Ksiaze niezlomny</u>, in his <u>Dziela</u>, Vol. IX, Warsaw, 1952, pp. 257-374.)

Ouaknine, Serge. "Alrededor de <u>El príncipe constante</u> por Grotowski." <u>Primer Acto</u>, No. 95 (1968), 28-43.

A detailed examination of the dramatic technique, staging, and acting in Grotowski's presentation of <u>El príncipe constante</u>.

Rivers, Elias L. "Fénix's Sonnet in Calderón's <u>Príncipe constante</u>." <u>HR</u>, 37 (1969), 452-58.

This article, "in belated homage to Otis H. Green," clarifies the antithesis, generally misunderstood, between Don Fernando and Fénix. Rivers explains that Fénix's comparison of human life with that of stars represents the immortality of the human soul and not the death of the human body.

Psalle et Sile

Wilson, Edward M. "A Key to Calderón's <u>Psalle et Sile</u>." In <u>Hispanic Studies in Honour of I. González Llubera</u>, Oxford, Dolphin, 1959, pp. 429-40.

Wilson analyses the poem (printed in 1662), and concludes that it is really a meditation based on the pattern established by St. Ignatius of Loyola.

El purgatorio de San Patricio

Livermore, Ann L. "The Magic Flute and Calderón." Music and
  Letters, No. 36 (1955), 7-16.

  Mrs. Livermore finds a surprising likeness to Calderón's El
  purgatorio de San Patricio in the libretto of Mozart's The
  Magic Flute.

Lionetti, Harold. "La preocupación..." (1958). See Studies —
  General.

Dinis, M. Vieira. "Loa para a comédia O purgatório de S.
  Patricio." In Actas do Colóquio de Estudos Etnográficos "Dr.
  Leite de Vasconcelos," 3, Oporto, 1960, pp. 211-24.

La púrpura de la rosa

Wilson, Edward M. "The Text of Calderón's La púrpura de la
  rosa." MLR, 54 (1959), 29-44.

  Wilson studies a previously unknown MS of La púrpura de la
  rosa, showing that it might be a copy of Calderón's autograph.
  At any rate, it provides an earlier text than the one printed
  in 1664.

Stevenson, Robert. "The First New-World Opera." Américas, 16
  (1964), 33-35.

  The article deals mainly with the composer, Tomás de Torrejón
  y Velasco (1644-1728), who made a second musical setting (the
  first, by an unknown composer, in Spain, ca. 1660) of
  Calderón's La púrpura de la rosa, performed in Lima, October
  19, 1701, and surviving in manuscript form in the National
  Library in Lima. The author praises the music.

Subirá, José. "Calderón de la Barca,..." (1965). See Studies —
  Individual Works (Celos aun del aire matan).

La selva confusa

Sloman, Albert E. "La selva confusa Restored to Calderón." HR, 20 (1952), 134-48.

Until 1929, there was only one text of La selva confusa known to exist, a manuscript signed by and in the hand of Calderón. A play of the same title, under the name of Lope de Vega, was said to be included in Parte XXVII, published in Barcelona in 1633, of which there was no known copy. It was assumed that Calderón's play was taken from Lope's. H. C. Heaton discovered a copy of the Barcelona Parte XXVII and, after a collation of the two texts, claimed (in "On La selva confusa attributed to Calderón," PMLA, 44, 1929, pp. 243-73) that the Parte text was Lope's and that Calderón's manuscript represented a mere copy, in which certain lines of his own were inserted and a few alterations made to cover up his theft. The same claim was made a year later, in 1930, by González Palencia, in his edition of La selva confusa for the New Academy edition of Lope's works. Sloman claims that a careful collation of the two versions supplies "conclusive proof that the text attributed to Lope is a corrected and amended version of Calderón's manuscript, that what has been interpreted as Calderón's misguided elaboration is an earlier form of the text that was pruned and shorn, perhaps by Calderón himself...." The versification studies of Morley and Bruerton and of Hilborn do not bear out the attribution to Lope suggested by Heaton; and Sloman argues his case convincingly. Sloman's argument is supported by the following major points: (a) in four instances at least the text of the Barcelona edition contains defective stanza forms which are complete in the manuscript; (b) difficult and sometimes meaningless passages in the printed text appear correctly in the manuscript; (c) superior versification in the shorter printed text suggests at once that it is the final rather than the first form; (d) lines wrongly ascribed in the printed text, inconsistency in cutting and in using in the printed text lines that had been crossed out in the manuscript. — All of this indicates the chronological precedence of the manuscript and certainly acquits Calderón of the charge of plagiary.

La sibila del oriente

Shervill, Robert N. The Old Testament Drama... (1958). See Studies-General.

Glaser, Edward. "Calderón's La sibila del oriente y gran reina de Sabá." RF, 72 (1960), 381-403.

A good study of the religious, scriptural and legendary background of the play, and of the use and adaptation of this material by Calderón.

El sitio de Bredá

Hesse, Everett W. "Calderón y Velázquez" (1951). See Studies — General.

Vosters, S. A. "Lope y Calderón, Vázquez y Hugo, Maastricht y Bredá." RL, 24 (1963), 127-36.

Observations on the relationship between Calderón's El sitio de Bredá and Lope's Los españoles de Flandes and El asalto de Mastrique, Padre Hugo's account of the siege of Bredá and Alonso Vázquez's Los sucesos de Flandes y Francia del tiempo de Alejandro Farnese, with a discussion of the character of Chavarría and the similarities and differences of El sitio and El asalto.

- "La rendición de Bredá en la literatura española." Cuad. de Hist. de España, 41-42 (1965), 224-98. (See especially pp. 230-54.)

In writing El sitio de Bredá, Calderón drew on Lope's El asalto de Mastrique, plus Alonso Vazquez's Los sucesos de Flandes y Francia en tiempo de Alejandro Farnese, 1577-1592, and Hermannus Hugo, S. J., Obsidio Bredana. Partly through the men's characters, and partly through the dramatists' different viewpoints, Calderón's Ambrosio Spínola is a more generous conqueror than Lope's Príncipe de Parma. The siege of Bredá was less eventful than that of Maastricht, though more than twice as long; but Calderón could no doubt have added "local colour" if he had been an eyewitness. Even so, Vosters considers El sitio de Bredá one of Calderón's fine plays, unfairly dismissed as a "drama juvenil" and clearly anticipating the "inmortal creador de La vida es sueño y de El alcalde de Zalamea."

Aubrun, Charles V. "De la chronique à la tragi-comédie: Le Siège de Bredá, par Calderón de la Barca." Actes des Journées Internationales d'Etude du Baroque (Montauban, Centre National de Recherches du Baroque), 2 (1967), 75-84.

Aubrun studies the technique used by Calderón to convert an epic account into a dramatic work: style, character presentation, changes in action, etc. The author insists on the typically Baroque treatment in the genesis of this play.

- "Dalla cronaca alla tragicommedia." Sipario, 24, Nos. 278-79 (1969), 5-10.

On El sitio de Bredá. (See above.)

Sueños hay que verdad son

Varey, J. E. "La mise en scène..." (1964). See Studies — General.

Glaser, Edward. "Calderón de la Barca's Sueños hay que verdad son." ZRP, 72 (1966), 41-77.

The auto owes much to the Joseph-Pharaoh-Jacob story in Genesis, 37, 39-45; but Calderón changed the sequence of events, and used the abstractions Castidad and Sueño to introduce and comment on the story. Predictably, he also imparts a Christian flavour to the auto, making Joseph resemble Jesus, and hinting at Redemption after Joseph and his brothers are reconciled. Pharaoh's dream of plenty and famine is equated to mankind's life before and after falling from grace. Calderón, then, has made the story his own, and turned it "into a typological cycle which illumines the central Mystery of Christianity."

Tan largo me lo fiáis

Wade, Gerald E. "The Fernández Edition of Tan largo me lo fiáis: A Review Article." BCom, 20, No. 2 (1968), 31-41.

This is a detailed review article of Xavier A. Fernández's edition of <u>Tan largo me lo fiáis</u> (D. Pedro Calderón), Madrid, <u>Revista Estudios,</u> 23, No. 79, Oct.-Dec., 1967, pp. 503-784 (Número monográfico). As Professor Wade writes, "The editor offers a brief history of the Calderonian attribution, as also of its refutation." Wade praises Fernández for his introduction, but takes issue with him for failing to reproduce faithfully the <u>suelta</u> text, for the use of Calderón's name as the play's author, and for his belief in the priority of the <u>Burlador</u>. "I am not at all convinced — writes Wade — of the Fernández thesis that <u>TL</u> came from the <u>Burlador</u> since the arguments in the other direction are, for me, overwhelming."

La torre de Babilonia

Foster, David W. "Calderón's <u>La torre de Babilonia</u> and Christian Allegory." <u>Criticism</u>, 9 (1967), 142-54.

Basing his study on Auerbach's definition of "Figura," Foster shows the connection which exists between the principle of medieval allegory and Calderón's Baroque drama. The example put forth is <u>La torre de Babilonia</u>.

Las tres justicias en una

Bomli, P. W. <u>La Femme...</u> (1950). See Studies — General.

Parker, Alexander A. "The Father-Son Conflict..." (1966). See Studies — General.

Olsina, Bartolomé. "Calderón de la Barca en Montauban." <u>Estudios Escénicos</u>, No. 12 (1967), 103-07.

A description of the "Festival barroco de Montauban, 1967," in which Calderón's <u>Las tres justicias en una</u> was performed.

Leavitt, S. E. "Scenes of Horror..." (1968). See Studies — General.

Los tres mayores prodigios

Viqueira, José Maria. "Temas clásicos..." (1959). See Studies — General.

Troya abrasada

Varey, J. E., and N. D. Shergold. "Sobre la fecha de Troya abrasada de Zabaleta y Calderón." In Miscellanea di Studi Ispanici (Pisa, Istituto di Letteratura Spagnola e Ispano-Americana), 6 (1963), 287-97.

By using contracts and actors' lists, the authors suggest the date of the estreno of the play as between Easter of 1643 and February 2, 1644, and make some conjectures as to composition date, which in the case of Zabaleta could have been in 1640 or even earlier, later retouched (first act) and rewritten (second and third acts) by Calderón.

Tu prójimo como a ti

Sánchez, Alberto. "Reminiscencias cervantinas..." (1957). See Studies — General.

Lorenz, Erika. "Tu prójimo como a ti. Bemerkungen zu einer Calderón-Edition in den Clásicos Castellanos." RJ, 16 (1965), 318-32.

A comparison of many passages in the 1957 edition with the autograph MS reveals many discrepancies — 15 more, in fact, than in the 1927 edition, due mainly to misprints in the newer one. Although Valbuena Prat says that he used the autograph, absolute accuracy was apparently not intended. Otherwise, so many distortions of both meaning and style would not be comprehensible.

La vacante general

Varey, J. E., and N. D. Shergold. "An autograph fragment of

Calderón's <u>La vacante general</u>." <u>Symposium</u>, 17 (1963), 165-82.

A printing of the 12 pages of the <u>auto</u> in Calderón's hand from the manuscript of the Biblioteca Municipal, Madrid, with the addition of essential punctuation and a list of variants to be found in three printed editions, and including the extensive stage directions of the poet himself. The authors believe that it was originally written for two carts, and these scenes re-written when the number of carts was increased to four in 1647, since the autograph appears complete in itself, but is not the entire <u>auto</u>.

El verdadero Dios Pan

Groult, P. "La <u>loa</u> de <u>El verdadero Dios Pan</u> de Calderón." <u>LR</u>, 9 (1955), 39-54.

Calderón is shown as primarily a poet, and only secondarily as a theologian.

La vida es sueño (auto)

Palacios, Leopoldo Eulogio. "<u>La Vie est un songe</u>..." (1951). See <u>La vida es sueño</u> (<u>comedia</u>).

Flasche, Hans. "Beitrag zu einer kritischen und kommentierten Ausgabe des <u>auto sacramental, La vida es sueño</u>." In <u>Homenaje a Johannes Vincke</u>, 2 (Madrid, 1963), 579-605.

The first 255 lines of the 1677 edition of Calderón's <u>auto</u> are presented with variants and detailed notes, commentary and suggestions, as a contribution to, and an example of, a critical and annotated edition.

- "Baustein zu einer kritischen und kommentierten Ausgabe Calderóns. (Vers 256-537 des <u>auto sacramental, La vida es sueño</u>.)" In <u>Gesammelte Aufsätze zur Kulturgeschichte Spaniens</u>, I (Spanische Forschungen der Görresgesellschaft, 21), Munster, 1963, pp. 309-26.
Rev: R. D. F. Pring-Mill, <u>BHS</u>, 45 (1968), 80-81 (Speaking of

the volume, the reviewer states: "Of the two dozen contributions, few come directly within the scope of this journal. In
the Spanish field, there is Hans Flasche's 'Baustein...' —
the second portion of his critical edition of the <u>auto</u> version
of <u>La vida es sueño</u>, whose publication by instalments has been
keeping Calderonian scholars tantalized, but full of admiration, for a number of years.") (See Flasche, 1963, above, and
1965.)

- "Baustein II zu einer kritischen und kommentierten Ausgabe
Calderóns. (Vers 538-802 des <u>auto sacramental, La vida es
sueño</u>.)" In <u>Gesammelte Aufsätze zur Kulturgeschichte Spaniens</u>,
III (Spanische Forschungen der Görresgesellschaft, 23),
Münster, 1965, pp. 223-50.
Rev: R. B. Tate, <u>BHS</u>, 45 (1968), 81-82 ("Hans Flasche continues
his earlier investigations into the text of Calderón's <u>auto
sacramental, La vida es sueño</u>, with a commentary on ll. 538-
802. His extensive notes embrace lexical, syntactical, seman-
tic, patristic and literary aspects. He insists that these
articles are merely an assemblage of materials to be fashioned
later into a full critical edition.")

- "Probleme der Syntax Calderóns in Lichte der Textkritik (<u>La
vida es sueño, auto sacramental</u>)." In <u>Actes du Xe Congrès
International de Linguistique et Philologie Romanes</u>, Paris,
Klincksieck, 1965, pp. 705-26.

Guided by editions of 1677 and 1717 and a manuscript of 1751,
Flasche examines 22 passages of the <u>auto</u> from the viewpoint
of the syntactical problems that they pose. Recalling his
opening warning that the difficulties of such a task are
considerable, he concludes that a thoroughly satisfactory
clarification of the work's 1935 lines is extremely hard to
come by, but it is worth the effort.

Gérard, Albert. "Pour une phénoménologie..." (1963). See
Studies — General.

Mitchell, Margarete Koch. <u>Die christliche...</u> (1965). See
Studies — General.

La vida es sueño (comedia)

Palacios, Leopoldo Eulogio. "La Vie est un songe (Essai sur le
sens philosophique du drame de Calderón)." Laval Théologique
et Philosophique, 7 (1951), 123-49.

Palacios notes that much more attention has been paid to the
subject of the sources and the literary antecedents of La
vida es sueño than to the intrinsic meaning of the play. He
attempts a refutation of prevalent interpretations of the
play, which he feels can be reduced to two: (a) the theory of
the play as a symbol of human life, understood completely only
when viewed in relation to the later auto of the same title
(the refutation is well stated: Palacios finds "indéniables
parallélismes," but insists on the need to distinguish between
the theological and philosophical dimensions of the two works,
and claims that the meaning of the comedia is universal and
intelligible to all men, Christian or not); (b) the theory
that the play represents the thesis of liberty against astrological fatality (here the refutation is equally acceptable).
Palacios' own interpretation is based on the two conflicting
conceptions of life, as expressed in the attitudes of man in
the exercise of political power: (a) life as pride; (b) life
as a dream. In the play, Segismundo reflects the first attitude prior to his reawakening in the tower, and the second
thereafter. He is in the first stage an example of the
Machiavellian prince; in the second, a model of "prudentialisme"
(see Palacios' La prudencia política, Madrid, 1946, for the
thematic opposition of Machiavellianism and "prudentialisme,"
and for the justification of the second term).

Reyes, Alfonso. "Un tema de La vida es sueño. El hombre y la
naturaleza en el monólogo de Segismundo." In Trazos de
historia literaria, Buenos Aires, Espasa-Calpe, 1951, pp. 11-
81 (Col. Austral, 1020); and in Obras completas, 6, Mexico,
1957, pp. 182-248.

These pages first appeared, bearing the same title, as an
article in RFE, 4, 1917, pp. 1-25 and 237-76. They are here
reprinted with five short appendices. As stated in the prologue, this study examines the formal structure of the comparison of man and nature with relation to the concept of liberty
for the purpose of determining the antecedents of the
celebrated first monologue of Segismundo. Reyes documents the

appearance of the theme in classical antiquity, its penetration into Spain through Pliny, and its development in Spain from a simple poetic theme to its masterful treatment by Calderón.

Sciacca, Michele Federico. "Verità e sogno (Interpretazione di La vida es sueño di Calderón de la Barca)." Humanitas (Brescia), 6 (1951), 472-85.

This is the Italian version of an article which appeared, as "Verdad y sueño en La vida es sueño, de Calderón," in Clav, 1, No. 2 (1950), 1-9. Sciacca, by his own admission a philosopher rather than an Hispanist, advances an interpretation of the sudden conversion of Segismundo which has been effected when he awakens to find himself once again a prisoner in the tower after his short-lived tenure in the palace. The prince's newly acquired and profound knowledge that all of life, particularly worldly power and glory and sensory experience, is no more than a dream is explained as the effect produced on him by the beauty of Rosaura and Estrella. Their beauty is platonic and, symbolizing external and perfect beauty, elevates Segismundo to an objective perspective which enables him to see that the life of men on earth is, in reality, a dream. (Cf. William M. Whitby, "Rosaura's Rôle in the Structure of La vida es sueño, HR, 28, 1960, pp. 16-27.)

Roaten and Sánchez y Escribano. Wölfflin's Principles... (1952). See Studies — General.

Dunn, Peter N. "The Horoscope Motif in La vida es sueño." Atlante, 1, No. 4 (1953), 187-201.

The article includes a good analysis of Basilio's character, but the study of the possible sources of the "horoscope motif" remains inconclusive.

Gómez de la Serna, Ramón. "La vida como sueño en Calderón y Unamuno." Cultura Universitaria (Caracas), No. 40 (1953), 5-20.

Hesse, Everett W. "La concepción calderoniana del príncipe perfecto en La vida es sueño." Clav, 4, No. 20 (1953), 4-12.

Hesse sees Segismundo as the Aristotelian-Thomist "perfect prince," but offers little new in his comments on the play.

Keller, John E. "A Tentative Classification..." (1953). See Studies — General.

Martínez Almendres, Gregorio. "La vida es sueño de Calderón y los problemas del existencialismo actual." Studium Generale (Porto), 1 (1953), 97-125.

Salazar Larraín, Arturo. "Segismundo y 'el hombre natural'." Mar del Sur, No. 26 (1953), 72-74.

The author briefly traces the concept of the noble savage or "hombre natural" in the period spanning the discovery of America to the writing of La vida es sueño, and points out that Segismundo is not devoid of personality and human reality, but is rather the slowly evolving character of an "hombre natural" into Segismundo who, through the use of his free will, achieves moral maturity.

Sloman, Albert E. "The Structure of Calderón's La vida es sueño." MLR, 48 (1953), 293-300. (Repub. in Wardropper, Critical Essays, New York, 1965, pp. 90-100.)

The play is composed of two dissimilar plots, and the strength of its structure depends on their combination and blending. Rosaura makes possible the conversion of Segismundo, and Segismundo is in turn responsible for the clearing of Rosaura's honour. The two plots fit together to form one dramatic movement.

Fucilla, Joseph G. Relaciones... (1953-54). See Studies — General.

Crocker, Lester G. "Hamlet, Don Quijote, La vida es sueño: The Quest for Values." PMLA, 69 (1954), 278-313.

The study contrasts Segismundo's final solution of the problem of evil and reality with the failure of Hamlet and Don Quijote.

Laubach, Jakob. <u>Hugo von Hofmannsthals Turm-Dichtungen</u>. Kempsten, 1954. Pp. 139.

A diss., Univ. of Freiburg, 1949. Contains a section of <u>La vida es sueño</u>.

Parker, J. H. "Una carta autógrafa de don Marcelino Menéndez y Pelayo al doctor Buchanan." <u>BBMP</u>, 30 (1954), 171-73.

Contains references to sources of <u>La vida es sueño</u>.

Qualia, Charles B. "A Note on the Popularity of Boissy's <u>La Vie est un songe</u>." <u>BCom</u>, 6, No. 2 (1954), 3-4.

A play first performed in 1732.

Whitby, William M. <u>Structural Symbolism...</u> (1954). See Studies — General.

May, T. E. "El sueño de Don Pablos, Don Quijote and Segismundo." <u>Atlante</u>, No. 4 (1955), 192-204.

Segismundo and Don Quijote applied to the study of Quevedo's Pablos.

Strzalkowa, Maria. Commentary, in the Edward Boyé translation of <u>La vida es sueño</u> (<u>Zycie snem</u>), Warsaw, 1956. (The vol. contains 176 pp.)

Anderson Imbert, Enrique. "Calderón y su Segismundo." In <u>Los grandes libros de Occidente y otros ensayos</u>, Mexico, De Andrea, 1957, pp. 75-79.

In this short essay, the author recalls common criticisms made of <u>La vida es sueño</u>, first by the "críticos románticos (que) creyeron que era una gran creación dramática, viva, libre..."; secondly by the "críticos realistas" who objected to psychological inverosimilitudes. In answer to the objections of the latter critics, although no one is specifically named, Anderson Imbert states that "En broma, en cambio, se les podría contestar que Calderón ... convirtió a Segismundo, no en un hombre, sino en un símbolo." As for the feminine characters, "son también símbolos: Rosaura, la Gracia; Estrella, la Monarquía." The author concludes his article comparing Segismundo with Shakespeare's Miranda (The Tempest), and points out that she is not a "símbolo parlante, como el barroco Segismundo, sino una mujer,...una muchacha enamorada." This brief essay, which is easily and pleasantly read, lacks originality and depth.

Bergamín, José. La corteza de la letra (palabras desnudas). Buenos Aires, Losada, 1957. Pp. 181.

"Don Juan y Segismundo," pp. 63-67.

Capelleti, Angel J. "Notas sobre tres dramas y una epopeya de la libertad." Universidad (Univ. Nac. del Litoral), No. 36 (1957), 237-49.

Capelleti's article starts with the background of Western philosophies and their concern with freedom, from the Greeks to modern times. Spain, however, " ha permanecido desde la aurora de los tiempos modernos al margen del quehacer especulativo de Europa, (pero) no ha eludido sin embargo, durante la Edad de Oro de la Nación, la meditación de la libertad." Capelleti points out that rather than the Spanish philosophers, or theologians or historians, the poets were the ones who dealt with the "tema de la libertad." The author states that "El problema de la libertad como negación es el problema de la libertad relativa." As such, there are three situations: "el sujeto que inquiere y requiere la libertad, el objeto de cuya negación surge la libertad y la relación que se presenta como una lucha entre sujeto y objeto...y son precisamente los tres más grandes dramaturgos de la época quienes asumen esas tres cuestiones." The first case is presented by Calderón in La vida es sueño, the second, by Lope de Vega in Fuenteovejuna, and the third, by Tirso de Molina in El condenado por desconfiado. Finally, the author states that the "batalla de la libertad absoluta" could not be dealt with in a play, but in the epic genre, and ends up his essay dealing with Don Quijote. This essay is an intuitional, rather than a scholarly, one; without a single footnote, despite the fact that there are abundant quotations from the authors. The treatment of La vida es sueño is wrapped in philosophical jargon, and the author does not add anything new to what had been already noted about Calderón's masterpiece.

Cioranescu, Alejandro. <u>El barroco...</u> (1957). See Studies — General.

Estrella Gutiérrez, Fermín. <u>Historia...</u> (1957). See Studies — General.

Jacquot, J. "<u>Le Théâtre du monde...</u>" (1957). See Studies — Individual Works (<u>El gran teatro del mundo</u>).

Kirk, Charles F. <u>A Critical Edition, with Introduction and Notes, of Vélez de Guevara's "Virtudes vencen señales."</u> (Unpub. doct. diss., Ohio State Univ., 1957. Pp. 350. (<u>DA</u>, 17, 1957, 2268ab.)

Kirk states in the dissertation abstract that in Part VI of his "Introduction" he makes "a detailed study of the similarities and parallelisms between <u>Virtudes vencen señales</u> and Calderón's <u>La vida es sueño</u>." And he ends his abstract with a final conclusion about the plays: "The relationship between <u>Virtudes vencen señales</u> and <u>La vida es sueño</u> was studied by Rudolph Schevill almost a quarter of a century ago (<u>HR</u>, 1, 1933, pp. 181-95). Although Calderón's play is a more polished, artistic literary product than is Vélez's, it is strikingly similar to the latter in character relationships, plot details, and diction." (See also Sloman's <u>Dramatic Craftsmanship</u>, 1958, pp. 250-77, where he studies the source of <u>La vida es sueño</u> as being the Calderón-Coello, <u>Yerros de naturaleza y aciertos de la fortuna</u>.)

Parker, Alexander A. <u>The Approach...</u> (1957). See Studies — General.

Parker, J. H. <u>Breve historia...</u> (1957). See Studies — General.

Smieja, Florian. "Nowe przeklady..." (1957). See Studies — General.

Lionetti, Harold. "La preocupación..." (1958). See Studies —
General.

Pérez Vila, Manuel. "Polémicas sobre representaciones dramáticas: 1775-1829." RNC, No. 127 (1958), 95-104.

The article refers to the prohibitions, decreed by the clergy
in Venezuela, of La vida es sueño. The author recalls that
the last performance in Maracaibo was the one of the play in
1760 in order to celebrate "la coronación de Carlos III." The
new governor, obeying his wife's wishes, also wanted to have
La vida es sueño performed in 1777, but Bishop Martí was
opposed to it. The governor had to write to the viceroy in
Bogotá and to the King himself. The King, in a decree, pro-
hibited the performance of new comedias; however, the old
ones, written "por poetas conocidos y de nota que se
representaban en los reinos de España" could be performed,
and it was not necessary to have new ecclesiastical approval.
Such was the case of Calderón's play. The article is written
in a live, humorous vein, and proves that Calderón was still
popular towards the end of the 18th century in the Spanish
colonies.

Piñera Llera, Humberto. "¿Descartes en Calderón?" La Torre
(Puerto Rico), 6 (1958), 145-65.

This article, couched in philosophical language, deals with
the coincidence in the thoughts of Calderón and Descartes
concerning the "indiscernibilidad entre lo real y lo ilusorio,
entre el sueño y la vigilia" in the writings of the French
philosopher and the similar preoccupation in Calderón's La
vida es sueño, which develops "el mismo tema de la existencia
como ilusión." Piñera quotes several passages from Descartes'
Discours de la Méthode and Méditations and also various
passages from La vida es sueño, and compares them with the
thoughts of the French philosopher. Then he asks: "¿Influencia
de uno en otro? Y en este caso, ¿quién el influyente y quién
el influido? O, tal vez, ¿coincidencias de orden histórico,
epocal?" The author rejects the first one, since La vida es
sueño was first published in 1636 and the Discours dates from
1637. Instead of any direct influence of one on the other, he
proposes as "más admisible ... la segunda hipótesis, es decir,
la de una cierta coetaneidad de las ideas de una época, esas
Ideas triunfantes y vigentes—como dice Ortega y Gasset—y en

las cuales flotan los individuos de una misma época." This
article lacks scholarly value, does not add anything to what
has been written about La vida es sueño, and the author, in
his preconceived pursuit to point out the similarity between
Calderón and Descartes with respect to the difficulty in
neatly separating illusion or dream from reality, fails to
be aware of the complex moral, philosophical and religious
background of Calderón's play.

Sloman, Albert E. The Dramatic Craftsmanship... (1958). See
Studies — General.

Bergamín, José. Lázaro, Don Juan y Segismundo. Madrid, Taurus,
1959. Pp. 186.

"Rosaura: Intriga y amor," pp. 83-87; "Segismundo," pp. 88-92.
Personal impressions and reflections on La vida es sueño and
its main characters.

Burbano, José Ignacio. "Dos ensayos. Probables nuevas fuentes
de dos obras maestras de la poesía castellana: Las Coplas de
Jorge Manrique y el primer monólogo de Segismundo, en La vida
es sueño de Calderón de la Barca." Rev. del Núcleo del Azuay
de la Casa de la Cultura Ecuatoriana (Cuenca, Ecuador), 7,
No. 13 (1959).

Granja, Fernando de la. "Origen árabe de un famoso cuento
español." Al-Andalus, 24 (1959), 317-33.

Gutiérrez García, Luisa. Bibliografía de "La vida es sueño" de
Calderón. Unpub. diss., Univ. de Madrid, 1959.

Peri, Hiram. Der Religionsdisput der Barlaam-Legende. Ein Motiv
abendländischer Dichtung. Salamanca, Univ. de Salamanca, 1959.
Pp. 274.
Rev: R. D. F. Pring-Mill, BHS, 38 (1961), 180.

Chapter VII, "Die spanischen Barock-Dramen," deals only very
briefly with La vida es sueño.

Schwarz, Egon. "La vida es sueño und Hofmannsthals Bearbeitung in Trochäen." Germanisch-Romanische Monatsschrift (Heidelberg), 9 (1959), 375-90.

See Egon Schwarz, Hofmannsthal und Calderón, 1962 (Studies — General).

Ariola, Paul M. "Two Baroque Heroes: Segismundo and Hamlet." Hisp, 43 (1960), 537-40.

An interesting article which proposes that Segismundo and Hamlet represent the Baroque as a symptom of emotional strain and personal anguish which could be the common denominator of Calderón and Shakespeare. This anguish would be the result of a universal unrest common to the seventeenth century. Segismundo is not sufficiently well analysed.

Aubrun, Charles V. "La Langue poétique de Calderón de la Barca notamment dans La vida es sueño." In Réalisme et poésie au théâtre, Paris, Centre National de la Recherche Scientifique, 1960, pp. 61-76. (2nd ed., 1967.)
Rev: G. Larrieu, Les Langues Néo-latines, 55, No. 3 (1961), 87-88.

Conférences du Théâtre des Nations (1957-59). Entretiens d'Arras 1958.

Carlisky, M. "Sueño y juego en Calderón." Revista di Estetica, 5, No. 1 (1960), 231-35.

Iriarte, Joaquín. "Calderón o la temática moderna" (1960). See Studies — General.

Julien, A. M. "La Mise en scène de La Vie est un songe." In Réalisme et poésie au théâtre, Paris, 1960, pp. 225-32. (See Aubrun, above.)

Norton, Richard W. Casuality in Calderón's "La vida es sueño". Unpub. doct. diss., Univ. of Illinois, 1960. (DA, 21, 1960, 1569.)

Analyses the apparent conflict between fatalism and free will
in terms of the two Catholic systems of theology in conflict
at the time of Calderón, Molinism and Thomism, and of the
pagan philosophy of Stoicism. The author concludes that
casuality in the play can most satisfactorily be explained in
terms of Molinism.

Palacios, Leopoldo Eugenio. "Don Quijote" y "La vida es sueño."
Madrid, Rialp, 1960. Pp. 88.
Rev: Antonio Gómez Galán, Arbor, 48, No. 182 (1961), 107-09.

Discusses the evolution of Segismundo as a prince, from pride
to tyranny, to desengaño, and to political prudence.

Strzalkowa, Maria. Studia... (1960). See Studies — General.

Wardropper, Bruce W. "'Apenas llega cuando llega a penas'." MP,
57 (1960), 240-44.

The symbolical significance of the first scene of La vida es
sueño.

Whitby, William M. "Rosaura's Rôle in the Structure of La vida
es sueño." HR, 28 (1960), 16-27. (Repub. in Wardropper, Critical Essays, New York, 1965, pp. 101-13.)

A fine analysis showing how the honour episode of Rosaura
parallels and blends into the main action, while her presence
awakens in Segismundo a consciousness of his dual nature as a
human being and brings about his conversion to good.

Casalduero, Joaquín de. "Sentido y forma de La vida es sueño."
CCLC, No. 51 (1961), 3-13. (Repub. in his Estudios sobre el
teatro español: Lope de Vega, Guillén de Castro, Cervantes,
Tirso de Molina, Ruiz de Alarcón, Calderón, Moratín, Duque de
Rivas, Madrid, Gredos, 1962, pp. 161-84; 2nd ed. aumentada,
1967, pp. 169-90.)
Rev (of the 1962 vol.): Carlos Ortigoza, Hisp, 47 (1964),
196-97.

A detailed stylistic analysis, showing how this play fits into

the structural world of the Baroque. "Como en toda obra del
barroco, nada es casual, nada es fortuito. Nuestro autor
llega a componer con un rigor extraordinario. Su arte tiene
algo de algebraico."

Salvador, A. "Concepción de la vida como sueño." <u>CHA</u>, 45 (1961),
370-76.

An exploration of Calderón's metaphysical-ethical concept of
life as seen through <u>La vida es sueño</u>. For Calderón, life is
only a dream, and death represents the awakening to true life;
therefore a hedonistic philosophy is not valid. "La concepción
de la vida como sueño no es una figura literaria, sino una
tesis metafísica. Es la razón misma la que habla por la boca
de Segismundo, conforme al tipo de hombre del siglo XVII: el
hombre pensamiento."

- "Vivencia de amor." <u>CHA</u>, 46 (1961), 201-07.

Analysis of the sentiment of love as felt by Segismundo for
Rosaura in <u>La vida es sueño</u>. The author begins with "intuición,"
and continues through "suspensión," "admiración," "rendición,"
to "sacrificio," stating that all of these aspects comprise
"la vivencia de amor" as presented in the play.

Ayala, Francisco. "'Porque no sepas que sé'." <u>Quaderni Ibero-
Americani</u>, 4, No. 28 (1962), 193-202.

An effort to reorient Calderonian criticism by correcting
certain errors in the opinions of Menéndez Pelayo concerning
<u>La vida es sueño</u>, by showing that Menéndez Pelayo was unable
to comprehend the Baroque aesthetic, since he judged Calderón
by 19th century standards. One must not look for "lo verosímil"
in the characters of this play, but, on the contrary, see them
as allegorical symbols. The characters of the play are
analysed in this light.

Sánchez Escribano, Federico. "Sobre el origen de 'el delito
mayor del hombre es haber nacido' (<u>La vida es sueño</u>, I, 111-
12)." <u>RomN</u>, 3 (1962), 50-51.

The idea in this quotation can be traced back to Ovid, through

Erasmus. The latter used it ironically, to satirize the stupidity and malevolence of human beings, whereas Calderón uses it to reflect "la desesperación vital del hombre de su tiempo."

Schwarz, Egon. <u>Hofmannsthal und Calderón</u> (1962). See Studies — General.

Abel, Lionel. "Metatheatre: Shakespeare and Calderón." In <u>Metatheatre: A New View of Dramatic Form</u>, New York, Hill and Wang, 1963, pp. 59-72.

Calderón is discussed on pp. 64-66, 71-72. The author classes as "metaplays" those in which a character is greater than the play itself, "all ... are theater pieces about life seen as already theatricalized." In this group he places <u>La vida es sueño</u> because the expected tragedy of Basilio's death and his country's ruin at the hands of Segismundo is changed by Basilio's substituting "for the play intended by fate, one of his own invention." Instead of the expected tragedy, we have "metatheatre."

Dam, C. F. A. van. "Balthazar Huydecoper en de Spaanse Letterkunde." <u>De Nieuwe Taalgids</u>, 56 (1963), 143-45.

The author refers to a recent dissertation on the 18th century philologist and a letter in which Huydecoper describes his return to his government post on an island after a visit to Amsterdam as like Sigismundus' awaking in his tower after his palace experience. Since the writer of the dissertation fails to do so, van Dam identifies Sigismundus as Segismundo of <u>La vida es sueño</u> and mentions the translation and popularity of the play in Huydecoper's time.

Fucilla, Joseph G. "<u>Un mundo breve</u> and <u>un breve cielo</u> (Calderón's <u>La vida es sueño</u>, Act II, verses 1565 and 1567)." <u>RomN</u>, 5 (1963), 53-54.

Fucilla points out that Calderón's source for the first could have been Castiglione's <u>Il Cortegiano</u>, translated by Boscán, and he refers to an anonymous poem of 1605 which has the antithesis "abreviado mundo, abreviado cielo."

Gérard, Albert. "Pour une phénoménologie..." (1963). See
    Studies — General.

Honig, Edwin. "Reading What's in La vida es sueño." Theater
    Annual, 20 (1963), 63-71.

The author considers the play a metaphysical and moral play
rather than a religious one, although sharing with many of
his religious plays and his comedies an anti-authoritarian
bias, a criticism of inflexible rule. To him, Segismundo is
the only one who emerges from the dream of life to the life
of consciousness. The other characters aid, block, and test
him. He then shows the relation of Segismundo to each.

Piper, Anson C. "Ribera's 'Jacob' and the Tragic Sense of Life."
    Hisp, 46 (1963), 279-82.

Ribera painted his picture four years after Calderón's La
vida es sueño, each creating "a work of art in which the central theme revolves around a world of dreams." This is the
only reference to Calderón.

Praag, J. A. van. "Otra vez la fuente de La vida es sueño." In
    Studia Philologica. Homenaje ofrecido a Dámaso Alonso, 3,
    Madrid, Gredos, 1963, pp. 551-62.

After describing how, in his book on Calderón's craftsmanship,
Sloman established the debt of La vida es sueño to Yerros de
naturaleza y aciertos de la fortuna and that of this play in
turn to Coello's La adúltera castigada, the author shows how
all three are based on the novel Eustorgio y Clorilene, by
Enrique Suárez de Mendoza. He outlines the similarities of
the four works. The basis of the novel was the Historia
pontifical católica of Luis de Bavia, which furnished Lope
with the idea for El gran duque de Moscovia.

Ruiz de Conde, Justina. "La revolución matrista de Segismundo."
    La Torre, 11, No. 44 (1963), 93-106.

Segismundo is considered as heading a "matristic" revolt
against a "patristic" group led by his father and including
Clotaldo and the slain servant. He is, moreover, influenced

232

by Rosaura, a woman, the first new person he sees at his
tower. The palace represents authoritarianism and the prison,
democracy; the battlefield is where the struggle is resolved.

Szondi, Peter. "La vida es sueño." Humboldt, 4, No. 16 (1963),
17-19.

A brief comparison of the similarities, but mainly the differences, between Oedipus Rex of Euripides and La vida es
sueño in the way that the prognostication is fulfilled in
the former and thwarted or changed in the latter.

ter Horst, Robert M. "La vida es sueño": The Rôle of Conflict.
Unpub. doct. diss., The Johns Hopkins Univ., 1963. Pp. 161.

An extremely detailed, rather rambling, analysis of the play
from a theological point of view. "The play represents the
nature and purpose of conflict through an analogy of the
imperfect with the perfect." For the author, conflict is the
major premise, the conflict between the imperfection and evil
of man and the perfections and graces of God ("man's constantly and necessarily troubled relationship with God") and his
salvation through Christ's sacrifice. He illustrates this
through a discussion of the words and actions of Segismundo,
Rosaura, and Basilio, and, to a lesser extent, Clotaldo and
Clarín. He considers Segismundo as the only true performer
and devotes about half of the thesis to him and his part in
the play as one who "presents living proof of God's
compassion."

Bader, Orlando. "Calderón en Nueva York." Mundo Hispánico, No.
194 (1964), 60-62.

A brief account of the establishing of the Teatro Español of
New York, and the impressive first performance of Calderón's
La vida es sueño under the direction of José Crespo. The
Teatro Español was also to offer the play in Roy Campbell's
English version. The article reproduces Howard Taubman's
review of the Spanish version. (See Reynolds, Hisp, 1965,
below.)

Cepeda Calzada, Pablo. La vida es sueño. Madrid, Librería
Editorial Augustinus, 1964. Pp. 240.

Rev: J. Yagüe, <u>Augustinus</u> (Madrid), 9 (1964), 509-15; J. A. S., <u>Razón y Fe</u>, 174 (1966), 134-35. ("Las citas de muchos pensadores coincidentes o discrepantes, antiguos y modernos, dan un sabor de actualismo y oportunidad a este sólido y bien construido estudio.").

The subtitle is "reflexiones sobre la conciencia española." This is a religious, philosophical work whose conception began with Calderón's <u>La vida es sueño</u> and which is more concerned with the ideas that the play presents (liberty, free will, responsibility, imagination, life as a theatre, disillusionment) than with the play itself. The author discusses also the ideas of such men as Descartes, Quevedo, Gracián, Schopenhauer, Pirandello, and others. He seems to see in the play a synthesis of the Spanish conscience and a guide. "Can man of today learn the lesson, the eternal lesson, to be derived from the Calderonian drama?"

Ehrgott, Ulrike. <u>Das Schicksal Calderóns in Deutschland. Unter besonderer Berüchsichtigung der Übersetzungen von "La vida es sueño"</u>. Diss., Univ. of Innsbruck, 1964. Pp. v, 309.

García Bacca, Juan David. <u>Introducción literaria a la filosofía</u>. 2nd ed. Caracas, Univ. Central de Venezuela, 1964. Pp. 327.

Contains a detailed analysis of <u>La vida es sueño</u>.

Hatzfeld, Helmut. <u>Estudios...</u> (1964). See Studies — General.

Seidler, Herbert. "Prunkreden..." (1964). See Studies — General.

Valbuena Briones, Angel. "Un preludio y tres interpretaciones de <u>La vida es sueño</u>." <u>Atlántida</u>, 2 (1964), 616-24.

The author calls the play a "Tragedia aristotélica a la española" and says that the origins of the theme are oriental, tracing them through the Old Testament, Plato, Seneca, and the Middle Ages (Barlaam and Josaphat, Juan Manuel) to the 17th century. Calderón gave it a philosophical consistency and used it to illustrate two philosophical problems which disturbed the thinkers of his generation: predestination of man and the

education of his character. Valbuena Briones continues with
his own interpretation of the play and suggests that its rich
construction invites others.

Borel, Jean-Paul. <u>Quelques aspects du songe dans la littérature</u>
<u>espagnole</u>. Neuchâtel, Editions de Baconnière, 1965. Pp. 75.
Rev: Robert Richard, <u>BH</u>, 69 (1967), 302; K. Piekarec,
<u>Kwartalnik Neofilologiezny</u>, 14 (1967), 320-21.

Contains references to Calderón's <u>La vida es sueño</u>.

Joly, Monique. "A propos d'une leçon erronée de <u>La vida es</u>
<u>sueño</u>." <u>Les Langues Néo-Latines</u>, 59, No. 174 (1965), 69-72.

Line 239, usually "fuera muerte desta suerte," should be
"fuera vida...," as Krenkel suspected, seconded by Northup,
Buchanan, and Riquer. Segismundo, speaking amorously, likens
Rosaura's absence to <u>life</u>, since his life to date is worse
than death would be for others.

Lawson, Richard H. "Grillparzer's Fragmentary Translation of
<u>La vida es sueño</u>." <u>RomN</u>, 7 (1965), 58-61.

Grillparzer did less than half of Act I, very poetically: not
a reworking, and "very likely the best translation ever
accorded Calderón in any language." His approach is a flexible
one; he does not always translate the same word the same way,
and he does not use the verse-forms that Calderón did. As a
poet himself, Grillparzer, "basing himself on a poetic sensi-
tivity to Calderón's language ... is translating poetry into
poetry."

Meca Ketterer, Alberto. "El sentido de lo barroco en <u>La vida es</u>
<u>sueño</u> de Calderón." <u>Poesía Española</u>, No. 147 (1965), 17-20.

The change of leadership in Europe, with the political centre
of gravity shifting from Spain to France, led to the <u>desengaño</u>
and pessimism of the 17th century, including Calderón; but he
shows no bitterness. On the contrary, <u>La vida es sueño</u> is,
over all, "una tremenda afirmación." The Baroque, born of the
collision of the <u>eterno-humano</u> and the <u>eterno-divino</u>, does
not carry its doubt to matters of dogma and faith; and neither
does Segismundo, despite his misgivings as to life's value.

Mitchell, Margarete Koch. *Die christliche...* (1965). See
Studies — General.

Moon, H. Kay. "Calderón and Casona." *Hisp*, 48 (1965), 37-42.

Casona especially resembles Calderón in treating the Devil
(a fallen angel who retains forbidden knowledge, as in *La
barca sin pescador*). Also, Pablo Saldaña, in *La tercera
palabra*, is like Segismundo in his isolation, initial failure,
and eventual success. (He has also thrown a man from a window!) As Rosaura greatly influences Segismundo, only Marga
can modify Pablo's reactions; but unlike Rosaura, she marries
Pablo. Of today's playwrights, Casona best combines modern
humour and realism with "... the poetic and ethical qualities
characteristic of the Golden Age."

Porqueras-Mayo, Alberto. "Más sobre Calderón: 'Pues el delito
mayor del hombre es haber nacido.' Contribución al estudio
de un *topos* literario en España." *Segismundo*, 1 (1965), 275-
99.

Going beyond Sánchez Escribano, who ascribes the lines to
Erasmian influence, the author finds the principal source in
Job, especially chapter III. This would of course have suf-
ficed for Calderón; but Fray Luis de León's commentaries on
Job, published by Quevedo in 1631, also helped.

Reynolds, John J. "*La vida es sueño* in New York." *Hisp*, 48
(1965), 499-501.

Alternate performances in Spanish and English (Roy Campbell
translation) were staged from March 17 to early May, 1964.
The Spanish version was preferred, and most reviewers were
favourably disposed, including critics of such stature as
Richard Watts and Walter Kerr. The latter, stressing the
play's influence on 20th-century thought, felt that "... we
should know it at least as well as we know *Hamlet*." (See
Bader, *Mundo Hispánico*, 1964, above.)

Wilson, Edward M. "On *La vida es sueño*." In Wardropper, *Critical
Essays*, New York, 1965, pp. 63-89. (The original version, "*La
vida es sueño*," in Spanish, appeared in *RUBA*, 3rd series, 7,
1946, pp. 61-78.)

The outstanding, and new, interpretation, of La vida es sueño.

Cascudo, Luis da Câmara. "O mais pobre dos dois..." Rev. de Dialectología y Tradiciones Populares, 22 (1966), 3-6.

Rosaura's famous décima ("Cuentan de un sabio...") seems to have an Oriental source, probably via the tenth ejemplo of the Conde Lucanor ("Lo que sucedió a un hombre que por pobreza y falta de otra cosa comía altramuces"). Later versions are cited, all stressing someone who eats another's discarded food.

Hesse, Everett W. "Some Observations on Imagery in La vida es sueño." Hisp, 49 (1966), 421-29.

Stresses "... animals, man-beast, buildings, nature, the court and light." When Segismundo uses his reason more and more, there is progressively less imagery; though of course reason and emotion overlap. Calderón's images need further study, in the hope of learning which ones he favoured, as well as which ones tended to become stylized.

López, Matilde Elena. "Hamlet, Don Quijote, Don Juan, Segismundo y Fausto, cinco grandes mitos del arte en la Edad Moderna." La Universidad (Univ. de El Salvador), 91, No. 2 (1966), 69-102.

May, T. E. "The Folly and Wit..." (1966). See Studies — Individual Works (A secreto agravio, secreta venganza).

Parker, Alexander A. "The Father-Son Conflict..." (1966). See Studies — General.

Quissac, Jean de. "Actualité du théâtre du Siècle d'Or." Rev. des Sciences Politiques, No. 17 (1966), 69-74.

Chiefly on La vida es sueño.

Salinas, Pedro. "The Acceptance of Reality..." (1966). See Studies — General.

Balbín, Rafael de. "Bécquer y Calderón." <u>Atlántida</u>, 5 (1967), 365-70.

A comparison of <u>Rima XXXII</u> with <u>La vida es sueño</u>, lines 1512-17. A possible influence of Calderón on Bécquer.

Bandera, Cesáreo. "El itinerario de Segismundo en <u>La vida es sueño</u>." <u>HR</u>, 35 (1967), 69-84.

Basing his study on a suggestion from Wardropper, that the beginning of <u>La vida es sueño</u> ("Hipogrifo violento...") is an allegory of giving birth (<u>parto</u>), the author continues his study to consider Segismundo as an allegorical figure, seen in the light of the patristic-scholastic tradition of platonic character, upon which Calderón's theological and philosophical training had great influence.

Díaz-Plaja, Guillermo. <u>Los monstruos y otras literaturas</u>. Barcelona, Plaza y Janés, 1967. Pp. 239.

Includes "Segismundo," pp. 135-39.

Hesse, Everett W. "El motivo del sueño en <u>La vida es sueño</u>." <u>Segismundo</u>, 3 (1967), 55-62.

Maurin, Margaret S. "The Monster, the Sepulchre and the Dark: Related Patterns of Imagery in <u>La vida es sueño</u>." <u>HR</u>, 35 (1967), 161-78.

The author studies the images of <u>La vida es sueño</u> as manifestations of the Baroque.

Bodini, Vittorio. <u>Segni e simboli nella "Vida es sueño"</u>. Bari, Adriatica, 1968. Pp. 212.
Rev: Georges Güntert, <u>FMod</u>, 8 (1968), 311-13. (Favourable. "... los signos, símbolos, personajes, paisajes o ambientes llegan a ser función de lo que Bodini llama 'dialéctica elemental,' o sea, de los cuatro elementos, según la cosmogonía aristotélico-ovidiana.").

An analysis of language, structure, symbols, characterization

and themes in La vida es sueño. No introduction or bibliography is included. The book has a sub-title "Dialettica
elementare del dramma calderoniano," and it is in the series
Biblioteca di Filologia Romanza, 11.

Hall, H. B. "Segismundo and the Rebel Soldier." BHS, 45 (1968),
189-200.

Studies Machiavelli's precepts as illustrated by Segismundo's
punishment of the treasonous soldier for reasons of state.

Hesse, Everett W. Análisis e interpretación... (1968). See
Studies — General.

Pring-Mill, R. D. F. "Los calderonistas de habla inglesa y La
vida es sueño: Métodos del análisis temático-estructural."
In Hans Flasche, Litterae hispanae et lusitanae, Munich,
1968, pp. 369-413. (See Flasche, 1968, Studies — General.)

A study of the major contributions of British and American
calderonistas, their methods of criticism and their significance to the scholarship of Calderón. An article of supreme
importance.

Samonà, Carmelo. Saggio di un commento a "La vida es sueño" di
Calderón de la Barca. Rome, Libreria Editrice E. De Santis,
1968. Pp. 133. (Università degli Studi di Roma. Facoltà di
Magistero; Anno accademico, 1966-67.)

Shergold, N. D. "La vida es sueño: Ses acteurs, son théâtre et
son public." In Jean Jacquot, Elie Konigson, and Marcel Oddon
(eds.), Dramaturgie et société. Rapports entre l'oeuvre
théâtrale, son interprétation et son public aux XVIe et XVIIe
siècles (Nancy, April 14-21, 1967), Paris, Centre National de
la Recherche Scientifique, 1968, pp. 93-109.
Rev (of vol.): TLS, July 10, 1969, p. 748; G. Boquet, Annales,
24 (1969), 1226-29; M. Scaduto, Archivum Historicum Societatis
Iesu, 38 (1969), 363-67.

Weiger, John C. "Rebirth in La vida es sueño." RomN, 10 (1968),
119-21.

Treats the significance of Segismundo's reawakening with
relation to Basilio's words in Act III:
> Hijo, que tan noble acción
> otra vez en mis entrañas
> te engendra, príncipe eres;

and refers to Sánchez Escribano, RomN, 1962, and to Porqueras-
Mayo, Segismundo, 1965.

Boullosa, Virginia. "La actitud conflictual en Segismundo y
Hamlet." In Cvitanovic (ed.), El sueño..., 1969, pp. 166-76.
See Studies — General.

Brody, Ervin C. "Poland in Calderón's Life Is a Dream: Poetic
Illusion or Historical Reality." Polish Review (New York),
14, No. 2 (1969), 21-62.

Cioranescu, A. "Letture barocche." Sipario, 24, Nos. 278-79
(1969), 13-16.

References to La vida es sueño.

Cotrait, René. "La vida es sueño de Calderón, source possible
de El hombre deshabitado de Rafael Alberti?" Bulletin
d'Information du Service de Documentation (Faculté des
Lettres et Sciences Humaines, Univ. de Grenoble), 21-22
(1969), 15-32.

Custodio, Alvaro. "La Edad de Oro del teatro en España y en
Inglaterra." La Torre, 17 (1969), 124-41.

For Calderón, there is reference above all to La vida es
sueño. ("La vida es sueño y Hamlet," pp. 137-41.)

Cvitanovic, Dinko. "Hipótesis sobre la significación del
sueño..." (1969). See Studies — General.

Iriarte, Raúl R. "El problema de la realidad en La vida es
sueño." In Cvitanovic (ed.), El sueño..., 1969, pp. 123-29.
See Studies — General.

240

Mercadé, Georgina Sábat. "A propósito de Sor Juana Inés de la Cruz: Tradición poética del tema 'sueño' en España." _MLN_, 84 (1969), 171-95.

Brief reference to _La vida es sueño_.

Parker, Alexander A. "Calderón's Rebel Soldier and Poetic Justice." _BHS_, 46 (1969), 120-27.

This article is a reply to "Segismundo and the Rebel Soldier" (_BHS_, 45, 1968, pp. 189-200), in which H. B. Hall has argued against an interpretation of _La vida es sueño_ which affirms that this play is the most notable manifestation of poetic justice in Spanish drama. Professor Parker argues that the evidence must be weighed in the light of the moral attitudes of Calderón's time, and not those of our own.

Hall, H. B. "Poetic Justice in _La vida es sueño_: A Further Comment." _BHS_, 46 (1969), 128-31.

In reply to the above article by Parker, Hall questions the assumption that Calderón accepted a uniform seventeenth-century attitude toward rebellion which had grown out of a similarly uniform sixteenth-century attitude.

Warnke, Frank J. "The World as Theatre: Baroque Variations on a Traditional Topos." In Bernhard Fabian and Ulrich Suerbaum (eds.), _Festschrift für Edgar Mertner_, Munich, Wilhelm Fink Verlag, 1969, pp. 185-200.

Reference, above all, to _La vida es sueño_.

I N D E X

Editors, Translators, Critics (but not reviewers of books) in
the "Annotated Bibliography" are presented by page references.
(Numbers in parentheses indicate multiple listings on a page.)